SPEAKING
CONFLICT

Books by David Buttrick

Speaking Jesus (2002)
Speaking Parables (2000)
Preaching the New and the Now (1998)
A Captive Voice (1994)
Proclamation Five: Easter (1993)
The Mystery and the Passion (1992)
Proclamation Four: Pentecost 3 (1989)
Preaching Jesus Christ (1988)
Homiletic (1987)
Proclamation Three: Epiphany (1985)
Proclamation Two: Pentecost B, with Donald H. Juel (1980)

Liturgical Writing and Editing

The Worshipbook (1970)
Book of Common Worship, Provisional Services (1966)
Service for the Lord's Day (1964)

Edited Volumes

Jesus and Man's Hope (1970)
Violence and Social Crisis (*Perspective*, Book Issue, 1966)

SPEAKING CONFLICT

Stories of a Controversial Jesus

David Buttrick

Westminster John Knox Press
LOUISVILLE • LONDON

Quotations of the Hebrew Scriptures are adapted from *Tanakh: The Holy Scriptures*, © 1985, published by The Jewish Publication Society with the permission of the publisher.

Quotations from the Christian Scriptures are the author's own translations.

Excerpts from *All My Sons* and *After the Fall* by Arthur Miller are reprinted by permission of International Creative Management. All rights reserved.

The amidah prayer from the Yizkor is reprinted from the *Mahzor for Rosh Hashana and Yom Kippur*, edited by Rabbi Jules Harlow, © 1972 by the Rabbinical Assembly, p. 137. All rights reserved.

Excerpt from *The Historical Figure of Jesus* by E. P. Sanders is reprinted by permission of Penguin Books, Ltd. All rights reserved.

Excerpt from "Mutual Admiration Society" is reprinted by permission. All rights reserved.

Excerpt from "On Marriage and the Marriage Service" by David Buttrick, in *Reformed Liturgy and Music* (Winter 1980), is reprinted by permission of the Office of Theology and Worship, Presbyterian Church (U.S.A.). All rights reserved.

Excerpt from "On Preaching from Romans 9–11" by David Buttrick, in *Ex Auditu* 4 (1989), is reprinted by permission of North Park Theological Seminary. All rights reserved.

Excerpt from "Preaching on the Family" by David Buttrick, in *Preaching In and Out of Season*, edited by Thomas G. Long and Neely Dixon McCarter, is reprinted by permission of Westminster John Knox Press. All rights reserved.

Excerpt from "Red Seed," in *Voice in the Circle* by Jeanne D'Orge, is reprinted by permission of Carl Cherry Center for the Arts. All rights reserved.

Excerpt from a sermon in *Homiletic: Moves and Structures* by David Buttrick is reprinted by permission of Augsburg Fortress. All rights reserved.

Book design by Sharon Adams
Cover design by Lisa Buckley

First edition
Published by Westminster John Knox Press
Louisville, Kentucky

This book is printed on acid-free paper that meets the American National Standards Institute Z39.48 standard. ♾

PRINTED IN THE UNITED STATES OF AMERICA

07 08 09 10 11 12 13 14 15 16 — 10 9 8 7 6 5 4 3 2 1

Library of Congress Cataloging-in-Publication Data

Buttrick, David.
   Speaking conflict : stories of a controversial Jesus / David Buttrick. — 1st ed.
      p. cm.
   Includes bibliographical references and indexes.
   ISBN 978-0-664-23089-0 (alk. paper)
  1. Jesus Christ—Conflicts. 2. Bible. N.T. Gospels Mark—Homiletical use. 3. Jesus Christ—Conflicts—Sermons. 4. Bible. N.T. Gospels Mark—Sermons. 5. Sermons, American. I. Title.
   BT303.B98 2007
   226.3'06—dc22

                                        2007003346

*I have taught students in
seminaries, schools of theology,
university divinity schools, colleges,
cathedrals, churches, retreat centers,
here and in other lands.*

*All my life I've lived with students,
and I salute them all.*

Contents

Preface

*H*ere is a book I had to finish. The book completes a project, namely, three books on the language of Jesus, attributed words that Christians treasure and preachers preach. In 2000, I wrote *Speaking Parables: A Homiletic Guide,* on interpreting the parables of Jesus. I followed with *Speaking Jesus: Homiletic Theology and the Sermon on the Mount,* a book that studied the inaugural teachings of Jesus found in Matthew and Luke. In addition to parables, teachings, and occasional aphorisms, there are conflict-pronouncement stories, most of which appear in the Gospel of Mark. So here is *Speaking Conflict: Stories of a Controversial Jesus.*

Little has been written about the conflict stories in the past forty years, except a fine book by Arland J. Hultgren, *Jesus and His Adversaries: The Form and Function of the Conflict Stories in the Synoptic Tradition* (1979). In addition, there is Joanna Dewey's dissertation, *Markan Public Debate: Literary Technique, Concentric Structure, and Theology in Mark 2:1–3:6* (1980), and Jack Dean Kingsbury's *Conflict in Mark: Jesus, Authorities, Disciples* (1989). But for the task of interpreting these odd stories in teaching and preaching, there is little. Perhaps the book you have begun to read will be useful in this regard.

I need to thank some people because, directly or indirectly, they have helped to produce these pages. Jennifer Hackett, all-a-flutter about getting married, has been lodged in our Nashville house, allowing me to finish writing these pages in northern Michigan. Cynthia Ann Curtis has completed my garbled indexing. Sandi Whiteford has been wonderfully adept as well as sweet. Instead of commenting on my spectacular computer stupidity, she has shown up and solved all the goofed-up problems with well-trained grace. There are others: Lee Arnold, an extraordinary chef and friend, has provided for evening parties away from the desk. Ketrina Martin has boosted morale and helped maintain creature comforts. And nearby, on the lake, there are Joyce and Walter Marcotte, neighbors now for fifteen friendly years.

Since I began writing books, I have had a grand editor, Stephanie Egnotovich. I followed her from one publishing house to another. She is wise, gracious, and always on-target with her comments and suggestions. Every writer should be so lucky.

I would like to thank congregations where I have worshiped while writing these pages: Brookmeade Congregational Church (UCC) in Nashville and the Evangelical Lutheran Church in East Jordan, Michigan. Theological professors do need congregations.

In every book, I have written tributes to Betty Allaben Buttrick. Side by side we have grown old together. ("Not old," she says firmly, "but older!") She thinks it may be time for me to write a profitable book, perhaps a risque romance novel, instead of "professor books." She's probably right. As always, I celebrate Betty, a wise, winsome lady, whom I dearly love and love more dearly year by year.

I seem to write for people who will teach or preach the gospel message, and for students, quick and always amusing, who are planning to do so. I hope these pages may be useful to them.

D.G.B.
On Six Mile Lake, Michigan

Introduction

Most of us Bible readers recognize the parables of Jesus. And we know miracle stories when we see them. In the Sermon on the Mount, we can pick out Beatitudes and recite the Golden Rule. We recognize different kinds of language by the way they are designed. But ask average Bible readers about conflict stories and probably they will not be sure what you mean. Let us begin with a discussion of form.

Forms of Speech

Forms of speech are the stock, familiar ways we speak to one another.[1] If you overhear two people talking, "Fifty dollars! Listen, I wouldn't give you five," you surmise they are bargaining. Or how about, "Hey, did you hear the one about the farmer's daughter and the traveling salesman?" If you overhear those words, you can guess a vulgar joke will follow. If at nightfall you overhear a mother reading to her little girl, "Once upon a time there was a beautiful lady who sat on a bench which, when the sun shone, seemed made of gold," you would suppose you were overhearing a fairy tale. These represent conventional ways of speaking that can be recognized.

Of course, there are familiar forms in written language as well. For example, if you receive a letter that begins, "Mr. and Mrs. J. Huffington Smith request the pleasure of your company," you know you are reading the formal invitation to a social event, probably a wedding. How about, "Dear Customer: In going over our past due accounts . . ."—oops, you have opened a dunning letter. But if a letter begins, "This letter is being sent to a select few persons who are sensitive to . . . ," you may guess you are being set up by an advertising agency. Someone is trying to sell you something, probably something expensive you don't need. Once again, we recognize the form at once.

Though these examples include just the first words of familiar forms, the full forms are as predictable. The joke about the farmer's daughter will develop a situation and end in a punch line. The formal invitation will state where-and-when details and then conclude with an RSVP statement. All cultures have such set ways of speaking—oral forms that may well end up as written conventions in more literate societies. Words are not simply a medium of exchange: I have a thought; I put it into words. You receive the words, decode them, and grasp my thought. No, most language is designed to do! Words bargain for a selling price, or make someone laugh raucously, or help a child to imagine another fairy world. Language gets us to pay our bills, to answer invitations, or, with flattery, to spend our money. In a way, language always both *means* and *does*. Language is purposeful. Familiar forms of language are ways of getting things done. Every society develops such conventional forms for use on different occasions or for particular purposes. If we try to understand the Bible, obviously we will ask what words mean, but also we must recognize what words may be trying to do. We must decipher both meaning and intentionality.

Forms orient us. When someone begins, "Did you hear the one about the traveling salesman and the farmer's daughter?" (in Britain, it's "the bishop and the actress," a tribute to the enduring influence of the Anglican tradition!), we brace ourselves to hear a dirty joke. We are handed a hermeneutic clue; we are told what kind of language we are going to hear and therefore how to respond when the punch line occurs—with laughter, groaning, annoyance, or prudery. Of course, we can be crossed up. Forms can be deliberately broken. The "one about the farmer's daughter" could turn into a lecture on agrarian reform. The fairy tale about "a beautiful lady who sat on a bench which, when the sun shone, seemed made of gold" could continue, "and her name was Hilda Glockenspiel, 2633 Grand Concourse Avenue, Bronx, New York." The suspension of temporal reality necessary for a fairy tale would be sabotaged. Often biblical forms are deliberately broken, for example, when surreal details disrupt the everyday reality of Jesus' parables. Good heavens, how could a "kingdom of God" be contained in everyday conventional language?

Scholarship

In the first third of the twentieth century, form critics noticed different forms within the biblical text. In the Christian Scriptures, there were parables, miracle stories, beatitudes, proverbial sayings, sign stories, creedal forms, liturgical acclamations, hymns, and others. Sometimes scholars noticed the same forms in wider Jewish usage or in the familiar rhetoric of the pagan world. Conservative Christians were appalled; it seemed to them that the uniqueness of Jesus the Christ was being undermined. But, actually, forms establish Jesus' full humanity; he lived in a human world where forms are a normal, indeed, useful way of conversing with one another. What is more interesting is to study how Jesus may have been modifying conventional forms for the sake of a new, surprising gospel message.

Early form critics noticed the conflict stories, which appear in bunches in the Gospel of Mark. People come up to Jesus with a question: "Do we pay taxes to Caesar?" "Is divorce an option?" "What is the great commandment?" Frequently Jesus replies with a counterquestion, after which there is a concluding epigrammatic saying. The form is distinctive and repeats with different questions. Early form critics—notably, Martin Albertz, Martin Dibelius, Rudolf Bultmann and, rather more cautiously, Vincent Taylor—all studied the conflict-pronouncement stories and, unfortunately, each developed a different terminology and each a separate scholarly focus. Albertz reduced the form to an introductory situation, a question, and a saying. He likened the stories to those of the Hebrew prophets contending with the kings and priests of Israel. Thus, he believed conflict stories were drawn from actual contending—prophetic Jesus versus Jewish leadership.[2] On the other hand, both Dibelius and Bultmann viewed the stories as products of early Christian communities.[3] Yes, Jesus undoubtedly engaged in controversy, but the stories were probably shaped as early Christians, in the midst of controversy, were questioned and answered with sayings from their founding figure, Jesus. Bultmann believed the form evolved from rabbinic dialogue. Dibelius, on the other hand, believed the forms were didactic, in effect teaching devices, designed for the church's mission in Hellenistic settings. Dibelius was also more interested in the sayings than in the question-counterquestion form. Taylor was much more cautious. He believed that many of the stories were remembered controversies in which Jesus was engaged, memories that in turn were triggered by situations in early Christian communities.[4] The "both/and" proposals seem most likely. Though Jesus was involved in controversy and the sayings may well be true to his positions, probably the stories we have were shaped as early Christians were questioned by surrounding critics, Jewish and Hellenistic.

Arland J. Hultgren's study is a more sophisticated work. While Jewish or Hellenistic speech forms may have conditioned the language of early Christianity, Hultgren argues that the forms are nonetheless distinctive, a new kind of language:

The conflict stories in the synoptic gospels have no formal dependence on other literary or popular forms of the period. They are as new in form as they are in content. They are presented in a form composed by early Christian storytellers specifically for the needs of the newly developing Christian movement.[5]

Thus, while first-century cultures did use dialogue—for example, in Aristotelean rhetorical debate and in Jewish rabbinic instruction—early Christianity developed its own distinctive forms involving questions and sayings. Hultgren offers examples of some conflict stories that seem to be in process of developing from earlier nondialogical source material. He then categorizes the stories as unitary and nonunitary. The unitary stories are those in which the concluding saying is directly related to the preceding dialogue. The nonunitary story appears to be an artificial construct surrounding a significant dominical saying. Hultgren's work is the most significant English language study of the conflict stories in the previous century and remains a major work on the subject.

There was a problem with early form criticism before Hultgren's work. Confronted with many somewhat varied examples of a particular form, scholars tended to reduce component parts to a recognizable minimum. For example, if there were variations in miracle stories—sometimes Jesus touches a person, other times he does not; sometimes Jesus warns people not to tell of their healing, other times there are no warnings—scholars tended to reduce the form to the bare minimum of the always recurring. Thus, miracle stories could be reduced to "someone is sick, they meet a healer, and someone is well," a definition that is not terribly helpful. By such a definition, all hospital medical records would qualify as miracle stories. Now that form criticism has morphed into contemporary literary or rhetorical criticism, we may want to describe a developed form, a "classic" model, rather than a reduction. In describing the conflict-pronouncement stories, I will try to do so.

Translations

I have provided translations of the stories. I hold no brief for my ability to transform a Greek text into speaker's English. While King James English may be breathtakingly beautiful at times, and even cadenced so as to be sung, nonetheless the King James Version misrepresents the accessibility of the biblical text. Koine Greek was the Greek of everyday conversation. Think of the mystery of God wrapped in everyday, almost casual, street language. Street language uses simple words, concrete images, and surprising metaphors, but seldom tries for erudition or parades complexity. No wonder that, as language changes—these days almost daily—we must retranslate biblical texts. I have tried to move toward contemporary speaker's language, but with some care so the texts are reliable for study.

A problem: How should I translate the complex but familiar term "Son of Man"? I wish to sidestep any hint of sexism. I could go with "child of humanity," a peculiar alternative. Or I could borrow "the Human One" as recommended in the National Council of Churches' *Inclusive Language Lectionary* (1983). With gratitude to the Jesus Seminar, I considered swiping their "son of Adam," recalling that the Hebrew word *adam* simply means "earthling." But with both "son" and "Adam," the term might seem very masculine indeed. Finally, I decided to go with the literal and quite awkward "son of humanity."

Another problem is "kingdom of God." The Greek *basileia,* though usually translated "kingdom," can be translated "realm" or "empire" just as well. "King" and "kingdom" are not specified. But though the term refers to a social order, it does not refer to a democracy. The *basileia* is definitely "of God." Thus, "kindom," a newly coined term, is not entirely helpful. The Jesus Seminar has chosen "God's Imperial Realm," which is okay, if a bit lumbering. I have used "kingdom" when referring to particular texts that are often so translated. Otherwise, I have tried to use terms such as "God's new order" or "God's social order."

I am not a guild biblical scholar. Therefore, I draw on the scholarship of others. Whenever we comment on biblical passages, we place ourselves in a progression of interpretation. We study the work of different scholars who themselves are drawing on the scholarship of those who have gone before them. Much scholarship is bound to be repetitive. I will be drawing on the work of many others. Where there is general agreement I will not document sources, but if I draw on a singular interpretation, I will cite a source. The bibliography lists the many books consulted. After each of the translated texts, mostly from the Gospel of Mark, I will mention variations to be found in other Gospels, if they are significant. Sometimes I will reverse the sequence, offering a text from Matthew or Luke and then looking back at an earlier version of the form in Mark.

Organization

Some years ago, I wrote a book on preaching the parables of Jesus. There I organized the parables by where they appear—in Mark, in Matthew, in Matthew and Luke, in Luke alone. This was easy and clear. But what about the controversies? I could try to distinguish controversies that seem historically likely within the life of Christ from those contrived amid later first-century conflicts, but this would be chancy guesswork at best. Or I could categorize based on the purpose of the controversies: those prompted by Jesus' behavior, those prompted by the disciples, those relating to the Christian life, and those occasioned by hot-potato social issues such as taxation. But again, while such divisions can be created, they might obscure the relationship between Mark's brilliant storytelling and the controversy material. Finally, I decided to present the stories in the sequential order of their appearance in Mark, but with some recognition of the groupings.

Sermons

Ministers like to have sermons included in their books, or so I am told by my publisher. Through the years, reluctantly, I have published a few sermons, originally in the old *Pulpit* magazine and then, almost exclusively, in the now defunct *Pulpit Digest*. I like the magazine's recent editor, splendid David Farmer. But in order to stock these pages with sermons, I have had to chase down some manuscripts, old and new, some published and others from file. A few go all the way back to days when, as the very young minister of a Presbyterian parish in Fredonia, New York, I was trying to learn how to preach. They were produced long before I wrote my *Homiletic* or considered the shape of biblical texts in any contemporary way. Most of them, though based on a biblical passage, distilled a general topic and then, in sections, made "points" and "subpoints." As a result, some of the sermons offend me now, and some have problems that clearly need correction. Therefore, I have followed each sermon with some critical notes. There are no perfect sermons, and we all can benefit from a backward glance at our ever imperfect products. Maybe we never do learn how to preach, which, of course, is what keeps homileticians busy.

Homiletics

Preachers sometimes suppose that all they need in order to preach is a limp Bible and the dramatic enabling of the Holy Spirit. But preaching requires theological smarts as well. The fascinating thing about the conflict-pronouncement stories is that they raise issues, perennial issues in Christian faith, that demand theological consideration. So after chasing down biblical information, we shall engage our theological brain cells before considering matters of homiletic construction. I regard the homiletic task as drawing on biblical study, theological reflection, cultural analysis, rhetorical strategy, pastoral sensitivity, poetics—so many different forms of wisdom!

Our Reformation forebears Luther and Calvin were firmly convinced that when preachers gathered such wisdom and spoke, they would convey God's "Word" to a congregation. The conviction has ebbed in an age when preachers can subscribe to precooked sermons and then reheat them in their own pulpits. The result: Our world suffers desperately from a dreadful silence of the true Word of God. Remember the prophet Amos:

A time is coming—declares my Lord God—when I will send a famine upon the land: not a hunger for bread or a thirst for water, but for hearing the words of the Lord. [People] shall wander from sea to sea and from north to east to seek the word of the Lord, but they shall not find it. (Amos 8:11–12)

Some months ago, I was asked to write a chapter on the question "What is the matter with preaching today?" a somewhat peculiar assignment.[6] I chased down some general concerns but finally came to the conclusion that for the most part mainline American preachers were frightened. Most local pulpits were silent when a bad war—indeed, a wicked, aggressive war such as the one in Iraq—was proposed, debated, and begun. Our silence was an indictment. Evidently our timid pulpits no longer dared to speak God's prophetic Word. If there is no Word of God, then people "wander from sea to sea," quite lost. The absence of the prophetic Word has condemned mainline American pulpits. As for "right-wing" pulpits that have fervently embraced the policies of a friendly president, I risk no comment. But current American policy both offshore and in-house, endorsed with uncritical enthusiasm by many American Christians, has begun to give our Christian faith a bad name.

The conflict stories we will be surveying raise issues, many of them still "hot issues" among Christian people. I will try to find ways to preach the passages with candor and yet concern for human sensibilities, and above all, I will try to learn from the controversy form a new and useful homiletic for the preaching of such passages.

Conflict-Pronouncement Stories in the Synoptic Gospels

Controversies over Healing	Matthew	Mark	Luke
Paralytic	9:1–8	**2:1–12**	5:17–26
Withered hand	12:9–14	**3:1–6**	6:6–11
Exorcism	12:22–37	**3:19b–30**	11:14–23
Woman bent from birth			13:10–17
Dropsical man			14:1–6

Controversies over Conduct			
Eating with sinners	9:10–13	**2:15–17**	5:29–32
Over fasting	9:14–17	**2:18–22**	5:33–39
Over plucking grain	12:1–8	**2:23–28**	6:1–5
True relatives	12:46–50	**3:31–35**	8:19–21
Over clean and unclean	15:1–20	**7:1–23**	
Demand for a sign	16:1–4	**8:11–13**	
Anointing at Bethany	26:6–13	**14:3–9**	
Woman at the feast			7:36–50

Controversies over Issues			
On divorce	19:1–12	**10:2–12**	
Over children	19:13–15	**10:13–16**	18:15–17
Rich young ruler	19:16–30	**10:17–31**	18:18–30
Sons of Zebedee	20:20–28	**10:35–45**	
Over authority	21:23–27	**11:27–33**	20:1–8
Tribute to Caesar	22:15–22	**12:13–17**	20:20–26
On the resurrection	22:23–33	**12:18–27**	20:27–40
The Great Commandment	22:34–40	**12:28–34**	10:25–28
David's son	22:41–46	**12:35–37**	20:41–44

Possible Controversies			
On John the Baptist	11:2–19		
Syrophoenician woman	15:21–28	**7:25–30**	
Coin in the fish	17:24–27		
Cursing a fig tree	21:18–22	**11:12–26**	

Chapter 1

The Shape of the Form

Many of us view the Gospel of Mark as a collection of miracle stories and, after the "Little Apocalypse" in chapter 13, a long passion narrative. Indeed, there are fifteen miracle stories in the first ten chapters of the Gospel, and the passion narrative does fill two long chapters. But we should not overlook the eighteen conflict-pronouncement stories that show up in bunches from chapter 2 through chapter 12. Actually the Gospel of Mark is made up of a mix of miracles and controversies followed by the Little Apocalypse and then an intense passion narrative. The conflict stories are a familiar, dramatic part of the homiletic canon, but they are especially difficult to interpret and to preach.

Though there is considerable variation in conflict-pronouncement stories, some with fewer parts, others with more, I will describe what might be termed a "classic" model:

1. A question is asked.
2. Jesus replies with a counterquestion.
3. Jesus delivers a concluding pronouncement.

Some scholars have reduced the form to no more than a question followed by a pronouncement, but the developed form almost always includes a counterquestion as well.

The Questions

The questions that initiate the conflict stories are many. Mostly they are asked by groups—scribes, Pharisees, elders, and so forth—less often by individuals. And behind every question is a situation and a controversy. Instead of a direct question, sometimes there is a statement that embodies a question or implies a controversial issue. For example, when Jesus' mother and brothers gather outside to corral him, the crowd says, "Look, your mother and your brothers and your sisters are outside wanting you." The implied question is "Why aren't you going to them?" Sometimes the situation implies a controversial issue, for example, when disciples try to prevent parents from bringing children to Jesus. Christian groups in the first century were concerned about the status of children within their communities. The question "What do we do with our young?" is lurking in the situation. But, for the most part, questions are actually spoken. Perhaps there's a way to catalog them all.

There are questions designed to trap Jesus. For example, in Mark 12:13–17, Pharisees and Herodians come "to trap him with his own words." So they ask, "Is it lawful to pay taxes to Caesar or not?" Because Roman tribute was demanded and despised, they are handing Jesus a no-win, loaded question. If Jesus says no, he might be subject to arrest; if he says yes, he will incur popular disapproval. Other issues generate other questions that are put to Jesus. When Jesus is asked to name the "great commandment" (Matt. 22:35–40), and again when he is quizzed on the subject of resurrection (Mark 12:18–27), he faces what appear to be no-win questions. Perhaps the question over divorce (Mark 10:2–12) was originally a troubling query, for there was sharp disagreement over grounds for divorce at the time of Christ. In every age, there are "hot-potato" issues, and Jesus was handed a few.

There are questions prompted by Jesus' own behavior. Jesus boldly announces a forgiveness of sins (Mark 2:1–12); he eats and drinks with known sinners (2:14–17); he heals on the Sabbath day (3:1–6); he seems to neglect his family (3:20, 31–35). Because of his free, unauthorized healing ministry, he is accused of serving Beelzebul (3:20–30). Then, after he initiates a prophetic disturbance in the Temple, he is quizzed over "authority" for his actions (11:27–33).

There are other questions prompted by the behavior of Jesus' disciples. The disciples do not fast regularly, as evidently did the disciples of John the Baptist (Mark 2:19–20); when walking through fields they pluck grain on the Sabbath day (2:23–28); and they eat at table without observing ritual cleanliness (7:1–23). Most of these stories may have been prompted by the activity of postresurrection Christian communities.

Finally, there appear to be questions prompted by controversy over the terms of Christian discipleship. Can people be wealthy and be Christian?—a valid question, particularly in capitalist America. As a result, there is the story of the "rich young ruler" (Mark 10:17–31). Can the Christian mission reach beyond Israel to Gentile lands? We get the great story of the Syrophoenician woman (7:24–30). Can Christians seek positions of power? There is the story of the sons of Zebedee wanting to be throned in triumph on either side of Jesus when God's new order arrives (10:35–45). Then there are different versions of the anointing at Bethany (14:1–9; Luke 7:36–50), which seem to raise an issue over the cost of pious devotion when there are poor folk in the land.

Of course, all these conflict stories are represented as happening within the lifetime of Jesus, whereas, in actuality, they may have been fabricated from later first-century controversy as an enlarging Christianity generated tension in Israel and then spread across the ancient Greco-Roman world. But, whatever the causes, Mark, or some previous source, seems to have collected conflict stories.

I have previously noted Arland J. Hultgren's *Jesus and His Adversaries* (1979). The book is the most comprehensive work on the conflict stories in the second half of the twentieth century. Hultgren draws a distinction between unitary and nonunitary stories. He argues that unitary stories may be primitive; indeed, a few may go back to Jesus. They are unitary because the final saying is directly related to the dialogue and the situation that has prompted dialogue. He lists the question over authority (Mark 11:27–33), which emerges quite naturally from the cleansing of the Temple (11:15–17), along with the cursing of the fig tree (11:20–26). He also concludes that the question of taxes to Caesar, the question of fasting, of healing on the Sabbath, and the story of the anointing by an unknown woman are all unitary stories. But Hultgren is drawing a *literary* distinction; he is not necessarily saying that some stories are connected with the historical Jesus while others are products of a subsequent Christian community. By contrast, nonunitary stories have dialogue and settings that appear somewhat artificial, as if designed specifically to present a dominical saying. The nonunitary stories he signals are the Beelzebul controversy (3:20–30), the healing of the paralytic (2:1–12), eating with tax collectors and sinners (2:14–17), plucking grain on the Sabbath (2:23–28), the "tradition of the elders" regarding hand washing (7:1–23), the controversy over divorce (10:1–11), and the debate over resurrection (12:18–27). Hultgren's literary-historical approach is cautious. Again, he is not trying to answer the historical question of which controversies might have occurred within the actual story of Jesus. Such a question is complicated and can only be ventured at best by educated guesswork.[1]

But all the conflict stories reflect situational issues, most of which are with us still. Thus, they all begin with a direct or an implied question.

The Counterquestions

Here's a theory: I believe the counterquestions asked directly or indirectly disclose the mind-set of Jesus' questioners. Almost all the controversies feature a counterquestion in reply to the question raised. A few of the stories have a countering statement, which most often could be rephrased as a question. There are only a few exceptions. For example, when Pharisees complain that Jesus is partying with riffraff, he answers with a proverb: "The healthy don't need a doctor, but the sick do." But the proverb also exposes the mind-set of Jesus' questioners: They view themselves as religiously healthy but regard Jesus' table guests as moral "sickies." A few times Jesus gives citations from Scripture, and some are phrased as questions—"Have you not read . . ."—but even when there is no actual question, Jesus' replies seem to disclose the orientation of his questioners. Let us look at a few examples of counterquestions:

> In a controversy over divorce, Jesus asks, "What does Moses tell you?" At once we realize that Jesus' opponents view divorce primarily as a legal issue. They are thinking within the law.
>
> Upon hearing that his mother and brothers are present and asking for him, Jesus counters with, "Who are my mother and my brothers?" We realize that Jesus' questioners are bound by kinship rules that he in turn is questioning from a much broader perspective.
>
> When the rich young man addresses Jesus as "good master," Jesus answers, "Why do you call me good? No one is good but God alone." We realize the young man is an unexamined moralist.
>
> In the debate over paying taxes, Jesus asks his opponents to show him a coin. They hold out an offensive Roman denarius hailing the divinity of Caesar rather than an inoffensive Jewish "denarius" decorated with temple symbols. Obviously, they are already financially involved with Rome.

Out of the more than twenty passages we will study, all but two contain a reply that can be said to disclose the mind of Jesus' questioners. Of the two, one is the brief passage about the children that disciples were trying to keep away from Jesus. His reply countermands their prohibition, and his remark "Of such is God's new order" certainly discloses an opposite mind-set. The other passage is the question of the Great Commandment, which Mark has turned into a sincere catechetical question. But Matthew, from his studied Jewishness, understands the request as a trick question and thus offers quite a different dialogue.

So those of us who interpret the controversy stories must stop and review Jesus' replies. Directly or indirectly, they will always disclose the mind-set of Jesus' opponents. Why is the discovery so crucial? Most of the stories label Jesus' questioners; they are Pharisees or scribes, Sadducees or Herodians, in effect, Jewish. In preaching, we are apt to label Jesus "Christian" and forget he is as Jewish as his contenders. Unfortunately, the same general mind-set is still with us and, more often than not, on display in our churches.

The counterquestions are crucial. Not only do they reveal the mind of Jesus' opponents, but frequently, by contrast, they tend to disclose Jesus' own position. Thus, they offer clues to the interpretation of pronouncements that follow. Though most scholars focus on the pronouncements—after all, they may have come from Jesus—I suspect the counterquestions are as significant.

The Pronouncements

Most of the pronouncements are epigrammatic in character. Usually they are brief and rhetorically striking. Here is a partial list:

> "The Sabbath was made for humanity, not humanity for the Sabbath."
> "Give to Caesar, Caesar's; [but] give to God, God's."
> "Whoever does the will of God is my mother, brother, sister."
> "What God has joined together, let no one rip apart."
> "Whoever wants to be great among you, must be your servant."
> "Who is forgiven little, loves little."
> "I didn't come to recruit the upright, but sinners."
> "No one puts new wine into old wineskins."
> "There is nothing from outside a person that can defile, but from inside a person are things that can defile."
> "Whoever will not accept God's rule like a child cannot enter the new order."
> "How hard it is for monied people to get into God's new order."
> "God is not a God of the dead, but of the living."

Above all, Jesus' pronouncements are nonlegal. They are not rules to obey. Instead, they might be termed a free wave toward the purposes of God. Because they are epigrammatic, they frequently force listeners to puzzle them out. But unpacked, they do seem to address the issues, invoke the presence of God and, at the same time, conclude the dialogue. For example, the enigmatic "Give to Caesar, Caesar's, and give to God, God's" may seem indistinct or even puzzling (it has puzzled church interpreters, draft boards, and politicians for centuries!). But Caesar distributed the Roman denarius, and minted coins were the property of the ruler who minted them, thus "Give to Caesar, Caesar's" is a blunt way of saying you got your money from Roman involvement, so you might as well pay off Caesar. But the parallel statement, "Give to God, God's" calls to mind the huge generosity of God—"The earth is the Lord's and the fullness thereof!" Another parallel construction appears in "The Sabbath was made for humanity, not humanity for the Sabbath." Sabbath observance is a gift of God, not only as it locates us worshipfully before God, but as it prevents a seven-day workweek, giving rest to weary workers. Strain on an unrested workforce is very much a problem in our world now. Above all, Sabbath regulation should set us free for God; it should never stifle or coerce.

There are some odd exceptions. There are three controversies over healing on the Sabbath: Mark 3:1–6, Luke 13:10–17, and 14:1–6. None of the stories conclude with a saying. In these cases, Jesus' immediate action to heal the person replaces any pronouncement. The story of Jesus and the Syrophoenician woman likewise ends abruptly with a healing.

The other interesting exception is a passage on authority—Mark 11:27–33. After the cleansing of the Temple, chief priests, scribes, and elders ask, "By what right do you do what you do? Who gave you authority?" Jesus hands them an implied counterquestion, saying, "If you'll answer me, I'll tell you by what authority I act." They refuse to answer him, so the passage ends dramatically without a pronouncement.

Pronouncements with Added Discussion

There are four cases where, at the end of a controversy story, there is an addendum, an additional discussion of issues, usually held privately between Jesus and his disciples. In some cases, these additional sections simply elaborate or clarify, as, for example, the material in Mark 7:17–23, 10:23–27, or 10:41–45. But there is one notable addition. The dispute over divorce ends with a saying, "What God has joined together, let no one rip apart." Then there is the usual reference to a separate conversation, Jesus alone with his disciples:

> In the house, the disciples asked him about this. And he said to them, "Whoever divorces his wife and marries another, commits adultery with her. And if she marries another after divorcing her husband, she commits adultery." (Mark 10:10–12)

Here we have a legal addition to the original controversy. The rules given are different between Mark and Matthew because of a specific ground for divorce that Matthew has added. But the language in both is legal. Subsequent church legislation has been added to a nonlegal pronouncement. But these exceptions prove the case. The pronouncements that conclude controversies are nonlegal in character. Instead, they are theological epigrams that call us to consider the mysterious purposes of God.

Ever since form critics first analyzed the controversy stories, they have tended to give special attention to these final sayings. Yes, some of the situational dialogue might seem contrived, but the sayings were accorded dominical status by some and thus were given a kind of scholarly priority. But, to be truthful, the pronouncements are more uncertain. Though some of the sayings are clever, crisp, and rhetorically well crafted, others seem labored or somewhat off-target given the preceding dialogue. Is style a giveaway?

Recent parable scholars have questioned some parables on the basis of style. Most of Jesus' parables begin in the everyday world but then include some sudden surreal detail—workers hired to work different hours are all paid the same, a spurned host invites street bums to a wedding banquet, a woman hunts all day to find a small lost coin but then throws a huge expensive party with neighbors in the middle of the night to celebrate her find. The stories are strange. But a few of the parables are positively plebeian, without much wit or surprise, and these parables scholars tend to view with suspicion. In like manner, most pronouncements are epigrammatic and sharp, but must we not wonder about those that are somewhat labored? Controversies within the life of the early Christian movement were very real and often heated, but what if there was no remembered saying of Jesus that seemed to apply? Did the community shape one? Having wrestled with the issue, did the community form a useful saying that they then attributed to their Lord? Likely, Jesus had a crisper style than his followers—and probably still does.

Groups of Sayings

Long ago, scholars noticed that the conflict stories came in bunches: (1) There are five of them from Mark 2:1 to Mark 3:6; (2) there seem to be four in chapter 10 from verse 1 to verse 45; and (3) there are four more in chapter 12 from verse 13 to verse 37. There are a few controversies scattered elsewhere, but these three sets appear to be deliberately organized.

Scholars have remarked that Mark 2:1–3:6 seems to be a package. Perhaps the stories came as a set from a separate source or, possibly, Mark crafted the material. The section begins and finally ends with a controversy over healing. In between, there are three conflict stories having to do with eating and drinking. So a rhetorical pattern emerges:

Healing (by Jesus)—2:1–12
   Eating (by Jesus)—2:14–17
      Fasting (disciples) vs. eating—2:18–20
   Eating (disciples) on the Sabbath—2:23–28
Healing (by Jesus) on the Sabbath—3:1–6

Joanna Dewey, whose dissertation, *Markan Public Debate*, has provided the most comprehensive study of the section, notes that all the stories are prompted by behavior—indeed, scandalous behavior—on the part of Jesus and his disciples.[2] What's more, the behavior in question is central to Jesus' ministry, namely, his healings and his inclusive meals. But they draw opposition. Jesus' unauthorized healing prompts criticism, and his meals offend those who cataloged sinners or required ritual purity.

The conflict stories in Mark 12 also have been studied. David Daube, in his *The New Testament and Rabbinic Judaism,* has an essay on the four types of questions involved in Mark's final controversies.[3] Daube argues that whoever put the stories together, presumably Mark or one of his sources, was familiar with a rabbinic tradition. The Talmud reports that Alexandrians put twelve questions to Rabbi Joshua ben Hananian, questions that could be grouped in four categories, three in each. There were three questions of *hokhma,* "wisdom," usually questions concerning points of law; three questions of *haggadah,* usually over contradictions in Scripture; three questions of *boruth,* "vulgarity," which were a mocking ridicule of beliefs; and finally three questions of *derekh 'eres,* about "the moral or successful life." The tradition of four types of questions also appears in the Passover Haggadah. In the Haggadah for the Seder, four sons ask questions: the first son asks a "wisdom" question over a point of law, the second son asks a scoffing question, the third son asks a simple pious question, but the fourth son doesn't know how to ask a question, so his father poses a question instead. Daube argues that the pattern underlies the four final controversies in Mark 12, and he makes a strong case for his contention: The conflict over taxes to Caesar is a matter of law; the ridiculous question over levirate marriage ridicules belief in resurrection; the question over the Great Commandment is asked in simple piety; and finally, Jesus himself poses a question about Messiah as a "Son of David."

What about the questions in Mark 10? They have been studied less probingly, but they are significant. These four questions all seem to have to do with the character of a disciple. Can disciples be divorced? Can children be considered disciples? Can disciples be rich? Can disciples desire to be powerful? Three of these controversies include additional private instruction for the disciples, and in a fourth, the question of children is provoked when the disciples attempt to exclude kids from the presence of Jesus. So these conflict stories do seem to be specifically designed to answer what today might be termed "church questions."

Situational Controversies

In studying the conflict stories, I have been struck by their perennial relevance. They express issues that through the centuries have surfaced repeatedly in religious communities, Christian and non-Christian alike. H. Richard Niebuhr's *Christ and Culture* offers a brilliant classification of options: How do our religious communities relate to their surrounding culture? (1) Do we go along, embracing a modified "culture religion"? (2) Do we oppose, regarding the world around as a contaminating danger? (3) Do we withdraw from social structures in an attempt to live strictly within some sort of alternative world? (4) Or, evangelically, do we seek to transform the world around us?[4] Tension between world and cult seems inevitable. Are the conflict stories perennial controversies that recur generation after generation within all religious communities? Perhaps. Maybe the struggle to love God and love neighbors in a sin-struck human world will always generate peculiar tensions and, thus, situational controversy. Certainly today in our changing world there are huge, unresolved religious issues. The conflict stories of Jesus can help us to understand and, perhaps, to meet such issues with graceful wisdom.

Chapter 2

Problems, Problems, Problems

*T*here are problems peculiar to preaching the conflict-pronouncement stories. Here are the most obvious:

> How can we preach stories of Jesus that may never have happened but were created by later Christian communities?
>
> What can we do to prevent stories of Jesus versus Jewish leaders from fanning the anti-Judaism that lives, mostly unacknowledged, in all our congregations?
>
> Can we make sense of the "Son of Man" phrase that appears in three of the conflict stories but, though unwritten, may underlie all?

Ministers may tend to ignore such problems, regarding them as nitpicky scholarly stuff that has little or nothing to do with preaching the gospel message. But, stop and think: What if Gospel authors themselves wrote anti-Judaism into our biblical texts? Then, in the name of the gospel message of God's generous covenant love, must we not correct Scripture with our preaching? And suppose we discover that a conflict story could not have happened and in fact is a caricature of the true Jesus. Do we hide the discovery from our congregation so as not to trouble their faith? What about the statement "The son of humanity is Lord of the Sabbath"? Is Jesus setting himself above God's Sabbath day, or is he saying that any child of humanity can decide how to honor the Sabbath, or what? The problems are anything but abstruse. They have a bearing on the kind of gospel message we preach.

Problems we face in the conflict stories are troubling. Here I will try to identify the full nature of each problem. In a subsequent chapter, I will seek solutions—practical, pulpit solutions.

The Problem of Authenticity

At the outset, there is the problem of authenticity. Long ago Rudolf Bultmann suggested that many of the conflict stories do not go back to actual situations involving Jesus but that Mark is drawing on later first-century controversies between a fledgling Christian movement and its Jewish origins.[1] Other scholars agreed that while some of the stories were uncertain historically or quite obviously contrived to frame pronouncements, the pronouncements themselves may be words of Jesus.[2] But generally, Bultmann's thesis has been accepted by many if not most scholars. When it comes to history, the stories are uncertain. If a number of the conflict stories have been retrojected—that is, written back into the life of Jesus—and thus did not actually happen, how can preachers preach? Do we tell our listeners that the stories are not certifiable history? Most preachers would rather not. When it comes to the Bible, most people in the pews tend to be quite literal. There is a kind of crypto-fundamentalism lurking in most congregations. People are apt to be deeply troubled by suggestions that, though the Bible says Jesus spoke or acted in certain ways, in fact he may have done neither.

At the outset, we should recognize that the problem is larger than conflict stories. Here is how 1 Timothy begins: "Paul, an apostle of Christ Jesus by the command of God our Savior and of Christ Jesus our hope, to Timothy, my loyal child in the faith." In spite of the ascription, almost all scholars doubt Paul was the author of the letter. The style, theology, and references to the life of the church reflect a different age. Presumably someone has written under the pseudonym of "Paul," probably around fifty years after Paul's martyrdom. The unknown author is saying, "If Paul were alive and writing today, this is what he would write to us." Such a practice was not uncommon in the ancient world.[3] So should we ignore scholarship and tell congregations that Paul wrote 1 and 2 Timothy? No. Above all, preachers ought to seek truth and, if possible, speak truthfully. Of course, we should "speak truth in love," but love should not dictate speaking untruth in order to protect people from their own untaught, immature faith. Can we not preface a Scripture reading from 1 Timothy with a brief explanation of pretended authorship? Is it too difficult to say, "whoever wrote Timothy," in our sermons? If we have been teaching the Bible properly in our congregations, a big *if* these days, there should be no problem. Admittedly, lately some denominational Bible study resources have taken an overly cautious approach and, quite unhelpfully, have catered to naive biblical literalism. After all, if they offend, they might lose sales. We do not need to play such games. Preaching may not be classroom teaching, but it should not ignore or contradict all-but-certain, majority scholarship.

Lately some conservative critics have complained that major theological faculties are ignoring conservative scholarship. The answer is twofold. Yes, most university divinity schools have not hired *very* conservative scholars, that is, fundamentalist scholars. Why would they? In the name of "fairness" should university geology departments hire faculty from the Flat Earth Society? Actually, there are many fine university divinity schools with theologically conservative faculty members. In the recent flap over the "historical Jesus," prompted in part by the work of the Jesus Seminar, most biblical scholars appear to be on the conservative side, that is, in general, they support biblical testimony. The other thing that must be noted is that American Christianity, like the nation, is politically split. The complaint that biblical scholarship is controlled by liberal faculties is about as silly as the idea that the press is "liberal"; repeatedly, such statements have been proven fanciful at best. Most news sources are owned by corporations, and corporate America has never been dangerously liberal about anything. But these days, in a culturally divided America, all areas of thought appear to be split into contending camps. At a time when the nation desperately needs an articulate Christianity, are we too subdivided to speak?

Of course, some preachers argue that scholars never agree and that, therefore, they should not presume to pick and choose among scholarly nuances. I confess I find the argument annoying. Are clergy not "theologians in residence" for a congregation? Have we not done some graduate study to prepare ourselves to interpret the faith? Actually, most of the time, on most basic biblical matters, scholars do agree. The notion that scholars are endlessly uncertain, divided, and contentious is a form of popular anti-intellectualism. Trained ministers are acquainted with biblical scholarship; thus, they should be able to make decisions in helping their people to understand Scripture. Of course, if we do opt for truth, we should never get our pulpit "kicks" out of debunking the traditional faith of the church. We need to be sensitive. Above all, we should be faithful to the gospel tradition. But let us not be afraid to shape a grown-up grasp of the Bible in our congregations.

Lately some Christians worry that such learning will undercut "the authority of Scripture." But protecting a notion of sovereign inerrancy is foolish; the Bible may be unfailing, but it is not inerrant. The Bible had human authors, and infallibility is not exactly a human attribute. Think of God's amazing grace in trusting the Word to us unreliable human creatures. So, first, let us regard the Bible as a good gift God has given us. If the Bible is a gift of God, it will establish its own credentials. Foolish efforts to protect "God's Word" will only lead to bibliolatry. Our task is not to protect but to interpret the Bible. Second, the whole notion of a dominating authority simply does not match the nature of our God, a God whose sovereignty is symbolically on display in the utter helplessness of the cross. Instead of a dominating authority model, can we not regard Scripture as a gift, a gift of God we can receive gratefully, enjoy, study, learn, love? Recent "Word of God" theology has not been helpful. If we label Scripture "Word of God," we may find it difficult to admit that Paul could not have scribbled 1 Timothy, that stories of Jesus may not have happened as reported, or that Gospel texts might express a degree of sneaky anti-Judaism. Maybe we should recall Luther. For him, gospel preaching was the Word of God, and the Bible could be labeled "Word of God" as well because it contains gospel preaching—not because it is a magic, infallible Godbook. With regard to the Bible, "contains" is always a better word than "is."

So what can we do? In every congregation we can teach our people how the Bible came to be. Clearly, God did not dictate every page to blank-brained, pre-programmed scribes. Nor did whole books drop from the sky on angel wings. Writing, collecting, copying, and editing, though prompted by the Spirit, were human actions and thus subject to human error and slanted human perspectives. Those who demand an inerrant Bible edge toward heresy, wanting to replace God, in whose mystery we "live and move and have our being," with a book. Clearly, the Bible contains "a saving knowledge of God" but also many different theologies, primitive cosmologies, peculiar notions of science, medicine, and psychology, as well as some thoroughly discredited social customs—for example, slavery, the subjection of women, and apparent anti-Judaism in some of the Gospel records. Historically, the Bible is a human product, drawn from oral tradition and written down over a thousand-year period. Nevertheless, in our communities of faith, we believe the Bible is a gift, a gift of grace for us all, containing a redeeming "knowledge of God."

The conflict stories, however, present a peculiar problem because they tell about Jesus, in debate with opponents, asking questions and saying sayings. In older Bibles, they would be "red letter" stories. Who wrote the two letters to Timothy is not a crucial question for most congregations. Nor will they care much if 2 Peter was not written by the author of 1 Peter and if neither author was the renowned disciple Peter. But stories of Jesus, what he did and what he said, are much more disturbing. Think of the stir kicked up among Christians by the Jesus Seminar. The Seminar published a translation of the Gospels in which the words of Jesus are color-coded according to probability—red, "Likely Jesus said them"; pink, "He probably said something similar"; gray, "Though Jesus didn't say them, the words are a useful contribution from a later Christian community"; black, "Nope, he never said such words." The Seminar has been attacked (often scurrilously), ridiculed, and resented by Christians even though much the same research was conducted years ago by scholars at the University of Chicago and elsewhere. The real problem: Leaders of the Seminar believe churches have kept parishioners in the dark on much recent biblical scholarship; therefore, the Seminar has deliberately publicized its findings. But what if we printed a Bible in which many of the conflict-pronouncement stories were printed in gray, some in black, and none with pink or red? We are dealing with a complicated problem.

Perhaps some conflict stories do reach back to the actual time of Jesus and do report controversies that may well have happened. But no trained scholar has been able to sort the stories successfully—this one is historical, this one is not. Stories that Hultgren labeled unitary may well go back to incidents in Jesus' life, their situations are vivid and coherent—but can we be absolutely sure? The early Christian movement might have provoked similar questions in similar contexts some years after Jesus' death and resurrection. Retrojection, the reading back of a present context into the past, is probable in many of the stories.

Obviously, Jesus stirred up opposition. But was most of Jesus' opposition Jewish? Probably not; crucifixion was a Roman practice. Jesus may have raised some eyebrows by welcoming ragtag, disreputable folk at table, and he may well have healed on the Sabbath, for there are several such stories. Possibly he did not maintain traditional days of fasting. Certainly he could have been alienated from his family. Would he have been questioned on taxation? Probably. But, again, the early Christian movement, adding Gentile members, may well have provoked similar questions and somewhat more stridently. There is evidence that early Christians may have dropped fasting and then, subsequently, reinstituted it on different days. Certainly, Gentile believers as well as social misfits were welcomed at eucharistic meals, and such inclusiveness might have seemed offensive to Jewish witnesses. What about "family values"? Evidently, early Christian leaders, busy spreading the gospel, were blamed for neglecting their families. As for Sabbath observance, historically the Sabbath was gradually demoted as "Lord's Day" worship became the norm. So, here's the question: Are situations the stories contain representative of Jesus, or of his subsequent followers? Some Jewish scholars have read the collection of controversies in Mark 2:1–3:6, stories that conclude dramatically with "Immediately, the Pharisees and Herodians went out and consulted against him, plotting to destroy him," and find the tag line most unlikely. After all, what is so scandalous about conflicts over food and Sabbath observance? They were matters under discussion among faithful Jews at the time of Christ. Certainly, they were never capital offenses. No one would want to plot Jesus' death for eating with sinners or healing on the Sabbath. But later, after Jesus' death and resurrection, as the fledgling Christian movement enlarged and loosened ties with the Jewish world, hostilities may have bristled on both sides. Moreover, such matters might have provoked the religious piety of devoutly religious "pagans" among Greeks and Romans as well.

The Problem: How can we preach conflict stories that may never have happened?

The Problem of Anti-Judaism

Here's another problem, a much more serious problem: The stories picture Jesus in sharp conflict with religious leaders of Israel; in effect, Jesus versus Jews.[4] Anti-Judaism began early and has haunted Christian history for centuries. But now we live in a post-Shoah world where Christian preachers have redoubled responsibility. They must be alert to guard against incautious language that might exacerbate congregational anti-Judaism. Such prejudice exists among Christian people and is expressed by us in different ways—from Jewish "profiling" to supersessionism—but is always intolerable, whether pictured in a Mel Gibson film or spoken in sermons. Anti-Judaism haunts most Christian congregations and, unfortunately, seems deeply embedded in the American social mind. Perhaps it is on the increase of late, for in the past two decades we have been shocked by swastikas scrawled on synagogue walls, by the desecration of Jewish cemeteries, and by air-headed remarks from some Christian leaders ("God doesn't hear Jewish prayers"). The rise of a fairly aggressive evangelical movement may have exacerbated the problem, but anti-Judaism has been with us since the early days of the American religious enterprise and, obviously, is with us today, expressed either by obtuseness or by indifference. So, if only for the sanctification of Christian people who may be captive to cultural anti-Judaism, we must address the issues.

The serious problem we face as Christians is the unacknowledged anti-Judaism of our own Gospels: Mark, Matthew, Luke, and John.[5] Some scholars insist that the Gospel records are neutral but that interpretation over the centuries has been bigoted.[6] They have documented such bigotry, which, unfortunately, is easy.[7] There is no doubt that our interpretations of Gospel texts and Pauline epistles have been skewed by unexamined prejudice, but are the Gospels and Epistles themselves free from anti-Jewish bias? The question is difficult to answer. Our Gospels, all written sometime between 60 CE and the dawning of the second century, may have been influenced by Jewish-Christian conflict and, of course, by a desire on the part of Gospel authors to accommodate an emerging Gentile constituency. No doubt Matthew's "Jesus synagogue" was assailed by nearby traditional Jewish synagogues. There was obvious bitterness.[8] At least one strand of the Gospel of John may reflect a similar conflict. As a result, the Fourth Gospel seems strident toward "the Jews."[9] Luke, writing for a Gentile audience, appears to blame Jewish leadership for the death of Christ, even though crucifixion was a Roman punishment and Pilate had a well-deserved reputation for precipitous cruelty.[10] But what about Mark?[11] In some ways Mark seems sensitive to Jewish people and to Jewish piety. Mark's Jesus maintains a Jewish prayer life, attends synagogue, endorses the Shema, and observes Passover. Moreover, his Jesus, even in controversy, seems familiar with discussions of halakah, the Jewish way of life involving prayer, fasting, almsgiving, Sabbath observance, ritual washing, and so forth. But Mark has collected conflict stories, which in turn have been picked up by Matthew and Luke. They pit Jesus against the religious leadership of Israel—scribes, Pharisees, Sadducees, priests. In Mark, the conflict stories seem to lead directly to the passion narrative, in which the same religious leaders are pictured as involved. There is a high level of bitterness tucked in the stories, and bitterness always seems contagious. Jesus may well have spoken with the flashing tough truth of a Jewish prophet, but subsequently his truth may have been reshaped out of bitterness during Christianity's transitional struggle from Jewish sectarian status to a Gentile religious movement. The conflict stories may well get at the essential posture of Christian moral freedom, but they have been mispreached and still are dangerous.

The Gospels have shaped Christian minds for centuries, especially as usual readings during annual celebrations of Holy Week. Intended or not, the Gospels have promoted anti-Judaism in Christian communities. Though we can explain how and why apparent hostility toward the Jews was written into the Gospels, such explanations do not ease the problem and seldom if ever trickle down to local parishes. In spite of enlightened criticism of the Gospels, scripturally shaped anti-Judaism is still very much a problem. Of late, it may be heightened by renewed assertions of biblical authority both from neofundamentalist groups and from widespread Barthian "Word of God" theology. If the Gospels are the literal "Word of God," then does God lay blame for Christ's death mostly on the Jewish community?

Since the mid-twentieth century, the problem of anti-Judaism in Christian communities has become particularly urgent. Now we preach in the shadow of the Holocaust, an event of such appalling cruelty as to call the gospel itself into question. Arthur Miller's *After the Fall* takes place on a bare, multileveled stage, which represents different levels of memory in the mind of a man named Quentin. But at the back of the stage, "rising above . . . and dominating the stage is the blasted stone tower of a German concentration camp," a symbol of the Holocaust. Throughout the two-act drama, Quentin speaks of the dark tower; he senses that the tower questions him: "'What do you believe as true as this? Yes! Believers built this, maybe that's the fright—and I, without belief, stand here disarmed." Later he admits, "What is the cure? Who can be innocent again on this mountain of skulls? . . . Our hearts have cut these stones! And what's the cure?"[12] Christian preachers must stand before the fact of the Holocaust and ask if the faith we declare, once scribbled down in somewhat anti-Jewish Gospel writings, can offer a "cure" or be "as true" as the Holocaust. Somehow or other we must speak so congregations may consider the deep issues of what is often termed "Jewish-Christian dialogue," a dialogue that takes place these days in the shadow of the same dark tower.

There is another, more complex level of the problem. The conflict-pronouncement stories have contributed to a theological theme: law versus grace. The theme is shaped by somewhat slanted interpretations of Paul's Letter to the Galatians, as well as the famous fifth chapter of his Letter to the Romans: those who are justified by grace through faith are free of the law. But Paul himself, born a Jew, *never* denigrates God's law; for Paul, God's law is just, and good, and holy.[13] Nevertheless, particularly in Protestantism, Martin Luther and Paul have shaped a theological hermeneutic that reads the conflict-pronouncement stories as law versus grace, with the grace of God in Christ Jesus triumphing every time. Preachers follow suit. Jewish champions of the law are pictured as rigid villains who are enemies of the liberating gospel Jesus has given us. Overstated, the theological position leads directly to the Marcionite heresy, namely, that the Jewish Bible preaches a God of law whereas Christian faith declares a good God of grace—in effect, two different Gods. Historically, there is no doubt that in his old age Luther became stridently hostile to the Jewish tradition.[14] Was anti-Judaism endemic to his thought all along? Calvin, equipped with legal training, was clearly much more sympathetic to the Hebrew tradition. But both Reformers read the controversies in the light of Protestantism's own struggles with an established Catholic Church—thus, as stories of a proto-Protestant Jesus in conflict with rigid representatives of repressive Catholic religion. Maybe, just maybe, we could teach congregations to sort through biblical texts to weed out anti-Judaism, but are ministers willing to modify theological traditions in which they live? If we are to escape our own anti-Judaism, we will have to do more than reinterpret biblical texts. We will have to reexamine and question our own theologies, a truly threatening task.

The Problem: How can we prevent anti-Judaism in our preaching?

The "Son of Humanity" Texts

In a way, the two "son of humanity" (NRSV, "Son of Man") texts may seem like a minor problem, but every Gospel shapes "son of humanity" texts differently, and controversy over their interpretation has gone on for centuries. Can the problem of meaning be solved? Probably not. But let us start with the basic problem of translation and see what we can discover. The title "son of humanity" (*ho huios tou anthropou*) requires some further investigation. The phrase seems to be used in several different ways in the Hebrew Scriptures:[15]

1. As a confession of our common humanity before God. Thus, Job 25:4–6 compares human impurity with God's perfect holiness:

> How can [a human] be in the right before God?
>   How can one born of woman be cleared of guilt?
> Even the moon is not bright,
>   and the stars are not pure in His sight;
> How much less a human being, a worm,
>   and the [son of Adam], a maggot.

In the parallel constructions of Hebrew poetry, "son of Adam" echoes "human being" in the previous line.

2. In the start of the book of Ezekiel, after an awesome vision of Glory, the prophet, left prostrate, hears a voice addressing him, "O son of Adam, stand up on your feet, that I may speak to you" (2:1). Thereafter the term is used repeatedly as the prophet's self-designation. *Tanakh* translates the term "O Mortal," supposing that, after the numinous vision of glory, a prophet would be acutely aware of his finite human nature.[16] The NRSV uses the same substitute.

3. But in Psalm 8:3–6 the title is used both to confess humanity's lowly status before God and, at the same time, as image of God, a God who has conferred authority on human beings:

> When I behold your heavens, the work of your fingers,
>   the moon and the stars that You set in place;
> What is human being that You have been mindful of him,
>   [son of Adam] that You have taken note of him?
> that You have made him a little less than divine,
>   and adorned him with glory and majesty;
> You have made him master over Your handiwork,
>   laying the world at his feet.

Notice the sharp contrast here: human beings seem insignificant beside the creative power of God, but, nonetheless, God honors humanity and designates human beings to manage creation. "Son of Adam" also appears in Psalm 80:17a: "Grant your help to the [son of adam] at Your right hand" (NRSV has "the one"), where the term seems to refer back to "the vine" of Israel.

4. Finally, the term shows up in the apocalyptic visions in Daniel 7:13–14:

> As I looked on, in the night vision,
> One like a [*son of Adam*]
> Came with the clouds of heaven;
> He reached the Ancient of Days

and was presented to Him.
Dominion, glory, and kingship were given to him;
All peoples and nations of every language must serve him.
His dominion is an everlasting dominion that shall not pass away,
and his kingship one that shall not be destroyed.

Usually scholars have supposed that early Christians grabbed the image from
Daniel and shaped it into "second coming" expectations. But recent scholar-
ship, drawing on the *Similitudes of Enoch* and *Pseudo-Ezra*, suggests that
Jewish messianic speculation had fixed on Daniel 7 before Christians arrived.

The "Son of Humanity" in Mark

In Mark, an apocalyptic Gospel, there are "son of humanity" texts that draw
on Daniel's vision depicting a heavenly cloud-borne figure coming to judge
the world (8:38; 13:26; 14:62). Though these references are put on the lips
of Christ, more likely they reflect second-coming convictions of an early
Christian community. Elsewhere Mark uses the term in connection with predictions of Jesus' suffering and death (8:31; 9:9, 12, 31; 10:33–34, 45; 14:21;
14:41). Finally, there are two uses of "son of humanity" in conflict stories: in
2:10 and subsequently in 2:28.[17] These uses would appear to reflect Psalm 8,
for though they acknowledge a common humanity before God, at the same
time they point to a conferred authority: "so you'll know the son of humanity has authority to forgive sins."

But here is the troubling question: Within the conflict stories, what does the
phrase mean?

> Is "son of humanity" an arrogant claim? "I, Jesus, as God's 'only begot-
> ten son,' have special conferred authority to announce the forgiveness
> of sins." Again, "I, Jesus, have special authority to regulate the Sab-
> bath day." Has Mark put a boldly overstated christological claim on
> Jesus' lips?
> Is "son of humanity" a term that affirms simple humanity? Is Jesus des-
> ignating himself as a human being among human beings? Therefore,
> by inference, does it mean that any human being can announce God's
> mercy, that any human being has authority over the observance of the
> Sabbath day?
> Is "son of humanity" a term referring to the notion of a "new humanity,"
> namely, members of God's coming social order? May Christian com-
> munities, as an "advance guard" of the coming new order, declare
> God's mercy and transform the Sabbath day?
> Is "son of humanity" a term that refers to authentic humanity—a true
> humanity that God intends and to which we should all aspire?

The issues are complex and are provoked by only two specific texts among the many conflict stories. But Jesus seems to speak as the son of humanity in all of the stories. So we are faced with a major interpretive decision.

The Problem: How are we to understand the "son of humanity" texts?

Problems and Church Programs

Can we solve these serious problems in the pulpit? Obviously, we are not supposed to give up whole sermons to such issues. Our mandate is to declare the good news of God. What we can do is to develop a somewhat multiphased strategy within our congregations.

We can teach. Most churches have one or many Bible study groups. Sometimes they examine passages prompted by the lectionary, sometimes they use "uniform lessons" provided by Bible societies or by denominations, and sometimes they work through particular Bible books a passage at a time. But frequently there is no general course on how the Bible came to be, on mysteries of authorship, on the where and when of composition. Though there are "introductions" to the various books in most Bibles, they are often overcautious. Thus, churches can avoid critical questions. We must begin to supplement Bible study circles with a more mature look at the whole Bible, its many different perspectives, its forms, redactions, and the like. Ministers have been trained for such a task.

With special regard to the issue of anti-Judaism, in addition to classroom study of the problem with post-Shoah sensitivity, we can and should inaugurate discussion with nearby synagogues.[18] But Jewish communities may not welcome you. Many have been victims of aggressive Christians trying to rush reconciliation while at the same time pushing Jesus on them. But communicant classes can visit synagogues. And interfaith dialogue can be part of every church's long-term purpose. With Judaism, we are seeking to restore what might be termed a family relationship, so eating together is a dandy suggestion. We should be starting such a program because responsibility for anti-Judaism for the most part has been a Christian disgrace.

We must be sure that worship always incorporates forms of praise drawn from the Psalms, as well as regular readings from Hebrew Scriptures. Lately, particularly in churches that use the lectionary, most ministers seem to be preaching from the "Gospel lessons." A theological tragedy![19] Not only should texts from the Hebrew Scriptures be read, they should be preached regularly. How can Christians understand themselves without hearing liberation stories of the exodus? Or how can we think theologically without profound stories from the first eleven chapters of Genesis? Or how can we grasp our own lives except in view of the mysterious interrelating of YHWH (whose name may not be spoken) and Israel? The neglect of our profound origins in Israel is a modern-day Christian scandal.

These are only a few ventured proposals to shape the life of all Christian communities. We will turn to discuss the particular problems of preaching conflict stories in the next chapter.

Chapter 3

Problem Solving

*H*ow can we preach the conflict stories? Problems are formidable. Yet the stories collected by Mark, revised and repeated by Matthew and Luke, are a substantial part of our Gospel record. They cannot be scrapped. If your church follows a lectionary, almost all of them will appear over a three-year cycle. The stories have been in the "homiletic canon" for centuries and, thus, for centuries sermons may have pitted Jesus against "the Jews." If we dare to admit that there might be unintended but quite potent anti-Jewish prejudice within our Holy Scripture, then the task of preaching will require both discernment and homiletic skill.

Scribes, Pharisees, Sadducees, and Herodians

We can help our congregations by choosing Scripture translations carefully or, if need be, providing substitute terminology, as when the Jesus Seminar changes "scribes" to "scholars." Most controversies seem to feature scribes and/or Pharisees. But there are other Jewish leaders that show up on occasion: Herodians, Sadducees, priests, chief priests, elders, and "a leader of the synagogue." A few times questions are posed by Jesus' own disciples, but they are often articulating usual social understandings. Thus, our problem: Most of the conflict stories seem to pit Jesus against Jews.

Friendly sparring partners might not be troubling, but in Mark Jewish leaders question Jesus with regard to his relationship to God's law and to the rituals of devout Jewish piety. Thus, the stories are not merely Jesus versus Jewish leaders, but seem to be Jesus versus Judaism. Because of the conflict stories, through the years Christian preaching has denigrated Jewish piety as obstructing God's true purposes. Pharisees and scribes are pictured as rigid, rather snide critics who are either unbearable legalists or are preoccupied with the morally trivial. Once stock understandings form, such scenarios tend to predetermine subsequent preaching. Sermons on the conflict stories are dangerous; not only may they misrepresent Judaism, but they may misrepresent Jesus, a faithful child of Israel, as well.

At the outset, we who preach should do our homework. Who are these different Jewish groups?[1] Descriptions are hard to come by. We have the works of Josephus, and in two of his writings he describes three politically important groups in Israel: Pharisees, Sadducees, and Essenes. But the descriptions are sketchy. He also refers to a "Fourth Philosophy," which apparently could include zealous Israelites who might have leaned toward insurrection. In addition to Josephus, there are rabbinic writings that look back to the time of the Pharisees. Of course, we also have references in Christian Scriptures: the Synoptic Gospels and the epistles of Paul, himself perhaps a one-time Pharisee. But in the sources, descriptions are scant and references shaped by very different perspectives.

The *scribes* (Greek, *grammateus*) are difficult to describe because there were many of them in the ancient world and they appear to have performed many different tasks. Among them were teachers and Scripture scholars but also managers, accountants, secretaries, record keepers, and governmental and temple bureaucrats; they were everywhere in the ancient world where reading and writing were needed. Though they served ruling structures in government, Temple, and finance, they were dependent on these same structures, for though they advised those who ruled, they were not rulers themselves. Even small villages might have had the services of a scribe as teacher, record keeper, and as a resource person for community religious life. Scribes ranged along the economic scale from poor village functionaries to those who served kings and thus might enjoy a higher level of status.

In Mark, scribes seem to be scholars who represent perspectives of the Jerusalem Temple. They are featured in many of the conflict stories, sometimes as "scribes down from Jerusalem," sometimes in tandem with Pharisees, and once as "the Pharisees' scribes." Recent scholarship suggests that some of them may have been Levites or even priests.[2] Nonetheless, in the controversies they are viewed as teachers who speak from scholarly learning. They are troubled by the actions of Jesus.

Sadducees seem to have been affluent pragmatic power people; they were from the ruling class. They were often high-level government people or perhaps high-level temple priests. Basically, they were social and political conservatives. They united in seeking to preserve traditions, in effect, to champion the status quo. Therefore, they were not a socially sizeable group. When it came to interpretation of Scripture, supposedly they were "strict constructionists." They supported traditional understandings, traditional rituals, and traditional social structures as God-given. If Scripture is a "light," they might have tended to see the light pointing down to form a circle in which we all should live and from which we should never wander. Their God is holy and transcendent but seems strangely distant from human affairs. Generally,

Sadducees opposed Pharisees, whom they viewed as favoring social change. Sadducees appear in only one of the conflict stories, where they challenge Jesus on the subject of the resurrection. Jesus and the Pharisees both affirm faith in resurrection; Sadducees do not.

The *Pharisees* (from the Hebrew *parus*, "separated") have gotten bad press in the modern world. We describe morally repressive people with scorn as "pharisaical," which one dictionary defines as "self-righteously obsessed with rules." The Pharisees were a religious-social-political group and, perhaps, a kind of pious luncheon club as well. In America we speak of a separation of church and state and suppose we can guard the distinction, but in the ancient world political, social, and religious concerns were not separable. Pharisees were numerically small, totaling not much more than a thousand, but they were often influential. Though Pharisees, unlike Sadducees, were not members of the ruling class, they sought to influence rulers and, if possible, to win support from rulers so as to influence society. Evidently they were social moderates with genuine religious concern for the poor. If Sadducees were almost never popular, Pharisees did enjoy considerable social approval. They were not rigid "strict constructionists" but sought with moral vigor to move law virtuously into many aspects of daily life. If the law is a light, they wanted it to illumine all of life. They were strong supporters of the Temple and the temple tithe. They had concern for ritual purity as a means to acknowledge God's holiness. But, at the same time, they seemed interested in what might be termed "liturgical renewal," out of a desire for ritual acknowledgments of God to become a prominent part of daily life. They expected that people would be held morally responsible for their actions, and they anticipated deserved rewards and punishments. Like Presbyterians, they lived in a paradox of moral freedom within God's determining purposes. They believed in life after death. All in all, Pharisees were devout, well-meaning people. They have been called "restorationists," meaning they supported social policies they hoped would restore Israel's covenant faithfulness. We must never portray Pharisees as repressive, self-righteous legalists. Pharisees were the kind of people we would feel fortunate to have as our religious leaders.

In Mark, the Pharisees seem to be active in Galilee (though Josephus supposes they are based mostly in Jerusalem). Apparently they are concerned with the observance of the Sabbath, with fasting, and with ritual cleanliness. If the Pharisees were "separated," they were separated by their pursuit of lifelong purity before the high holiness of God.

Herodians were not a defined group. Like Sadducees, they appear only once as direct questioners of Jesus. Along with Pharisees, they come to "trap Jesus" in a discussion of taxation. But they are mentioned earlier, for after

Jesus has healed a crippled man on the Sabbath in a Capernaum synagogue, Mark reports, "Immediately, the Pharisees and the Herodians went out and consulted together against him, plotting to destroy him" (3:6). Both references imply access to political power. The Herodians were not primarily a religious group; they were political supporters of Herod Antipas's carefully orchestrated political accommodation with Rome. In conquered Israel they were not popular people, and they are not popular with the Gospel writers.

When we preach the conflict stories, we tend to set up contending characters—Jesus and opponents. But the minute we represent scribes and Pharisees as opponents, we place them in a peculiar light. To us Christians, Jesus is truthful and morally in the right. Thus, inevitably, we cast his questioners as devious and in the wrong. To avoid the problem, we may want to describe the situations in which questions were asked, rather than the contenders who were involved. In our world, devout religious people divide over issues, often without any sure sense of who may be right or wrong. At the time of Jesus, many such issues were open to debate among devout Jewish believers. The Mishnah can guide Christians through impressive Jewish reasoned debate over moral issues.[3] Though the rabbis cited in the Mishnah came much later, after the destruction of the Temple, such modes of reasoning were alive at the time of Jesus. Matthew and Luke represent the debates in further detail than does Mark. A Jewish scholar who has analyzed the conflict stories describes Mark bluntly: "Mark understood religion to be defined by confrontation. Jesus and the Pharisees were enemies."[4] But as the earliest Gospel, Mark's presentation of the conflict stories has been formative. Contemporary Jewish scholars reviewing the stories cite evidence showing that many of the issues involved were freely discussed—Sabbath laws, food laws, fasting, grounds for divorce, the uses of wealth—and different positions defined before the time of Jesus. Thus, Jesus is not so disturbingly unique as Mark supposes. Mark pictures Jesus and the Pharisees as outright enemies, but again and again Jesus' teachings—for example, in the Sermon on the Mount—seem to parallel Pharisaic positions.

We should try to depict Jesus' questioners positively. They are not villains. They are not evil just because they question our Jesus. Scribes were not nasty know-it-all types. Pharisees were not unbearably self-righteous. Even the Sadducees are recognizable—in frightened America these days, they might be corporate CEOs or even Cabinet members. Unless we understand that Jesus' questioners are legitimate members of society, people like ourselves, we will never understand why he is being questioned or what his own commitments may be. If Jesus were known to be partying with a local pub crowd in our town today, we might wonder if he was much of a religious leader. If he picked up a reputation as an impromptu "faith healer" among down-and-out people, from a medical standpoint, wouldn't we "mainline" types be suspicious? The scribes and Pharisees are asking questions we would ask. Thus, an able preacher should be capable of forging congregational sympathy for scribes and Pharisees. After all, they appear to have been "our kind of people."

Perennial Issues and Identifications

At the outset, let us recognize that most of the issues involved are still more or less with us. Are there not Christians still troubled by what is or isn't appropriate on "the Sabbath day"? Or, Christians who worry that a general "declaration of pardon" in worship is presumptuous? And are there not Christians who approve fasting out of solidarity with the hungry of the world, not only during Lent after "Fat Tuesday" but on a regular basis? Because of our "family values," many Christians may be disturbed by Jesus' apparent lack of regard for his immediate family. In most Christian communities, we still debate the morality of divorce, the role of children in common worship, the legitimacy of Christian political ambition, and, once in a long while, moral limits in the pursuit of wealth. Almost without exception, the conflict stories pose perennial issues, issues that face religious communities everywhere.

Therefore, again and again, our homiletic strategy must be to quickly shift the focus of the sermon from first-century history to analogous issues in the present day. Then we become the questioners who are bringing issues to Jesus. In effect, homiletically, we ourselves will displace the scribes or Pharisees in asking Jesus to please give us an answer. Such a shift is not difficult to perform:

> Listen to the scribes, will you? They're asking our questions. They are not being difficult; their questions are important, and what's more, important to us. Wouldn't we worry over local faith healers who may be preying on poor, less educated people, and doing so without any real medical training?[5]

Sometimes the shift can be accomplished with an introduction:

> Some years ago there was scandal in a Philadelphia church. Right in the middle of a Sunday service, as the minister was moving toward a Communion table for the Lord's Supper, three people ran up from the congregation, threw Communion bread on the floor, and tipped over the chalice of wine. Later church officers asked the protesters, "Why did you disrupt our worship?" No wonder scribes cornered Jesus: "By what authority do you do what you're doing?" It's a legitimate question—a question we'd ask.

If we shift immediately from the Bible to present-day issues, there are benefits. At the outset, we will avoid the all-too-often excursions into biblical background: "Scholars tell us that . . . ," followed by a weighty bundle of infor-mation gleaned from Bible dictionaries. Such excursions are frequently tedious. But the big advantage is that by shifting from the biblical past to our present, we are able to bypass Mark's depiction of scribes and Pharisees as confrontational enemies. We ourselves become Jesus' questioners so that, when he answers with a counterquestion, he questions us.

Of course, the other homiletic strategy is to describe Jesus' questioners with positive metaphors and images drawn from our contemporary world. Notice, in the paragraphs above on Pharisees, I used familiar phrases: "luncheon club," "strict constructionists," "liturgical renewal," and "our kind of peo-ple." All these terms have contemporary reference. Earlier I also used time-bridging examples such as "If Jesus were known to be partying with a local pub crowd in our town today, we might well wonder if he was much of a reli-gious leader." Such homiletic strategies are easily designed. By inference they identify Pharisees by moving them into our field of contemporary experience.

Finally, though there are many homiletic ways to short-circuit Mark's anti-Judaism as well as our own, I suspect there is one procedure we must keep strictly. I see no reason to use the word "Jews" of Jesus' questioners, particu-larly when Christian preachers almost never use the word "Jew" to describe Jesus! We should never say, "Jesus and the Jews," as if they were categori-cally different. Thus, we must not add "Jewish" as a modifier—Jewish scribes, Jewish priests, Jewish Pharisees—as if singling out a distinction. All the evi-dence we have says that Jesus was emphatically Jewish. He talked, thought, and lived like a faithful Jew. His faith was not "Christian" but was shaped in Israel. His God, and our God, is the God of Israel, YHWH. We must deliber-ately and assiduously guard the Jewishness of Jesus.

What about "Made-up" Stories?

Did Mark suspect the conflict stories were not historically true? Probably not. Some of them were given to Mark by sources. The stories in 2:1–3:6 appear to be a unit, probably including the contentious verse 3:6. Likewise the four conflict stories in 12:13–37 are possibly from still another source. A third group of stories, in 10:2–45, all of which focus on discipleship, if they were not deliberately grouped and edited by Mark, may also be from yet another source. In addition to these blocks of material, there are a few important con-flict stories to be found in chapter 7, and one or two others that seem to relate to Mark's overall narrative design. But sources are no guarantee of historic-ity. Mark chose stories that related to the issues and problems faced by his own community.

What are the reasons for scholarly suspicion? In the first group of stories, some are quite unlikely. In the healing of the paralytic, Jesus says, "Your sins are forgiven," a phrase often labeled a "reverential passive," a way of indirectly implying an action of God without using a holy name. He is saying, "God has forgiven your sins." Therefore, the scribe's accusation of blasphemy would be ridiculous. The story of picking grain on the Sabbath is also contrived. The disciples and Jesus are wandering through a grain field when out of nowhere Pharisees pop up to accuse them of laboring on the Sabbath day. These two stories do seem to reflect later controversy. Finally, there is verse 3:6 at the conclusion of the healing in the synagogue. As a number of scholars, both Jewish and Christian, have observed, no one in Galilee at the time would have felt the controversies involved in 2:1–3:6 could have stirred an urge to kill Jesus. The issues were under debate, but in no way were they serious enough to provoke grounds for assassination, particularly from devout Pharisees. Jesus eating with tax officials and "sinners" might have stirred a moral censure in many minds, but lifted eyebrows would not generate or justify murderous anger. So the conflict stories in the second chapter of Mark seem contrived and, though they are designed to build with intensity, leading to 3:6, the issues under debate were not of such weight as to warrant a plot to kill Jesus.

E. P. Sanders, a scholar who is anything but incautious, assesses the stories:

> [We cannot] say that they all really took place. I have suggested that they reveal the signs of retrojection: later disputes have been thrust back into the lifetime of Jesus. The later Christian church, or at least sections of it, did disagree with the Pharisees and their successors, the rabbis, about the law. It is noteworthy that twice in this collection it is the followers who are accused, not Jesus himself (plucking grain; fasting). These disciples could represent the post-resurrection church, with the dispute retrojected into the lifetime of Jesus. The disputes may have taken place, but not between Jesus and the scribes and Pharisees.[6]

Did Mark want to picture Jesus at odds with Jewish leaders over the law? Apparently. Was there an appeal to Gentiles involved? Certainly Gentiles would have delighted in a Jesus who was willing to forego parts of the law. Mark does seem to be encouraging a Gentile mission.

The four stories on discipleship, in 10:2–45, also appear to be concerned with issues that would naturally arise within emerging Christian communities. They all involve the disciples in one way or another. After the pronouncement on divorce, there is an additional discussion of the issue for disciples. The same sort of added instruction is tacked on the stories of the rich young man and the ambitious sons of Zebedee. The story of Jesus welcoming children is precipitated by disciples trying to shoo them away. But all of these stories seem to address issues of a developed Christian community. So again, we have a group of stories in which retrojection would appear to be involved. We will examine the plausibility of the conflict stories as we study them separately.

Retrojection is more common in the Gospels than we might wish to admit. In a way, the process is quite wonderful. Do we not wish we could place our difficult situations before Jesus? Imaginatively we can, by retrojection. By doing so we put together our troubles and Jesus' remembered words. If we cannot recall a saying, we can draw on our understanding of his message and think one up. The early Christians were not hung up over historicity. They believed that, through preaching, the Lord Jesus still spoke to his people—a people who were gathered in the same Spirit that was with Jesus. Are we not in a similar situation?

But how do we handle congregations who may be troubled by a lack of historicity? Why not try honesty? Historicity took on greater importance in the nineteenth century after David Friedrich Strauss wrote *The Life of Jesus* (1835).[7] Strauss considered the virgin birth, most of the miracles, and the resurrection stories to be "myth," by which he meant nonhistorical. Most church leaders were aghast. The more conservative scholars rallied, working hard to document the historicity of the scriptural record. In the twentieth century, history took on additional importance as a locus for revelation. If scientists described the natural world without recourse to a notion of God, and psychologists studied human experience similarly, then nature and human nature were no longer reliable fields for general revelation. Instead, the church turned to "holy history" as a record of God's mighty acts and the foundation for biblical faith. Thus, "historical" seemed to become an ultimate definition of truth.[8] When philosophers remarked that our readings of history are inevitably slanted—the notion of objective history does seem to be an oxymoron—we began talking of "our history," with emphasis on "story" as a source of our precious faith-identity. The historical has become an overloaded category in local congregations. Yet since Strauss in the mid-nineteenth century, we have discovered the profound truth in "myths," for example, Paul Ricoeur's brilliant reading of the myth of the fall in Genesis 2.[9] And we have discovered sociology of knowledge and come to see that social symbols may mediate revelation as much as historical events.[10] But these options do not seem to have reached most Protestant congregations. For Protestants, the Bible remains the authoritative Word of God, and, therefore, its objective truthfulness is crucial.

Christians must learn the Bible not only by studying separate passages Sunday after Sunday in age-group circles but by studying how the Bible came to be—from oral sources to written sources, to an assembling of sources, to the editing and selecting of writings. Though God generated revelation, the tasks of gathering, grasping, transmitting, and so forth, were in the hands of fallible human beings like ourselves who, though no doubt stirred by the Spirit, were nonetheless emphatically human—and, "To err is human." Without some basic understanding of the Bible, the crypto-fundamentalism of American Protestant congregations will not be dented.

Here's another form of education: the church bulletin. From time to time, pastors can displace some of the usual notices in bulletins so as to include a paragraph of biblical background on a passage to be preached. Years ago I was preaching a series of sermons on sections from the initial chapters of Revelation. St. Augustine was right, we need great care when interpreting Revelation. Therefore, each week for the bulletin I wrote a paragraph of background on the passage to be preached. People were delighted, and thereafter the practice was welcomed whenever useful. We can use space in the church bulletins for orientation when we intend to preach difficult passages.

Are there other means to ease the problem of stories that seem to be the product of retrojection? Sometimes a brief explanation (and it must be brief) before the reading of Scripture will help. Even in congregations that stand for the Gospel reading and brace the reading with sung responses, the formality of liturgical practice does not, or at least should not, inhibit a brief preface before the reading of Scripture.

But what can we do within our sermons? Sometimes the introduction of the sermon itself can orient a congregation:

> Some years ago, teenage Christians started wearing bracelets. Remember the cloth bracelets with WWJD—What Would Jesus Do?—printed on them. They had the idea that they could imagine "what Jesus would do" in moments of moral indecision. Well, the custom isn't new. Way back in the first century, when early Christians bumped into trouble, they would imagine what Jesus would say to them. And they wrote their stories down for us, later generation Christians, who face many of the same problems. So let's hear their testimony, and imagine how Jesus would speak to us.

Or even something bolder:

> Years ago, first-century school children were taught to remember the sayings of famous speakers by making up stories to surround quoted words. Scholars have dug up schoolroom exercises in which a phrase from someone like Alexander the Great has been woven into a story so students could remember the words. Maybe early Christians picked up the practice. Did they write stories of their own lives and then have Jesus speak to them in the middle of

the stories? Maybe, for here's a story that happened long after Jesus in which he is still speaking. What's more, Jesus is still speaking to us.

Introductions are designed for specific sermons. There is no such thing as an all-purpose introduction for sermons on conflict stories. A sermon's structural movement should be determined before attempting to sketch an introduction. But these made-up introductions may spur your creative smarts as well as homiletic craft.

The other strategy is to use a paragraph within the sermon itself to explain. Such explanations had better be both honest and crafted into ordinary, every-day language—that is, they should not be weighty:

> Can you ask a blunt question? Did Jesus bump into a covey of Pharisees while walking in fields with his disciples? Did it all happen just the way it's reported? To tell the truth, the story sounds a bit shaky. Yes, we have walked fields, and yes, we've rubbed grain in our hands and licked the granules. People in the countryside eat grain as absent-mindedly. But then how did a group of Pharisees suddenly leap out of nowhere to raise an objection? The story seems somewhat contrived. But look, what a great story to tell in the midst of fighting over what's right or wrong on the Sabbath day. Let's not worry over how and why the story is told. Let's listen and learn God's will for us.

What these examples are doing is explaining and refocusing the biblical passages. We see explanations that help us to understand how the stories came to be, while at the same time aiming meaning at our own lives.

But brief homiletic strategies are not much of a solution. The real issue is pastoral education. We must teach our people how to read the Bible. We must continually bring them up to date on scholarship—they must understand what they are reading. Preaching is never separated from teaching or from pastoral sensitivity. We need not remain infants in our faith, a faith that always will and should seek understanding. We can all be more mature in our reading of Scripture.

What a Way to Refer to Oneself!

What do we do with the "son of humanity"? It seems a most peculiar way of speaking of oneself. Is it like the regal "we" that sidesteps the personal pronoun "I"? By itself, *ho huios tou anthropou* means exactly the same thing as the Hebrew *ben 'adam* and the Aramaic *bar enasha*, namely, "human being." Jesus appears to use the phrase to acknowledge his common humanity, and perhaps to affirm a prophetic vocation as well. We have seen that Mark's Jesus uses the phrase primarily in passion predictions, except for the few odd allusions to Daniel that occur in chapters 13 and 14, and, of course, the use of the term twice in the first group of conflict stories. Thus, we are concerned with only two specific texts:[11]

2:10

"But so you'll know the son of humanity has authority [on earth] to forgive sins," he said to the paralytic, "You, I say get up, pick up your mat and go home!"

2:27–28

He said to them, "The Sabbath was created for humanity, not humanity for the Sabbath. The son of humanity is lord even over the Sabbath."

Although the term "son of humanity" shows up in Mark as an apocalyptic text (8:38; 13:26; 14:62), it is not likely that an apocalyptic meaning is being written back into the conflict stories. Similarly, these texts are quite different from the intense passion predictions that also use the phrase. Because they are so different, one almost wonders if the son-of-humanity citations in Mark's second chapter didn't come from some other source.

Let's consider two options:

1. Is Jesus saying that any human being can announce God's mercy and any human being is free to determine Sabbath-day practices?
2. Is Jesus saying, "Though I am a human among human beings, I have been given special authority by God to announce mercy and to teach proper Sabbath-day disciplines"?

These options seem obvious because, after all, "son of humanity" does mean simply "human being." Mark obviously believes that Jesus is distinctive, indeed a "Son of God," but in chapter 2 his true identity is yet to be disclosed. The leper in 1:40–42 is told not to broadcast his miraculous cure but to go and have his skin checked by priests as required by law. Jesus' true identity begins to reveal itself with Peter's brazen announcement, "You are the Christ!" (8:29), where it is immediately countered with a passion prediction. In fact, every hint of triumph in chapters 8–10 is at once corrected by passion predictions. Mark is too good a writer to tip his hand early in the story. Unless you want to argue that "son of humanity" is a specific messianic title that has been written back into the conflict stories—a code word for eager early Christians to decipher—we are down to the two options outlined.

The first option may seem radical to most of us who have inherited a high Christology from twentieth-century theological education. But the option has much to commend it. The story of the paralytic shows up in Mark 2 but also in Matthew 9:1–8, where Matthew has added a key sentence to Mark's concluding "they glorified God." Matthew adds, "who has given such authority to human beings." Matthew uses the plural, "to human beings," meaning all human beings and not just Jesus. Apparently Matthew seems to understand "the son of humanity has authority to forgive sins" to mean that any person may declare God's mercy.

If the story is a product of retrojection, as seems likely, did Mark's community practice some sort of forgiveness ritual that might seem offensive to some? There are scholars who suppose that Paul's repeated injunction "Greet one another with a holy kiss" may refer to some liturgical practice, essentially an act of reconciliation affirming The Mercy in which we all live. Therefore, Jesus' inclusive "the son of humanity has authority to forgive sins" might be rallied to justify the practice.

Though the phrase may have been understood in Matthew's manner to mean that we all have authority to declare God's mercy, doesn't the phrase need qualification? Can anybody, indeed everybody, run around pronouncing God's forgiveness? Surely there are grounds to justify limiting such announcements to a priesthood or at least to those equipped with an approved grasp of the gospel message. Do not some churches preface a declaration of pardon with words such as, "As a called and ordained minister of the church of Christ, and by His authority, I therefore declare to you the entire forgiveness of all your sins"?[12] After all, human beings who declare God's forgiveness presumably will have some level of faith in God, and specifically in a God who is merciful. But does the text grant authority to forgive sins only to the ecclesiastically authorized? Hardly. Though some sort of faith in a merciful God would seem to be requisite, why would there have to be any other regimenting authority?

Of course, churches have the right to set up restrictions on who is authorized to perform rituals. Most churches, both Catholic and Protestant, carefully guard who may conduct Eucharist. After all, right understandings of Eucharist ought to accompany practices and govern their conduct. Probably most of us would be horrified if local bartenders assumed a priestly prerogative and advertised eucharistic cocktail hours for their cheerful clientele. Likewise, if a declaration of pardon is a formal liturgical announcement, churches have every right to regulate the practice.

But suppose there's something very different going on in these two texts. Jesus' preaching was a dramatic announcement of God's new order, and the message guided his speech and his actions. Given the images of the Hebrew Bible, would not *basileia* refer to a time when everyone would know the Lord and gladly serve one another as children of God? Surely such an image would involve mutual forgiveness as we live together in The Mercy. Though we may insist that God's new order in its fullness has not yet arrived, we must remember that Jesus was clearly inviting us to enter God's realm ahead of time and to live as citizens of God here and now. We tend to view *basileia* as a visionary future-perfect and thus to toss the notion into an eschatological file labeled "Hold for the Future." A theological error. Because God *is now*, the coming of the new order also *is now*. God's purposed realm is a "happening" that we are living in with good cheer and eagerness. Is the message of the new order an underlying clue to the conflict stories? Yes. Therefore, a broad "son of humanity" is probably implied in them all.

The second text is even more telling:

2:27–28

He said to them, "The Sabbath was created for humanity, not humanity for the Sabbath. The son of humanity is lord even over the Sabbath."

The creation of a Sabbath day is commanded in Exodus 16:22–30. Requirements governing the seventh day appear subsequently in Exodus 20:8–11. They deserve attention:

Remember the sabbath day and keep it holy. Six days you shall labor and do all your work, but the seventh day is a sabbath of the LORD your God; you shall not do any work—you, your son or daughter, your male or female slave, or your cattle, or the stranger who is within your settlements. For in six days the LORD made heaven and earth and sea, and all that is in them, and He rested the seventh day; therefore the LORD blessed the sabbath day and hallowed it.

Sabbath regulations ought be greeted with enthusiasm—no more work! For people who had been slaves in Egypt, the Sabbath was liberation. We are not meant to work all the time—not us, or our children, or our employees, or our migrant workers. Thank God! The Sabbath is a good gift of God, a time to consider the wonders of creation that are renewed for us providentially day by day. The Sabbath also has political significance for our labor laws and for ecological legislation. Profitability should not determine labor policy; the image of a God who rested after shaping the world should.

But how do we keep a feast day holy? The command was given to Israel and was not a personal option. In America, we tend to read the Ten Commandments as if they are primarily personal ethics. They are not. They are intended to transform the social order. If a commandment tells us to honor our father and our mother, it does not just mean that we should be nice to our parents; rather, it is a call to provide social security for everyone's parents. Likewise, the Sabbath command has a similar social purpose, which these days seems steadily eroding. Sabbath regulations should guarantee sufficient time off from labor. All of the commandments are framed for the transformation of the social order.

But we have a peculiar American problem. Driven by a demand for corporate profits, we work many more hours than workers in other nations. As a result, we have no time left, not only for one another, but for exploring the meaning of our own lives. If you are a day laborer, hustling cement bags or doing something equally strenuous, exhaustion defines your free time. If you are a corporate employee trying to get ahead, you will discover you are enlarging your company time. In America, our lives are ruled by a strange alien god—the stock market. So how can we keep a day to explore the meaning of our lives and to celebrate with festival the goodness of God, our creator? Because we are communities of faith and not a scatter of vaguely associated individuals who have tumbled haphazardly into church pews, we tend to set up governing rules for our mutual well-being before God. Because such regulations are connected with liberation, we ought to accept them gladly.

But rules can be accepted cheerfully or they can be imposed, often with unconsidered or even ill-considered strictness. When Christians attempted to impose Sabbath regulations on Sunday, without a proper Jewish social theology, the result was an unholy mess. Christians put on sober clothing, curbed games, banned movies, ate cautiously, discussed sacred subjects, and even restrained their pets (no indiscriminate tail wagging, please). Protestant personalism turned social transformation into individual bylaws that inevitably became coercive. Laws imposed externally or by the more pernicious inward demands of conscience can become both arbitrary and harsh.

Jesus had regard for the law of God. He was a faithful Jew. Does he not call the rich young man to obey a recital of the law (Mark 10:19)? And does he not condemn calculated evasions of the law (Mark 7:9–12)? With Jesus, the law is always regarded as a good, helpful gift of God. We may assume that Jesus was not cavalier about Sabbath observance or about temple worship. The issues that arose had to do with the imposition of Sabbath law to restrict concern for neighbors who might hunger or desperately cry out for healing. Should law restrict doing good on the Sabbath day? The issue is discussed in the Mishnah, indicating that Jesus was not alone in raising such questions.

The problems reflected in the conflict stories arose as the early Christian movement stepped out into Gentile territories. Paul's letters reflect ongoing controversy among Christians over the traditional readings of Torah. Circumcision was not the only issue; fasting, sacrifice, food laws, ritual washing, and Sabbath regulation were also points of contention. Were Gentiles required to become Jews in order to bow before Israel's God—the one and only God? As Christian faith expanded into the empire, gradually Christianity became a Gentile evangelical movement. Complicated issues provoked internal debate among Christians. Sabbath laws became an issue. What made the issue so complicated was the gradual shift to Lord's Day worship. By nature, as well as by the precedent of Jesus' resurrection, Christianity, with its message of God's new order, was an "eighth day" sectarian group. Did Christians simply drop all Sabbath regulations? Apparently not. There is evidence that, at first, Christians may have observed both days in tandem. The separation was gradual and complicated. Authentic Christianity (as the Gospel of Matthew knows) is never antinomian. But what and how to apply regulations became the issue. Christians still struggle with the discussion of the Sabbath and Sunday.

But again, what is going on in the difficult text—"The Sabbath was created for humanity, not humanity for the Sabbath. The son of humanity is lord even over the Sabbath"? The first sentence can be read much as we read the previous text: that human beings will fulfill and govern Sabbath law. The Sabbath was "created for humanity"; the statement is irrefutable. Not only are we liberated from cruel ungoverned slavery, but we are free to celebrate God our creator and in so doing discover who we are as people of God. But again, the statement seems to be aimed at Jesus' understanding of God's new humanity, where we will live, all of us, in the promise of an ultimate "Great Sabbath." The words must be understood with reference to God's new order.

What about the second sentence, *"The Son of Humanity is lord even over the Sabbath"*? No faithful Jew would suggest that though God has commanded the Sabbath celebration we human beings can do what we wish with the day. Jesus was a faithful Jew. Some scholars suppose that, as with Hebrew poetry, the second sentence is simply a reiteration of the first. Others have argued that the sentence was added to justify the Christian drift away from the Sabbath to a "Lord's Day" observance. Still others seem to read the text as triumphant Christology.[13] Whatever the second sentence is, it cannot mean that honoring God is an option governed by human whim and fancy. There is a famous extra teaching of Jesus in a late fifth-century codex: "On the same day, seeing someone working on the sabbath, Jesus said, 'You, if you know what you're doing, you are blessed; but if you do not, you are cursed and a transgressor of the law.'" "Blessed are you if you know what you're doing" seems to rule out whim and fancy. Instead, the words call for a deep understanding of our true humanity before God, the Creator, who has given us a good seventh day.

Can we read the son of humanity texts in Mark as invitations to join a new humanity? Yes, as long as we don't restrict new humanity to Christian auspices. "Humanity" is a larger term than "Christian." Hope of a new redeemed humanity, a true humanity before God, has animated all the children of Adam since the gift of time began. Maybe the idea of an ultimate Sabbath is a fine symbol of redemption. We would serve neighbors as our own kin, delight in the numinous wonders of a new creation, and, in immense gratefulness, enjoy God forever.

Chapter 4

An Inaugural Set

Conflict over the Forgiveness of Sins (2:1–12)
Conflict over Eating with Sinners (2:13–17)
Conflict over Fasting (2:18–20)
Conflict over Picking Grain on the Sabbath (2:23–28)
Conflict over Healing on the Sabbath (3:1–6)

*T*he five stories from Mark 2:1 to 3:6 are a set that Mark seems to have installed in his Gospel from some other source. They are rhetorically ordered with a chiasmic design: a, b, c, b, a.[1] Thus, there is (a) a healing story followed by (b) an eating story, then by (c) the new wine–fasting story, then back to (b) an eating story, concluding with (a) another healing story. Moreover, the stories build with intensity to the final conclusion in 3:6, which is a plot to kill Jesus. The questioners are scribes, then Pharisees, then disciples of John with Pharisees, then Pharisees again, then a synagogue crowd. Finally, in verse 3:6, Pharisees meet with Herodians and plan to kill Jesus.

CONFLICT OVER THE FORGIVENESS OF SINS

Mark 2:1–12 (also Matthew 9:1–8 and Luke 5:17–26)

[1]After a while, word got around that [Jesus] had come back to Capernaum. [2]When people heard he was at home, they crowded in to hear him speak, blocking the doorway. [3]A paralytic came carried by four men, [4]but because of the crowd, they couldn't get in, so they removed the roof over where [Jesus] was and, digging out an opening, lowered the mat on which the paralytic was lying. [5]When Jesus saw their faith, he said to the paralytic, "Child, your sins are forgiven."

[6]Some of the scribes were sitting there thinking to themselves, [7]"How can this fellow say what he just said; he's blaspheming. Who can forgive sins but God alone?" [8]Right away Jesus sensed in his spirit what they were thinking among themselves. He said to them, "Why are you asking these kinds of questions? [9]Which is easier to say to the paralytic, Your sins are

forgiven, or Get up, pick up your mat, and walk? [10]But so you'll know the son of humanity has authority [on earth] to forgive sins," he said to the paralytic, "You, I say get up, pick up your mat, and go home!"

[12]He got up right away, picked up his mat and, in front of everybody, he walked out. So they were all astounded and, glorifying God, were saying, "We've never seen anything like this before!"

Other Versions

Matthew 9:1–8 abbreviates the story by leaving out the description of the crowded house, the four men, and the removal of the roofing. But Matthew adds an astonishing last line to the story, reporting that the crowd glorified God "who had given such authority to human beings" (Matt. 9:8). Amusingly enough, in Luke 5:17–26 we are told that roof tiles were removed, though a tile roof would have been unlikely in Capernaum. Luke also has "Your sins have been forgiven." There is even a strange story in John 5:1–9 in which a paralytic is healed when Jesus says, "Get up, pick up your mat, and walk around." The richness of detail in Mark, as well as the many versions, does suggest that the story of the paralytic may go back to some particular event. Nevertheless, most scholars suppose that here two forms have been combined—a miracle story and an inserted controversy. If so, as both Calvin and Luther argued, Mark's rewriting of the source is remarkably cohesive.

Mark's Story

Prior to the story of the paralytic, Jesus heals a leper who, though warned by Jesus to say nothing, spreads word of his cure so that "people were coming to him from every direction" (1:45). When Jesus returns to Capernaum, his chosen base of operations, the house is instantly jammed with a crowd come to listen. There is some indication that Mark's word for "crowd" (*ochlos* rather than *laos*) indicates a lower-class crowd of the poor and the alienated. The house where Jesus is staying is humble, with an earthen roof that must be dug out. When Jesus sees the paralytic lowered into the midst of the crowd, he says, "Child [*teknon*], your sins are forgiven." The word "forgiven" is in the present tense, implying immediacy—right here and now your sins have been absolved. But Jesus does not say, "I forgive." The words should be read as a reverential passive, implying the mercy of God. Thus, Jesus' words appear to be a formal declaration of pardon. The scribes are jarred by Jesus' pronouncement. They begin to mull over a charge of blasphemy, imagining that Jesus has usurped the prerogatives of God (see Ps. 51:1–4; Isa. 43:25).

The Controversy

Some scholars argue that the story was told because questions had been raised by early Christians who were offering forgiveness freely. Was there some liturgical practice, a formal announcement of forgiveness, in connection with Eucharist or baptism that provoked such questioning? Such a form in worship might well have been early. Even today, when a priest or minister announces a bold assurance of pardon, some contemporary observers have been known to raise the same objection. In the past, querulous Protestants have complained about the Catholic rite of Penance. But the argument in the story of the paralytic is a strong refutation of accusing questioners—the son of humanity (the key word is "humanity") has authority to forgive sins! Though the whole story appears to be a conflation of two sources, its structure is typical of the conflict story formula:

> *Question:* Who can forgive sins but God alone?
> *Counterquestion:* Which is easier to say . . . ?
> *Pronouncement:* On the authority to forgive.

The scribes' silent question is actually an accusation: Jesus is a blasphemer because, though an ordinary human being, he is usurping God's role. God alone has power to commute our sins. There is also a hint of scholarly snideness involved. Jesus, an untaught peasant, is brashly declaring God's mercy, a subject scribes have studied and therefore consider understood and under control. We scribes can delineate the nature of sin, and we scribes can recommend appropriate sacrifice.

Jesus' counterquestion—"Which is easier to say to the paralytic, Your sins are forgiven, or Get up, pick up your mat, and walk?"—exposes the mind-set of his questioners. They accept the general notion of a link between sin and physical ailment. Sin is something that should not be; it is a violation of God's creation. So is physical impairment. No wonder that the lame were often shunned. The link made between illness, sin, and the resulting social disapprobation was a cruel "Catch-22." Jesus, an unauthorized healer, seems as concerned with social restoration as with the burden of the ailment. On hearing the counterquestion, we realize that the declaration of mercy, even if presumptive, seems a good deal easier to say than effective words of cure. The scribes suppose Jesus is not only ignorant of Torah but incapable of producing a cure. He is unauthorized in both respects. Then, suddenly, Jesus speaks: "But so you'll know the son of humanity has authority [on earth] to forgive sins: 'You, I say get up, pick up your mat, and go home!'" (The bracketed phrase "on earth" does not appear in all manuscripts and is probably a later addition.) If Jesus successfully heals the paralytic, he has called upon the power of God, thus validating his declaration of pardon.

What about the final pronouncement, "the son of humanity has authority to forgive sins"? Is Jesus saying, "I myself have been given authority to forgive sins"? A high Christology will so read the words. Or does the statement have a more inclusive meaning, declaring that all humans can forgive one another? Perhaps interpretation may lie in between. Most form critics have argued that controversy passages are probably products of early Christian communities. If early Christian practice included some sort of formal declarations of pardon, were opponents scandalized? The story does seem designed to answer such a complaint. If so, then "son of humanity" does imply an inclusive meaning: In God's name we, *representatives of God's new humanity*, can announce forgiveness.

Homiletic Theology

Liberation from the burden of guilt is central to Christian proclamation. Further, the acknowledgment of sin is understood as a form of evangelical honesty. But the nature of sin, categories of mortal sinfulness, catalogs of sins, and the like have been matters of debate. Likewise, the means of mercy—who may qualify and who may declare—have also been a subject of continuing controversy. Within Catholic tradition, forgiveness of sin usually has been understood to be vested in the church, the living body of Christ, and closely connected to the sacramental rite of Penance. But within some free-church Protestant bodies, mercy is conveyed through the preaching of the gospel and is understood to be ratified by the grace of inward believing. Other Protestant traditions vest the declaration of the gospel message with ordained clergy. While we may wish to broaden the positions, nonetheless the notion of conferred mercy does seem to be a proclivity of God's *new* humanity, for, in general, our common humanity does not enjoy forgiving.

Some problems stem from biblical inconsistencies. There are texts that imply confession; indeed, heartfelt confession is a prerequisite to gaining mercy. But there are other texts where forgiveness is undeserved and even unexpected. There are some texts that suggest that mercy is a conditional transaction. The conditions may vary: We must also be merciful lest forgiveness be nullified. Or we must rectify our lives to demonstrate a proper repentance. But there are other texts that seem to say mercy is a free grant—we have been forgiven, even if we may not realize or even choose to receive the gift. If we are to interpret such texts, we will need some sort of considered theological position.

First, let us try to step out of a transactional model, particularly any model that tends to set up regulations or conditional clauses that might diminish the free wonder of God's mercy. Can we not say that God's nature is mercy, The Mercy, "in whom we live and move and have our being." In other words we are all related, interfaced if you will, to a God whose nature is mercy. If so, our unwillingness to forgive neighbors or even our refusal to forgive ourselves is an astonishing form of defiant unreality. What's more, even when we forgive a neighbor we are not doing the forgiving; rather, we are acknowledging The Mercy, which we all live within. Thus, to refuse to forgive a neighbor, or an enemy, or ourselves is an attempt to displace God and deny God's sovereign grace. Of course, to understand and accept The Mercy requires a realistic awareness of our own sin—else why bother?—as well as faith in God.

Who can declare God's mercy? Many Protestants balk at the idea of Church = Christ. But even free-church Protestants can argue that a declaration of pardon is a form of speaking the gospel. We also can affirm that those who know they are forgiven sinners, undeservedly forgiven, are qualified to speak. The self-righteous are usually silent on the subject of free mercy. In France, the Reformed Church has an interesting practice. Instead of a ministerial act, one side of the congregation absolves the other and then reverses the action. As Matthew's version says, "Such authority is given to human beings."

If we live in The Mercy, mutual forgiveness would seem to be a way of life for all human beings. Thus, we may be uneasy over churches that claim exclusive rights to pronounce or withhold forgiveness. As Jean-Paul Sartre once suggested, churches may encourage guilt in order to keep themselves in the business of dispensing pardon.[2] But our own age, which views guilt as an abnormal psychological problem, is blind to both systemic evil and the majesty of God's mercy. After the Holocaust no human being can ever be innocent, but in God's amazing grace we "wretches" all live in The Mercy.

There is a secondary problem in the passage: the assumption that sin and sickness are connected. Though we tend nowadays to separate the two, are we being glib? In Luke 13:1–9, Jesus seems to refuse a connection between sin and calamity. In John 9:2–3, disciples see a blind man, and ask, "Rabbi, who sinned? The man, or his parents that he was born blind?" Jesus' reply seems to reject any cause-effect relationship between sin and a physical handicap: "Neither this man nor his parents sinned, but so the works of God may be manifest in him." But here in the story of the paralytic a connection between sin and sickness seems to be assumed.

The connection between sin and sickness is a biblical notion. For example, in Psalm 107:17 there is a clear connection assumed: "Some were sick through their sinful ways." In Psalm 103:3, the parallel pattern of Hebrew poetry demonstrates a tie between mercy and healing:

Bless the Lord, O my soul
   and do not forget all his benefits—
Who forgives all your iniquity,
   who heals all your diseases.

We must be cautious, never glib. Some years ago a top cancer researcher announced somewhat bitterly, "All cancers are caused by human beings." Though he backed off from "all," he was talking of cigarettes, the smog of auto emissions, the spills of industrial waste, and the like. In his perception, cancer could be labeled a "social disease," for our social behavior is clearly involved. What of any link between psychiatric problems and sickness? Anxiety can freeze the self and depression box-in the soul and, in both cases, cause physical concomitants. Helen Flanders Dunbar argued that psychological dispositions seem to parallel certain types of illness.[3] More recently, theologian Edward Farley has brooded on the issue profoundly.[4] All we need to know here is that, whatever Jesus may or may not have believed, the ancient popular assumption putting together sin and sickness explains Jesus' relationship to the paralytic. Here, in what may be a particular case, Jesus appears to put the two together.

Speaking the Passage

Because the passage has a split-focus—a miracle merged with a controversy—you may want to use a brief description of the scene as your introduction. But the body of your interpretation must focus on the controversy. Controversies almost preach themselves because usually they are still live issues. A first move can be launched from "Who can forgive but God alone?" Immediately you can remark, "It's still a good question," and move discussion into the contemporary world. Preaching need not, indeed should not, remain in the biblical world. Yes, we intone absolution in our worship, but isn't it cheap grace, because after all we are not God. A second move can take off from Jesus' counterquestion, exposing our minds: We church people are apt to suppose that we and we alone have authority to forgive. What's more, we add all sorts of "ifs" to granting forgiveness. A little sawdust and salt tears, please, to show proper repentance. Or, can you demonstrate amendment of life?—no point in our forgiving you if you go on sinning! How can someone not even acknowledged by the church go around forgiving? You might mention an old play in which a bartender, listening to all the sloshy confessions of his customers like a priest, suddenly recites words of absolution formally. But then work from the surprise of Jesus healing the paralytic. Here a preacher can say that while sin does not cause illness, nonetheless, forgiveness is a healing of the whole self. Now the sermon can move toward a theology of mercy, The Mercy. Thus, we human beings in a priesthood of believers must announce The Mercy to one another.

A Sermon

The sermon comes from way back in 1960. I preached it to a Presbyterian congregation in Fredonia, New York. The sermon was part of a Lenten series based on seven passages in which people are "amazed" at Jesus.

Introduction   Suppose you were sick and sent for a doctor. And suppose that when the doctor came, instead of writing a prescription or counting out pills, he turned to you and said, "Your sins are forgiven!" What would you do? Report him to the local medical society? But this is exactly what happened one day when they brought a paralytic on his bed to Jesus. Christ looked at the paralyzed man and said simply, "Son, your sins are forgiven." The scribes who witnessed the scene were incensed: "Why does this man speak thus? Blasphemy! Who can forgive sins but God alone?" Had Jesus simply healed the man there would have been no complaint. Instead, Jesus saw the deeper need and offered pardon. More than prescriptions, more than pills, the human heart cries out for mercy. Said Jesus to the paralytic, "Son, your sins are forgiven." The scribes were astonished. They were amazed at his mercy.

I

1a Let us begin by facing the fact of human guilt. Even in our world, where for many God seems gone away, folk still feel strangely guilty. Writes Erich Fromm, "People feel guilty about hundreds of things; for not having worked hard enough, for having been too protective toward their children, for not having done enough for mother, or even for having been too kind hearted. It's almost as if they had to find something to feel guilty about."[5] Maybe it is. Guilt may be exaggerated, explained, displaced, or dimly felt; nevertheless, all human beings struggle with a sense of guilt, else they have ceased to be human. Guilt is a fact as much as a complex. Did you see that cartoon that shows a burly, bruised criminal facing a prison psychiatrist? The psychiatrist says to the criminal brightly, "I know what's the matter with you. You've got a guilt complex." Our modern world may have a guilt complex—just possibly because we're guilty.

1b *Guilt is paralyzing.* The guilty man lives in terrible tension between what he is and what he feels he ought to be. He feels he ought to be perfect, and yet he cannot be perfect. In fact, there's nothing he can do or say that will not add to the sum of his guilt. Nor can he do nothing, step out of life, and destroy himself, for that too would be a sin. Unable to live with himself, unable to die, he is spiritually paralyzed. Some years ago a popular television program offered a man one thousand dollars if he could spend half an hour on a city street without inadvertently breaking some law. At first the man began by walking back and forth down the sidewalk. But it occurred to him that he might stumble into another pedestrian, so he stopped walking and stood still. Then he remembered that he could be arrested for loitering. So unable to decide what to do, he broke out in a cold sweat. You can't live with guilt, and yet you can't live without guilt. Guilt is paralyzing.

1c *Guilt is stubborn.* You cannot get rid of it at all. Rationalize it, psychoanalyze it, even tranquilize it—still, guilt is guilt. Project it, reject it, protect it—there's no solution. No matter how we try to hide guilt, it will not go away. In some lone, unguarded moment, guilt comes again to trouble us. There was a poem we used to recite as children:

> Chop it, cream it, boil it, bake it,
> No matter how you make it
> It's still spinach.

No matter how we disguise it, guilt is still guilt. The great human problem: What do we do to be rid of guiltiness? To whom shall we go? Let us acknowledge the hard fact of guilt.

II

In the story, friends brought the paralytic to Jesus. Let us face the fact of Jesus Christ, God's mercy and the answer to the paralytic's longing. "Who can forgive sins but God alone?" They questioned Christ and so do we.

2a *How can Jesus forgive us?* After all, he's ancient history; what good is his forgiveness? Still, who else have we? Not a priest, a preacher, a confessional box, or a public admission—not even Ann Landers. There's no one whose mercy can dissolve our guilt. Poet Jeanne D'Orge sings her complaint:

> I wish there were someone
> Who would hear confession
> Not a priest—I do not want to be told of my sins
> Not a Father—I do not want to give sorrow
> Not a friend—she wouldn't know enough
> Not a lover—he would be partial
> Not a God—He is far away
> But someone who would be friend, lover, priest, God—all in one.[6]

The answer to her longing is Jesus Christ, friend of our flesh, lover and priest, all in one. Who can forgive sins but God alone? The answer to the question is the God who is with Jesus Christ.

2b *Christ can forgive us because he takes sin seriously.* Easy forgiveness is always too easy; like whitewash, it wears off. W. H. Auden's "Christmas Oratorio" states it sharply: "I like committing crimes. God likes forgiving them. Really the world is admirably arranged."[7] But God's mercy isn't easy. There is still the cross to catch our sight and stab our souls awake. Forgiveness isn't easy; forgiveness involves suffering. Did not Christ on the cross bear the sting of our angers, the cut of our cruelty? But from the cross, in his suffering, he spoke, saying, "Father, forgive them." Forgiveness doesn't come easy; it comes from a cross.

2c *Christ can forgive us because he redeems our sin.* Suppose he did say, "Father forgive"—so what? Suppose his mercy falls upon us, like morning dew to renew our wilted lives—what's the use? Forgiveness doesn't right the wrongs, or remove the deeds; once done they're done. Perhaps the state of California will save Caryl Chessman from the gas chamber—I hope so, lest murder punish murder—perhaps the governor will grant clemency. But clemency won't change the fact that an injured girl remains in a mental hospital. It won't give life to the grave-gone men he throttled. What's the use of mercy if it cannot change the past, erase the stain, make right the wrong? What of Christ if a cross remains to slaughter others after he was tumbled into a stone tomb? Let Judas repent and Peter regret—they can't bring back Christ from the dead or make the crucifixion not have happened. But Jesus Christ is risen and in his rising has guaranteed the forgiveness of our sins. God has power to rewrite the human story. "My son," said Jesus to the paralytic, "your sins are forgiven." And they were.

III

3a Are you ready to face *the fact of your own forgiveness*? Listen, Jesus' words are spoken directly to you: "My child, your sins are forgiven." Forgiveness is a free-for-all gift; all you have to do is to receive. But, oh, how hard it is for us to accept God's mercy. We hear it preached and prayed and, week after week, we're handed an "assurance of pardon," but we can't seem to believe it's real. Performing needless penance, we go on tormenting ourselves with remorse. Like that prisoner who was granted freedom by President Wilson but who brought his case to the Supreme Court begging to be hung, we seem to prefer punishment to pardon. Why? Perhaps because if we accept mercy we'll have to admit our sinfulness. Or maybe we reject mercy because we would have to let God be God and bow before the glory. Charles

Peguy has a poem in which he imagines God watching a man at prayer. The little man, on bended knee, heaps up huge blame, over and over condemning himself until God laughs out loud. "Look at that little man," God says. "He asked for forgiveness, and I forgave him long ago. Yet he goes on confessing his sins."[8] The scribes questioned Christ, saying, "Blasphemy." But the paralytic heard the words of mercy, stood up straight and walked away free. Mercy is free, but you do have to receive.

3b *You can live your life trusting the mercy of God*, a God you know in Jesus Christ. God's pardon has set us free from paralyzing guilt and can be the climate in which we live our lives. Look, we are sinners. Even after we have been forgiven, we will sin again simply because we are human. Human choice is never between a clear-cut good versus obvious evil, no crisp right versus wrong. Instead, every decision is a choice among contaminated ambiguities.[9] We sin; inevitably we sin. But as Luther said, we can "sin bravely," confident in the continuing mercy of God. We live in The Mercy and can trust our merciful God to be merciful. Listen, we're not God. We must do our best as God guides us and leave our sins to The Mercy. A submarine commander in World War II put it bluntly: "You must go and do what you have to do and say your prayers." A fair description of the Christian life! We live as we can, say our prayers, and trust the everlasting mercy of God. We live in mercy like a bird in the sky or a fish in the blue sea. We Protestant people call it being "justified by grace."

IV

They brought a paralytic to Jesus. Jesus said, "My son, your sins are forgiven." Take time to look beyond the pulpit or the television screen— look into your own souls. Come face to face with your own guilt. We have all lost our innocence; it's the human story. Now turn from yourself to Christ and hear him speak: "My child," he says, "your sins are forgiven." Let his words be your faith: Say, "O my Lord, I really am forgiven." And step lightly, free and filled with the secret laughter of those who will accept the word "sinner" but know they have walked out from under the label and into grace.

Discussion

The sermon was written long ago by a young preacher, just a step beyond his twenties, who was still learning how to preach. Notice the 1, 2, 3, a, b, c sort of design that, happily, I have long since junked. Categorical development is intrinsically tedious and, worse, trivializing. One conceptual idea on top of another encourages a sense of repetition, thus tedium. Do we ever use lists to convey our deepest, most personal concerns? Of course not. We list errands to run, laundry to sort—trivial things—but we do not list the meaning of our lives! Categorical arrangement can always be avoided. But in spite of problems in design, let's review the sermon, section by section.

Introduction   The introduction works pretty well except for the last sentence, which shifts focus. It was added to tie into the "amazement" series but was still an error.

1   Section 1 includes three subsections: (a) We are guilty; (b) guilt is paralyzing; (c) guilt is stubborn. I probably could have explained the idea that we feel guilty over all sorts of different things without quoting from Fromm. Citations don't help unless we need expert support, and they are apt to intrude on our own language. The subsection on "guilt is paralyzing" seems to work, but the sexist use of "man" and "he" in 1960 was inexcusable. The third subsection is a problem. The jingle about spinach is cute, but that's the problem. Here I was trying to convey the desperation of those who are trying to be rid of guilt and, carelessly, I destroyed the building mood of desperation with cuteness. Dumb.

2   Section 2 contains three subsections. Subsection a poses a question, "How can Christ forgive us?" which subsections b and c try to answer. Upon rereading the material, I must conclude that both question and answers seem rather contrived. The poem in subsection a is powerful but does not support the question being raised. The next subsection seems to answer an accusation of cheap grace. The final subsection deals with a notorious trial and conviction then filling the newspapers.

3   Section 3 has two subsections, the first saying, "We have already been forgiven," and the second adding, "We can trust The Mercy in whom we live and move and have our being."

Conclusion   The Conclusion, though it returns to the text, may be the best thing in the sermon, which otherwise is labored and categorically wearing. The conventional point-making design prevents the sermon from matching the question-counterquestion-pronouncement pattern of the passage. Clearly, I should have thought out a different way to design a sermon.

CONFLICT OVER EATING WITH SINNERS

Mark 2:13–17 (also Matthew 9:9–13 and Luke 5:27–32)
   [13]Again he went out by the sea, where a huge crowd gathered for him to teach them.

¹⁴Walking along, [Jesus] saw Levi, son of Alphaeus, sitting in the toll office. And he said to him, "Follow me." Getting up, [Levi] followed him.
    ¹⁵And as he was reclining at table in [Levi's] house, toll collectors and sinners happened to be at table with Jesus and his disciples. (There were many who were following him.) ¹⁶The Pharisees' scribes, seeing him eating with sinners and toll collectors, said to the disciples, "Toll collectors and sinners—he eats with them?" ¹⁷Overhearing, Jesus said to them, "The healthy don't need a doctor, but the sick do. I didn't come to recruit the upright, but sinners."

Other Versions

The passage in Mark rambles. Verse 13 is a transitional verse moving us from the setting where the paralytic was healed to the seashore where, earlier, fishermen were called to be disciples. Verse 14 tells of the call of a toll collector, Levi. Verses 15–17 define the actual controversy. Matthew skips verse 13, and Luke reduces it to a phrase: "After this, he went out." Matthew changes the toll collector's name from Levi to Matthew. In the controversy, Matthew 9:13 adds a biblical citation to Jesus' reply: "Go learn what this means, 'I desire mercy instead of sacrifice'" (Hos. 6:6). Luke adds two words to Jesus' pronouncement: "I didn't come to recruit the righteous, but sinners *to repentance*" (Luke 5:32). The sequence of repentance then forgiveness appears to be a Lukan evangelical formula.

Mark's Story

In a way, Mark's story is mostly a juxtaposition; he has put together the call of Levi, a toll collector, with a controversy—Why does Jesus party with toll collectors and sinners? Levi, said to be a son of Alphaeus, is called in exactly the same way as, previously, fishermen were recruited (see Mark 1:16–20). But the name "Levi" is baffling because he does not appear in the list of the disciples in Mark 3:16–19, where the name "James" is given as the son of Alphaeus. In the Hebrew Bible (Num. 1:48–49), the Levites are not counted among the twelve tribes because they are servants of the tabernacle and, subsequently, of the Temple. Certainly "Levi" is an ironic name for a toll collector. No wonder, to straighten out confusion, the Gospel of Matthew renames him "Matthew."
    In Galilee, there were land taxes and then a host of other kinds of taxes. (In addition, all Jews were subject to a half-shekel temple tax.) Tax collectors received major land taxes, while the toll collectors were bureaucratic Jews

appointed by Herod Antipas or, worse, by Rome. The toll collectors were despised. From custom stations, they taxed shipping on trade routes in and out of districts and, by add-on fees, could become notoriously wealthy. The Mishnah likens them to robbers and murderers. In our day, perhaps we would call them racketeers.

To the account of Levi's recruitment, Mark tacks on the controversy over Jesus' open table fellowship. Not only does Jesus attract the corrupt, but he dines with them. Eating together was a virtual pledge of unity, one with another. So to eat with toll collectors and sinners would cast doubt on Jesus' moral judgment.

The Controversy

Mark's story is somewhat contrived. Jesus is having a meal in a house. He and his disciples are relaxing at table with "toll collectors and sinners." Mark does not tell us where or when. We can guess Jesus has been invited to Levi's house. Mark also throws in a parenthetical comment telling us that many toll collectors and sinners were following Jesus. Though the story is contrived, it involves a question, a statement, and a pronouncement. The question is asked by scholars of the Pharisees: "Toll collectors and sinners—he eats with them?" They are aghast. After all, eating meals together with pious regard for ritual purity was a central feature of pharisaic life. With sinners, food laws might be waived carelessly and required cleanliness ignored, but the issue is probably not ritual purity at table per se. The issue is more likely, What kind of religious leader shares table fellowship with people known to be brazenly corrupt and socially seamy? How could he welcome the company of people such as toll collectors, who bypass the law of God?

In reply, Jesus quotes a familiar proverb: "The healthy don't need a doctor, but the sick do." No doubt the Pharisees nodded their agreement; they would view themselves as religiously healthy. As a student once observed, "They certainly don't want to be called 'sickies'!" Neither do we. We are perfectly willing to use the term "sinners," an in-church term where, after all, we pray about things like "sin," but "sickies," particularly psychological sickies—never.

Then Jesus adds a pronouncement: "I didn't come to recruit the upright, but sinners." The Jesus Seminar translates the phrase, "I did not come to enlist religious folks but sinners!" and the translation is apt. The word *dikaious* can be translated "righteous," but here the word is used to describe those who would consider themselves righteous and, indeed, who would separate themselves from others they would label sinners. The upright Pharisees have excluded themselves from Jesus' partying company. They can only observe at a distance.

Homiletic Theology

I have used the word "recruit" in translating Jesus' pronouncement: "I didn't come to recruit the upright, but sinners." The word is usually translated "call," which, though correct, has become associated with religious vocation. In defining himself Jesus is specifically not being conventionally religious. Our problem is that we tend to justify Jesus' dinner parties with crooks and low-lifes as missionary activity. Surely Jesus would rather be spending time with us in our church fellowship halls, but isn't he brave to be out there rubbing flesh with sinners who do so need to be saved? The Gospel of Luke seems to support such a position. Probably we should begin by admitting that Jesus was no doubt enjoying the company he kept, namely, sold-out white-collar criminals and those too poor to be religious.

Underlying the pronouncement is the notion of God's new social order, or what most of our Bibles label the "kingdom of God."[10] There were many persons who were looking toward the future, who believed that someday, perhaps spelled SOMEDAY, there would be a grand feast on Mount Zion (Isa. 25:6–10). But Pharisees seemed to suppose that only the morally meritorious would find their names on place cards. If Jesus' meals were in any sense proleptic—that is, ahead-of-time celebrations of God's new order—then Jesus anticipated that God's new order would be inclusive rather than exclusive. After all, The Mercy will be host at Zion's feast. In Mark, Jesus himself never seems to ask sinners to repent. He never spells out how sinners must shift from sinfulness over to righteousness under the law. He simply welcomes them all to God's future feast.

Here is an additional symbol: Jesus was baptized among sinners. We should not suppose that Jesus said to himself, "Gee whiz, though I am sinless I ought to go into the Jordan anyway." All human beings experience guilt simply because we are interrelated children of God and, no matter what, inevitably we fail one another. Moreover, we belong to an age, like it or not, and every social age, to borrow a biblical phrase, is "an evil generation." Jesus willingly counted himself among sinners. He did not stand separated by his faith, nor with any sense of moral superiority.

Speaking the Passage

Some years ago, a sometime theologian argued that whenever preachers preached on Jesus' friendship with "tax collectors and harlots," these sinners were not real sinners. Because Jesus loved them, preachers supposed all the sinners had hidden hearts of gold. Will any preacher claim that Jesus actually liked awful people? No, the author said, probably not. As a result, he argued, we never hear the radical nature of the gospel message: God loves sinners. The advice is solid gold. If you preach about Jesus and sinners, the sinners must be certifiably sinful or congregations will not hear the gospel. So toll collectors are slick, sleazy, sold-out, dedicated racketeers. Did many of them have hired muscle to protect them while walking the streets? Probably. As for harlots (who are not in this passage), we had better be truthful. Whatever their sad history as social victims, they were probably hard-eyed, tight-rumped, and venial. Many of those cataloged as sinners simply didn't give a damn; they lived outside the law of God. So preachers, be wary; do not succumb to the whore-with-a-heart-of-gold syndrome.

A Sermon

The sermon was written in the 1980s and is very different in design from the older sermon on forgiving the paralytic. Sermon design is no longer comprised of a topic developed in categorical "points," but of "moves" in a movement of thought. The sermon appears in my book *Homiletic: Moves and Structures* (Philadelphia: Fortress Press, 1987), where I use it to demonstrate and discuss varieties of rhetorical point-of-view. The sermon does do all kinds of tricks with point-of-view. But here we will review the sermon simply as a sermon on a conflict story.

Introduction   In the chancel of a Pittsburgh church, there's a painting. The painting pictures Jesus at table with his disciples. There's Jesus in the center of the picture, dressed in white, and around him are disciples in stained-glass poses as if they were in church. A man came in, looked at the picture, and exclaimed, "Well, where are the sinners?" he said, "Didn't Jesus eat and drink with sinners?" Well, according to the New Testament that's exactly what Jesus did, not once but repeatedly. He ate and drank with sinners—no white linen, no silver chalice, but in some boozy back room in Capernaum. The story repeats in every Gospel, is told and retold with lifted eyebrows. Jesus, our Jesus, ate and drank with sinners.

1 Now make no mistake, *when the Bible says "sinners," the Bible means "sinners"!* Unvarnished, unrepentant, dyed-in-the-wool sinners. The Bible isn't talking about nice people gone astray, the good-at-heart prostitute, or the down-deep-they're-really-religious tax collectors. No, in the Bible, sinners are real sinners. Take tax collectors, for example; they were members of a social "Mafia," bagmen for the Roman conquerors, who gouged their own brothers and sisters for cash down. They had been crooks so long, with such absolute dedication, that the rabbis labeled them beyond redemption. Nowadays they'd be written up like Tony Pro or Mickey Cohen. And as for prostitutes, they were not misguided hometown girls gone astray in the big city; they were wised-up, tight-rumped, any-trick-for-a-buck, venial people. So who were the sinners in the Bible? As they say of pornographic films, they were "totally without redeeming social value." Listen, when the Bible says sinners, it means real honest-to-badness sinners. Jesus, our Jesus, ate and drank with sinners.

2   Well, *times have changed, for here we are at table.* We may not be the best people on earth, God knows, but by no stretch of the imagination are we the worst. And here we are at Christ's table. No, we're not going to pretend we're saints—we're not. But, on the other hand, to be honest, we're not all that bad! Yes, we lose our tempers, and we know we don't love enough, and at the end of the year when we flip through our check stubs, we admit that we haven't given enough away to charity. But to be truthful, we're not big-time sinners, and we're not going to pretend we are just to make a prayer of confession sound good. There's a poem about a man draped in sackcloth, beating his breast, and crying, "O Lord, my heart is black with guile, / Of sinners I am chief." To which a guardian angel replies, "Vanity my little man, / You're nothing of the kind."[11] Well, there is a kind of vanity in pretending we are awful sinners. We're not. We know we're not the best people on earth— no pretense—but we're not the worst. Times have changed, for here we are at Christ's table.

3   *But what was it Jesus said? He said, "I've not come to invite the righteous, but sinners."* I have not come for those in the right, but sinners. Well, he did. See him down in dirty Jordan water, baptized with sinners, or condemned by the Pharisees as an impure sinner, or hauled into court, judged and jailed, as a sinner. See him hung on a cross between thieves as a common crook— crucified as a sinner. All his life he lived with sinners, eating and drinking with sinners. Have you seen those picture books for sale at Christmas, "The Life of Christ in Christian Art"? You leaf the pages and you find pictures of Jesus as a boy in the Temple, Jesus preaching on the mountain, Jesus praying in the garden. You look in vain for a picture of Jesus whooping it up with sinners. Perhaps we do not want to see the picture, but we can. We can stand on lower Broadway. Stare through the smokey window into the barroom, where the flat-eyed men line the bar nursing their beers and the girls with the too-loud laughter dance to the juke box, and see, there's Jesus with them. He lived his life and he died his death

among sinners. What was it Jesus said? "I have not come for the righteous, but for sinners." He did not come for the righteous. He came for sinners.

4 Now, do you know where we are? *On the outside, looking in.* We're standing outside holding on to our chill righteousness while Jesus is inside, in the rosy warm room, partying with his friends, the sinners. On the outside, looking in! Like the little girl they found standing outside the banquet hall in a big hotel where they were holding a dinner for handicapped children. "I can't get in," she wailed. "There's nothing the matter with me!" So we're holding on to our righteousness but missing a party. Our righteousness shows up in little ways, in our everyday conversation: "Well at least I'm not . . ." "Well, at least I'm not a racist like Charlie," Or "At least I spend some time with my kids," "At least my house isn't a pigsty." "At least, I'm not . . . ," we say, and distance ourselves from others and from Jesus. For Jesus is in the bright room celebrating with his special friends, sinners. And where are we? We're on the outside looking in, holding on to our righteousness, out in the cold, while Jesus is somewhere else.

5 So what can we do? *Well, we can come to Christ as forgiven sinners.* Come as forgiven sinners, there's no other way. Look, it's not a matter of salt tears and grief, or sawdust down the aisle. We cannot earn Christ's mercy by our guiltiness. All we can do is to come as we are—forgiven sinners. Past tense, forgiven. The old at-least-I'm-not pride is tossed away, and we line up with sinners gladly, forgiven sinners. There's a wonderful story of an old evangelist who threw a party for all the riffraff in town, a wild, spilling-out-into-the-street party for sinners. There were champagne cocktails, trays of food, and a rock band beating out sweet-Jesus hymns—a happy party. A policeman walked by the door as a wreathy blonde danced out into the street. "Every bum in town is in there," sneered the policeman. "There's room for more, officer," sang the girl. "There's room for more."[12] Well, there is all the room in the world in the wideness of God's mercy. So what can we do? Simple. We can join the party as forgiven sinners!

Conclusion   Here we are together in church. Come if you wish, come as you are. The table's set. Perhaps you can hear the glad words of Christ echoing in your mind. He says to you, "Welcome. The party's begun, the joyful feast of the forgiven." The feast of the forgiven!

Discussion

The sermon is not set up with a 1, 2, 3, a, b, c categorical design. Instead, the sermon has a kind of sequential movement. The shift in methodology allowed me to orient us all as if we were those who looked at Jesus partying with sinners.

Introduction The introduction works nicely, abruptly shaking us from our churchiness to a truer picture of Jesus with sinners "in some boozy back room in Capernaum."

1 The first move looks at biblical sinners but does so with language and images drawn from our contemporary world: "Mafia" and "bagmen." The references to Tony Pro and Mickey Cohen were drawn from current newspaper stories describing major racket bosses. The same strategy is used describing prostitutes, with language on the edge of offensive: "wised-up, tight-rumped, any-trick-for-a-buck, venial." In a way, I am replicating the introduction by trying to dump churchy depictions of biblical sinners.

2 The second move swings from looking at the biblical world to the self-awareness of minister and congregation: "Here we are. . . ." The shape of the move is different; it is circled around the central poem, like people around a table. Generally, each move in a sermon should feature different internal construction. The language of the move is normal conversational phrasing for our modest and usual self-righteousness.

3 Here is a tricky move. The move begins by recalling Jesus' words and remembering moments in his life when he was emphatical with sinners. Then we realize that we never picture Jesus with sinners (the Christmas book image functions like the painting in the introduction). Then we deliberately do so, positioning ourselves to look into a barroom on "lower Broadway," which listeners in Nashville would recognize as their own city. The move ends with us on the outside looking in the window. Probably the move is overloaded and, thus, difficult to handle.

4 Move 4 begins with us recognizing where we are: "We're standing outside holding on to our chilly righteousness while Jesus is inside." Then there is the little girl who "can't get in because there's nothing the matter with me." The illustration is followed by our attempts to justify ourselves with "At least I'm not . . ." language.

5 The final move answers, "What can we do?" Instead of calling for repentance (no "salt tears and grief, or sawdust down the aisle"), the move simply lifts us into the community of sinners and, at the same time, announces our having been forgiven. The party image that follows (prompted by a reworked Frederick Buechner scene) is a strong, inviting, indeed gleeful, conclusion.

Conclusion The brief conclusion picks up the "Come on in" invitation and links it with the Eucharist.

Overall, except for a too-tricky third move that relies too much on delivery, the sermon works pretty well. It attempts to do what I think the passage itself is trying to do.

CONFLICT OVER FASTING

Mark 2:18–20 (also Matthew 9:14–17 and Luke 5:33–39)

[18]John's disciples and the Pharisees were fasting. People came to [Jesus] saying, "Why do the disciples of John and the disciples of the Pharisees fast, but your disciples don't?" [19]And [Jesus] said to them, "The groom's companions can't fast while the groom is with them, can they? As long as the groom is with them, they won't fast, [20]but the days will come when he is taken from them, and on that day, then they will fast.

[21]"No one sews an unshrunk cloth patch on an old garment, otherwise the patch will pull away, the new from the old, and there will be a worse tear. [22]And no one puts new wine into old wineskins, otherwise the wine will burst the wineskins and both wine and skins will be destroyed. Instead, new wine into new wineskins!"

Other Versions

The passage appears to be patched together from sources. There is a question on fasting to which Mark has added two brief parables, one on patching an old fabric, another on new wine and wineskins. The section on fasting seems occasional; the disciples of John are fasting, and Jesus' disciples are not. Matthew and Luke make the question of fasting a general issue, and Luke adds a peculiar verse 39: "No one who has drunk old wine wants the new, but says, 'The old is fine.'" The additional verse, though true enough, is inexplicable because it undercuts previous new/old metaphors.

Mark's Story

Again, Mark's story is less than a story but is rather a merging of disparate materials. The question of fasting (v. 18b) contrasts behavior: John's disciples fast, and Jesus' disciples do not. The reference to Pharisees (v. 18a) may have been inserted to tie the issue of fasting with the previous account of Jesus' feasting with sinners; both stories involve Pharisees who were concerned with patterns of eating. Though Mark imagines Jesus being accused and replying, the passage probably reflects contention over fasting some years after the resurrection when there may well have been some competition between the followers of John and the disciples of Jesus.

The Hebrew Bible requires fasting only on Yom Kippur, the day of repentance (Lev. 16:29–31). Thus, fasting was an expression of heartfelt repentance. But fasting was also a way of amplifying prayer. According to the *Didache*,

Pharisees fasted twice a week, on Mondays and Thursdays. By the end of the first century, Christians were resuming the tradition of fasting and, for them, the *Didache* recommended Wednesdays and Fridays (*Did.* 8:1). But while Jesus was in Galilee, apparently his followers may not have fasted. There is a verse from Q that may reflect similar tensions: "John the Baptist came not eating bread nor drinking wine, and you say, 'He's crazy'; the son of humanity came eating and drinking, and you say, 'He's a glutton and a drunk'"(Luke 7:33–34). John the Baptist preached a coming judgment that would inaugurate the kingdom of God. Thus, people were urged to repent and change their ways. Evidently, the changes involved self-denials appropriate to repentance. In contrast, the disciples of Jesus apparently didn't fast. Though Jesus also announced the coming new order of God, he did so with glad anticipation. In the new order, the poor would prosper, the hungry would feast, the powerless would be empowered, and those who wept for the way of the world would laugh for joy. No wonder cheerful table fellowship was central to the Jesus movement.

The Controversy

Here we have a question asked of John's disciples in tandem with Pharisees: They fast; why don't you fast? Jesus asks the counterquestion: "The groom's companions can't fast while the groom is with them, can they?" Marriage was an expression of covenant faith, and therefore attendance was obligatory. After all, marriage could ensure God's covenant promise to Abraham, "I will make you exceedingly numerous." Thus, though death deserved mourning in Jewish piety, with tears and fasting, weddings were much more important, with requisite festive partying. The counterquestion exposes the mind-set of the disciples of John. For them, the primary significance of the coming new order was judgment. Apparently, with Jesus, the metaphor "God's new order" conveyed liberation and thus celebration. The second part of the counterquestion seems to have been added by subsequent Christian experience, perhaps as a justification for resumed fasting: "The days will come when he is taken from them, and on that day, then they will fast."

We have a question and a counterquestion but no final pronouncement. Instead, Mark has added two brief parabolic sayings. The first is probably a folk saying about patching old clothing, which doesn't exactly fit the context. If the analogy is that fasting equals old custom and the Jesus movement equals a new patch, the only way to avoid tearing the fabric would seem to be either using a safe, old, cloth patch, or an entirely new garment which, unfortunately, is not mentioned. On the other hand, the saying about new wine is more appropriate and possibly could go back to Jesus: "No one puts new wine into old wineskins, otherwise the wine will burst the wineskins and both wine and skins will be destroyed. Instead, new wine into new wineskins!" While the new-wine parable is not exactly an epigrammatic pronouncement, it serves to complete the structure of a controversy form. The final verse, 22b, is quite epigrammatic.

Homiletic Theology

What about fasting? Given our national struggle with obesity, a little fasting might be in order, particularly in a world where most people are ill-fed and chronically hungry. As a personal discipline, helping us to bring our lives under God's control, fasting might be a good thing. Devotional fasting has been a feature of most religions. But if fasting becomes a work to cash in on salvation, it could lead to spiritual anorexia. Nevertheless, as part of a whole, ordered Christian life, fasting should not be ruled out.

When it comes to fasting, the Hebrew Bible offers prophetic warnings (Isa. 58:6–7):

> This is the fast I desire:
> To unlock the fetters of wickedness,
> And untie the cords of the yoke
> To let the oppressed go free;
> To break off every yoke.
> It is to share your bread with the hungry,
> And to take the wretched poor into your home.

If we are going to fast, perhaps we should recite Isaiah 58:6–7 every hour on the hour until our fasting is done. The only advice on fasting attributed to Jesus is in the Sermon on the Mount where Jesus suggests that those who fast do so without public display. Instead, they should wash their faces and anoint themselves in the usual every-morning manner (Matt. 6:16–18).

Through the centuries, Christianity seems to have been expressed in different ways. The ways have been labeled "the Way of Negation" and "the Way of Affirmation."[13] Negation involves denial, often heroic self-denial, to cancel all other loves but the love of God alone. The stuff of the world, including food and drink, are considered distractions that turn us from our true focus, namely, the holy mystery of God. The Way of Affirmation involves loving God through the gifts God gives: earthly gifts, domestic gifts, the modest flower, the cheerful cup, the sweet marital bed. Both modes of life seem to show up as a kind of alternating current in Christianity—St. John of the Cross versus Dame Julian of Norwich. Maybe neither way is an only way, but together they may be a useful alternating current. Isaiah's poetry (58:6–7) is a useful reminder that justice and compassion for neighbors is the overriding concern that must correct excesses of either way. A spirituality that is religiously self-serving is perverse. There are two sides to the Great Commandment, yet they are one.

What is interesting in the passage from Mark is the degree of flippancy with respect to religious exercises. No wonder that early Christians were scornfully labeled *atheoi,* "godless," by pious pagans. Christians seemed to be a good deal less than scrupulous, indeed irreligious, when it came to observing personal ritual practices. The substantial section in the Sermon on the Mount on personal piety (Matt. 6:1–18) does not deny the value of prayer, almsgiving, and fasting—the basic Jewish pattern of piety—but offers warnings. Piety must never be ostentatious or a source of spiritual pride. Nor should religious practice be self-demeaning. The prayer Jesus taught his disciples was unusual in its brevity, a quick everyday sort of prayer. Otherwise, Jesus did not seem to offer us spiritual exercises. The one central activity was eating together and welcoming others to the common table—partying as the antithesis of fasting.

What about the little parable of the new wine? At least obliquely, the parable relates to the question; wine is a celebrative drink. But as new wine continues to ferment within the usual goatskin containers, old containers can burst and wine be lost. New wine requires new wineskins. Thus Christianity, though it should never denigrate its Hebrew heritage, will seek new modes of common life appropriate to the evangelical gospel message. The word *kainos,* "new," is radical. It does not describe the merely novel, such as a new product or a new dress style, for products and dress styles are still very much at home in our social order. Here "new" refers to ways of life in God's new order. All Jesus' parables are new order parables.

American religious individualism tends to read the word "new" as personal inward renewal; with God we can be happy new people inside ourselves. Each one of us Christian types can be filled with the heady wine of the Spirit. But "kingdom" is a social model, wine is a happily shared social drink, and Christian understanding of the Holy Spirit among us is social. The newness Christianity announces is the promise of a new society—God's new social world involving all humanity. "New" does not describe something renewed but a replacing of an old, wearied social order with the world God intends.

Speaking the Passage

You may wish to overlook the first little analogy about unshrunk cloth. The usual image for a Christian life was new clothes, such as a new baptismal robe to replace the old clothes of an old life. But here we are told not to sew a new patch on an old garment. Maybe the idea is that patching some old garb is ridiculous when it's time for a completely new outfit. Unfortunately, as the analogy stands, there is nothing about a new garment. It's all about patching. Though the two little analogies are paired, they don't quite match. Preachers in constructing a sermon may simply skip the first analogy and concentrate on the new wine image. Or if preachers wish to hold tight to the biblical text, they may skip the old/new patch image and preach the foolishness of patching up ourselves when a total new life is required. Maybe preachers would be rhetorically smart to simply choose one or the other image to develop. The wine image seems more useful because of its eucharistic associations.

But the big issue is newness. The idea of a "kingdom of God" is not personal but is a metaphor for a completely new social order, God's social order. So the gospel of the "kingdom" calls for living together in new ways and not merely with a little more niceness. So how can we be new-wine people in an old, change-resistant social order?

The passage can be preached in several ways. We can brood over the problems we have with old strategies and old customs; how can we ever break out of the repetitions of sin? Most of our therapies are "patching," so most of our renewals fade like New Year's resolutions. How can we live together in new ways beyond competition, beyond limited loyalties like patriotism or family pride, beyond the profound everyday failures of our halfway loves? In other words, we can set up an awareness of our old ways and of our stale compromising. Repentance, if it is simply regret, is not much use. We can then image what we know we need, as well as the fears that hold us back. Finally, we can hear the promise of new clothes or new wine.

Another option is to focus on the image of fasting. Certainly our bloated society needs to be lean and loving in a hungry world. Fasting is not a personal spiritual achievement for our own self-development. And it is never to be on display. Every Christian exercise is connected to neighbor love. Besides, we live in the sure mercy of God. Does fasting look back ruefully? True Christianity has a festive spirit, ever looking toward the future promises of God—promises that are happening now. The passage begins with the question of fasting and answers with a marriage image: how can anyone fast when the bridegroom is present? Then there are the two little parables. These three images—the marriage feast, the patched garment, the new wine—offer different ways to get at a sermon. All we need is theology and imagination.

CONFLICT OVER PICKING GRAIN ON THE SABBATH

Mark 2:23–28 (also Matthew 12:1–8 and Luke 6:1–5)

²³On the Sabbath, [Jesus] happened to be walking through grain fields. As they were going along, his disciples began picking heads of grain.

²⁴The Pharisees said to him, "Look, why are they doing what's forbidden on the Sabbath?" ²⁵And Jesus said to them, "Haven't you read what David did when he and his companions were hungry? During the days of High Priest Abiathar, ²⁶he went into the house of God and ate the Bread of the Presence, which only priests were permitted to eat. What's more, he gave some to those who were with him."

²⁷He said to them, "The Sabbath was created for humanity, not humanity for the Sabbath. ²⁸The son of humanity is lord even over the Sabbath."

Other Versions

Mark's memory of 1 Samuel 21:1–8 is faulty. The priest involved was not Abiathar but his father Ahimelech. Matthew and Luke correct Mark's mistake by deleting the reference to Abiathar. But both Matthew and Luke also remove Jesus' statement, "The Sabbath was created for humanity, not humanity for the Sabbath." Are they disturbed by the saying? Could occasional human hungers overrule God's Torah? Matthew substitutes three verses to replace the troubling saying:

> Or, haven't you read in the law that, on Sabbath days, priests in the Temple break the Sabbath, but are considered blameless. Yet, I'm telling you something greater than the Temple is here. If you had understood, "I desire mercy, not sacrifice," you would not have condemned those who are blameless. (Matt. 12:5–7)

Matthew has added the same quotation here—"I desire mercy, not sacrifice" (Hos. 6:6)—that he did to the story of Jesus' feasting with toll collectors and sinners (Matt. 9:13).

There is an odd variant reading in a manuscript of Luke that replaces 6:5: "On the same day, seeing someone at work on the Sabbath, Jesus said, 'Man, blessed are you if you know what you're doing; but if you don't, you're condemned and a law breaker'" (Codex Bezae). The extra "beatitude" certainly sounds like Jesus.

Mark's Story

As Jesus and his disciples are wading through a grain field, the disciples rather innocently are picking off heads of grain and, after rubbing them in the palms of their hands, eat some. Looking on, Pharisees (What could they be doing hiding out in a remote grain field?) raise their accusation, supposing rubbing of the grain, equivalent to threshing and harvesting, was labor on the Sabbath day. In reply, Jesus cites the case of hungry David and his followers who, abetted by a priest, ate the consecrated Bread of the Presence. According to Leviticus 24:5–9, every Sabbath, priests set twelve loaves of fresh bread in the tabernacle as an offering to God. When the bread was replaced on the next Sabbath, priests alone were to consume the old loaves. The idea of the citation seems to be that the Torah itself tells of an exception to the Sabbath-day commandment, a very Jewish argument.

But Mark's grasp of Sabbath law is not learned and is seldom accurate. Deuteronomy 23:26 permits the plucking of grain: "If you go into your neighbor's standing grain, you may pluck the ears with your hand, but you shall not put a sickle to your neighbor's standing grain."[14] Jewish legal interpretation does make a distinction between real harvesting and the casual plucking of grain heads. With the case of David and his men, Jewish interpreters recognized the overwhelming need of the hungry even on the Sabbath.[15] In other words, Mark's story is deliberately overdrawn.

The Controversy

The controversy is shaped nicely—question, counterquestion, and pronouncement. Though the citation with regard to David seems somewhat oblique and too sophisticated for Jesus from Nazareth, it does expose a Pharisaic mind-set. The Pharisees are reading the commandments of the Torah as absolutely binding on every form of human behavior. The story of David and Ahimelech demonstrates that Pharisees are more rigorous than Scripture, for Scripture tells of an exception to the commandment. Note the caricature that is already forming in the conflict stories.

The big problem is the meaning of the two-verse pronouncement: Would Jesus have announced that human beings are "lords" over the Sabbath day? Surely God alone is Lord of the Sabbath! The saying obviously troubled Matthew and Luke, who dropped the verse. Jewish Sabbath law is based on Genesis 2:1–3:[16]

> Thus the heavens and the earth were finished, and all their multitude. And on the seventh day God finished the work he had done, and he rested on the seventh day from all the work that he had done. So God blessed the seventh day and hallowed it, because on it God rested from all the work he had done in creation.

On the Sabbath day, God sat back and rested. Creation was complete, and "God saw all that he had made, and found it very good" (Gen. 1:31). "Very good" is understatement; creation was Edenic, with beauty and lush provision, food to eat and share, enough for all God's children, and wonder, awe-some wonder, to hush the human soul. Of course, God blessed the Sabbath day—a very good work complete. So, quite simply, if God rested and con-templated the good creation, we, God's own people, should do likewise. Notice what is involved in keeping the day holy: contemplation of creation—its wonder, loving provision, numinous beauty—all with delight and gratitude to God. According to the Westminster Shorter Catechism, human beings exist to glorify and enjoy God forever.[17] A fine definition of the Sabbath day.

Of course, the Sabbath was also connected with the exodus tradition as a liberation from slavery. Therefore, all work was stopped:

> Mark that the LORD has given you the Sabbath; therefore he gives you two days' food on the sixth day. Let everyone remain where he is: let no one leave his place on the seventh day. (Exod. 16:29)

So the children of Israel did their baking and boiling on the sixth day. On the Sabbath they feasted, sharing food and wine, without going to work, and with leisure considered the gifts of God's good creation and providential care.

But a third passage, Leviticus 25:1–7, extends Sabbath theology:

> The LORD spoke to Moses on Mount Sinai, saying: Speak to the Israelite people and say to them: When you enter the land that I assign to you, the land shall observe a sabbath of the LORD. Six years you may sow your field, and six years you may prune your vineyard and gather in the yield. But in the seventh year, the land shall have a sabbath of complete rest, a sabbath of the LORD: you shall not sow your field or prune your vineyard. You shall not reap the aftergrowth of your harvest or gather the grapes of your untrimmed vines; it shall be a year of complete rest for the land. But you may eat whatever the land during its Sabbath will produce—you, your male and female slaves, the hired and bound laborers who live with you, and your cattle and the beasts in your land may eat all its yield.

The idea of a Sabbath is extended not simply for people but for the land, domes-tic animals, and wild animals. Thus, the Sabbath is an ecological celebration of God's goodness in the creation. In the same chapter of Leviticus, the Sab-bath is multiplied "seven times seven years" to create a fiftieth year, the jubilee year. During the jubilee, there shall be a kind of amnesty. If poverty has forced a sale of property, the property shall be recovered. If people fall into financial want, you shall support them without taking profit. In other words, there is an attempt to restore the good freedom of the created world that was true on the original seventh day. The Sabbath is a day to celebrate the goodness of God by serving one another in joyful holy community. The Sabbath day is scarcely repressive. American Christians don't seem to realize that Jews look forward to the Sabbath, as a time to enjoy creation, serve one another with affection, relax, and remember that they are no longer slaves.

But as we all know, laws written to ensure mutual concern and release from oppression can swing around and seem to repress. Perhaps that happened in the midst of the conflict between an emerging Christianity and a parent Jewish community. Were laws accusingly applied and then defiantly shrugged off? Probably. Christianity was busy sliding out from under Sabbath ritual, and "Lord's Day" Eucharists were taking hold. Plus, many of the new Gentile Christians may have been slaves (remember Onesimus?) and unable to enjoy any kind of "day of rest."

Let's turn now to the pronouncement "The Sabbath was created for humanity, not humanity for the Sabbath. The son of humanity is lord even over the Sabbath." Mark has reported what was probably an original saying. What does it mean? Here are four options.

First, the saying could mean what it says, namely, that the commandment is for human beings, who should have one day of rest free from labor. Exodus 34:21, a Yahwist text, is specific: "Six days you shall work, but on the seventh day you shall cease from labor; even at plowing time and harvest time." Keeping the seventh day seems to have been a compassionate law so that workers, employees, slaves, and livestock could rest from labor. Thus, the Sabbath day commandment is a gift of grace.

Second, just as human beings have been given stewardship over the creation, so also they have stewardship even over the Sabbath day. Genesis 1:26 is sweeping: "Then God said, 'Let us make [humankind] in our image, after our likeness. They shall rule the fish of the sea, the birds of the sky, the cattle, the whole earth, and all the creeping things that creep on earth.'" In Genesis 1, human beings are created before the Sabbath is established. Here "son of humanity" is not an apocalyptic title but could refer to any human being.

Third, some scholars suppose that the original saying was "The Sabbath was created for the son of humanity, not the son of humanity for the Sabbath." Thus, "son of humanity" is a messianic title (after all, rabbis affirmed that the world was created for the Messiah). Such a reading is, I think, unlikely.

Fourth, other scholars interpret the text from a high Christology and suppose the verse means that the risen, regnant Christ is Lord even over the Sabbath. Such an interpretation might launch us in the direction of a supersessionism in which the church's Lord's Day displaces the Jewish Sabbath completely. But the big problem with high Christology here is that such a claim would severely undercut the passion pronouncements soon to come.

We faced the same question in interpreting the controversy connected to the healing of the paralytic: "The son of humanity has authority to forgive sins." Does the verse mean that Christ has authority, that a new humanity in Christ has authority, or that any human being has authority? Paul, who says that "the saints will judge the world" (1 Cor. 6:2), seems to suppose that representatives of the new humanity, themselves forgiven sinners, have authority to judge and forgive. But perhaps Paul's argument should be extended: *Any forgiven sinner living in The Mercy can forgive.*

Here the options are very much the same. What exactly is meant by "son of humanity"? Does Mark's apocalyptic theology govern interpretation? Does verse 28 interpret verse 27, or does verse 27 interpret verse 28? Is Sabbath behavior under human governance? Are children of the new humanity no longer under Sabbath legal regulation? Certainly love can transcend rules of piety on the Sabbath day.

Homiletic Theology

Observance of the Sabbath goes back before Israel's monarchy to the settling of Canaan. Originally it seems to have been a rest from work. Supporting the idea of the Sabbath were stories of creation, for, according to Genesis 1, God rested on the seventh day. God also liberated Israel from enslavement as workers in Egypt (Deut. 5:14–15). The Sabbath was a special sign connected with Israel's identity as God's chosen people (Exod. 31:15–17), so keeping the day holy was an obligation and was strictly maintained by Essenes, Sadducees, and Pharisees. Thus, a day of rest for laborers was reshaped into a day of religious obligation.

At first, Christians seem to have observed the Sabbath, soon adding a celebration of resurrection at dawn on the following day. Gradually the two days separated into the Sabbath and the Lord's Day. The separating of the two days may underlie the controversy. Clearly, Christians no longer felt bound by Sabbath regulations: "Don't let anyone judge you over what you eat and drink or over special days, new moons, or Sabbaths" (Col. 2:16). But, just as with fasting, gradually a tendency toward ritual regulation crept back into Christianity all over again. In 331 CE, the Emperor Constantine established Sunday as the official day of rest, thus pleasing both Christians and pagans (for whom the day of the Sun God had religious significance). Sunday as an official day soon gathered sanction.

Many of us grew up in homes with family rules about card playing and movies on Sunday. Such rules were soon shattered as television screens and video games invaded our lives. In addition, we have watched commercial pressures encourage fashionable brunches, the opening of stores, and the scheduling of pro football games on Sunday. How do we honor a proper recognition of God and still prevent "holy day" regulation from wrapping love's freedom in guiltiness? The extra beatitude that didn't get into Luke speaks to us: "Blessed are you if you know what you're doing; but if you don't, you're condemned and a law breaker." Neighbor love may transcend restrictions of holiness, but consumer greed for Sunday sales surely deserves condemnation.

Though the passage is concerned with keeping the Sabbath holy, issues underlying the passage are profound. Yes, we need to honor the sovereignty of the holy God with devout obedience. Therefore, a casual reading of "The Sabbath was created for humanity, not humanity for the Sabbath" may trouble us. Are we, willful and idolatrous creatures, to decide where and when we will honor God? Admittedly, we do determine how to use the day, whether as a Sabbath or a Lord's Day. Though ritual rules may help guide us, they cannot ultimately bind our freedom.

Actually, the matter is more complex. Individuals are not necessarily free deciders; society often has tacit regulations and patterns of behavior that determine us. For example, Hannah Arendt argued in 1958 that American workers are so overworked that they do not have leisure to consider deeper matters, indeed, to think over the meaning of their lives or the mystery of God.[18] Since Arendt wrote her remarks, the pressure on American workers by corporate managers has only multiplied. Has the all-American lust for corporate profit determined how we understand the Sabbath? Probably. Setting aside a day, any day, as a sacred day is obviously a good idea in a profit-driven culture; workers can and should rest. One day out of seven should be possible for all and, for religious believers, should afford time to praise God and meet together. Maybe Christianity's newness could turn Sunday into a day for enjoying others as well as the Other. Perhaps the true Christian symbol for Sunday is the glad eucharistic feast.

Speaking the Passage

We must be careful. The passage is contrived to portray Pharisees as sneaky, hypercritical people. We must not take the bait. Instead, we must move immediately into our own century and our own Lord's Day problems. We should not discuss first-century Jewish practices or prohibitions. We will be helped by recalling the Jewish theology of the Sabbath. Still, the passage can be a trap for preachers. We must not end up setting our Lord's Day against their Sabbath, particularly when we have defaced our day with football frenzy, local discount store sales, and, on the national level, ecological exploitation and antilabor legislation.

My first impulse is to let the Pharisees' question question us: "Why are you defacing your holy day?" We can then take a long look at what live-by-the-dollar America has done to Sunday. A next move might help us to recall what the Lord's Day is meant to be—— a time for neighbor love, a time for celebrating the creator God with those around us, a time to enjoy the good world as a gift. We might end with Jesus' words: "The day was meant for humanity"! If then we take the second half of the phrase, "not humanity for the day," we could worry over the problem of religious regulation. Communities of faith have every right to protect the holiness of their day, but inevitably there are exceptions and thus more laws are created. But we can then turn to the truth: as a society we determine the Lord's Day—we poor sinners. No wonder the day has been corrupted. For Christians, the Lord's Day was an "eighth day," a day to become new "kingdom" people of God in The Mercy of God.

CONFLICT OVER HEALING ON THE SABBATH

Mark 3:1–6 (also Matthew 12:9–14 and Luke 6:6–11)

[1]Jesus went into the synagogue again, where there was a man with a withered hand. [2]They were eyeing him to see if he would heal the man on the Sabbath so they could accuse him.

[3]And [Jesus] said to the man with the withered hand, "Stand up here so everyone can see you." [4]Then he asked them, "On the Sabbath, is it permitted to do good or evil; to save life or to kill?" They were silent. [5]He glared at them with anger, grieved by their hardness of heart. Then Jesus said to the man, "Stretch out your hand." He stretched, and his hand was restored.

[6]Immediately, the Pharisees and the Herodians went out and consulted together against him, plotting to destroy him.

Other Versions

Both Matthew and Luke have removed the references to Jesus' human emotions of anger and grieving. Matthew also has deleted Jesus' challenging the Pharisees by standing the handicapped man in front of them with a sharp counterquestion. Instead, Matthew introduces an argument: "If any of you has a single sheep who falls into a pit on the Sabbath day, won't you grab him and pull him out? A human being is much more valuable than a sheep." Matthew then turns Jesus' sharp query into a statement: "It is legal to do good on the Sabbath." Both Matthew and Luke drop any reference to the Herodians, as they were no longer a factor for their respective audiences. Luke has two other healing-on-the-Sabbath stories that essentially have the same plot as the man with the withered hand: the woman bent from birth (13:10–17) and the dropsical man (14:1–6).

Mark's Story

Our series of five conflict stories is preceded by the story of a leper healed by Jesus (1:40–45). The man is told to say nothing to others but to go and present himself before a priest with the prescribed offering, "as a testimony for them." Though Jesus has healed the man out of compassion, he may also be announcing his action to the priests with a touch of defiance. Thereafter, we have five conflict stories, one after another, with the scribes and Pharisees. Finally, the sequence ends climactically with another healing, prompting Pharisees to consult with Herodians about destroying Jesus.

The story of the man with the withered hand is brief. There is no exchange between Jesus and the man and no further description of the man's plight. He only functions as an object lesson. Presumably, he has an injured hand. The Pharisees (who are not named until the final verse) are in the synagogue to see if Jesus will break the Sabbath rule. Abruptly, Jesus tells the man to "stand up here so everyone can see you." Then, facing his critics, Jesus asks, "On the Sabbath, is it permitted to do good or evil; to save life or to kill?"

The issue in Mark's story has to do with Sabbath laws that might or might not permit healing. If a medical matter is urgent, healing must take precedence over scribal law. If an animal is in pain, has fallen in a well (Luke 14:1–6), or is thirsty (Luke 13:10–17), compassionate concern for the animal's plight sets a priority.[19] The problem in Mark's story is that the man's hand appears to have been crippled for a long time. Could healing wait a few hours? Probably. In Greek, the man's hand is described as "completely withered"; thus, most likely, he suffers from a permanent condition. Later rabbinic teaching, particularly of Hillel the Elder, seems to have agreed with Jesus. The rabbis lifted scribal restrictions and considered all healing as lifesaving and, therefore, allowable on the Sabbath.[20] Thus, Jesus' reply was not scandalous and certainly would not have provoked any murderous intent on the part of Herodians and Pharisees. Has Mark allowed the bitterness of his own controversial context to color his writing, or has the offending verse 3:6 come from the source of all five stories? We cannot say. But we can say that the reported meeting of Herodians and Pharisees simply would not have been provoked by eating grain heads or healing on a Sabbath day. The verse is unfortunate.

The Controversy

The form is partial. There is an implied question: "They were eyeing him to see if he would heal the man on the Sabbath so they could accuse him." There is also a direct counterquestion: "On the Sabbath, is it permitted to do good or evil; to save life or to kill?" But there is no final pronouncement. Instead, the man's hand is healed. We can assume that, as with the paralyzed man, the man's hand would be construed as evidence of God's disapproval; the man would be considered an obvious sinner. But forgiving sin is not the issue here. Because the story is attached to the previous passage, we can suppose that "the son of humanity is lord even over the Sabbath" covers the healing as well. But there is no final pronouncement.

Instead, the passage concludes with the Pharisees and Herodians plotting Jesus' final fate. The sudden coalition of Herodians and Pharisees is odd. Pietists and politicos together; they appear to be unusual co-conspirators, but actually they are not. Here, if the verse is not from a source, we may be viewing a touch of Markan irony. The newness of the Jesus movement creates unity among unlikely colleagues of the old order.

Homiletic Theology

The passage is climactic because it finally speaks the crucial question: "On the Sabbath, is it permitted to do good or evil; to save life or to kill?" If religious laws prevent charity, acts of love or liberation, simple times of being together and enjoying one another, cheerful partying at Sunday dinner, and the like, can they be justified? Guarding a sense of the sacred may seem important, but religious legislation is a clear danger. Religious legislation that stymies acts of neighbor love is essentially irreligious.

Of late, many of our churches seem to be torn in two. There are those in every congregation pushing social concern, while others champion spirituality. The conflict seems to be setting one term of the Great Commandment against the other. The Shema—a call to love God with heart, soul, and mind—is pitted against the Levitical call to love neighbors as our own. Both sides of the argument are right, and yet both are wrong. We live in a nation careless of God. And a busy impiousness that overlooks the holiness of God has crept into many of our full-service, over-busy churches. We need to cultivate holiness. But the failure of churches to see beyond the stained-glass barrier is also distressing; the gospel is preached as personal therapy, and social issues are frequently overlooked as potentially divisive. The prophetic voice of the church has been silenced. But charity has lagged as well; simple human concern for the poor, the disenfranchised, and the socially oppressed *is* gospel.[21] So both positions are right. But both are wrong in that they have split the Great Commandment with partisan spirit. If piety prevents neighbor love, it is not true piety. And if neighbor love interferes with our remembering God, it will soon burn out. Recall C. S. Lewis's wonderful description of a woman driven by concern for neighbors: "She's the sort of woman who lives for others—you can always tell the others by their hunted expression."[22]

Of course, the other issue here is the holiness of the Sabbath day, which Pharisees did seek to guard. But if we are created to serve one another in exchanges of love, then religious regulations that restrict neighbor love are simply inappropriate.

Speaking the Passage

At the outset, let us agree to ban reference to verse 3:6 from our preaching. The concluding verse should not be included in any homiletic concern, for it can only be labeled anti-Judaism. The only issue for designing a sermon is this: How can we restore the contending positions? The idea of healing on the Sabbath will win approval from any congregation. Along with Jesus, we're all for healing. Therefore, we will have to raise questions about respecting the holiness of God to give legitimacy to Jesus' opponents. "Hallowed be thy name" is still recited by most Christian congregations, and the only way to "hallow" is to create symbolic times and places for the reverencing of God. In Jesus' day, the time was the Sabbath, the place was the synagogue. From such a general argument we can step into Sabbath-day theology—a time and a place set aside to honor the holy God, the God of creation, the God of our lives. How do we guard times and places of reverence? Unless we can restore credibility to Jesus' opposition, we will not be able to grasp the full meaning of the passage. In the section on homiletic theology, we turned to the conflict between the two parts of the Great Commandment as a lively current issue. "Doing good" is an everyday responsibility, but what about honoring God? Is not honoring God also something for every day? If we cannot restore the integrity of the positions involved, we can easily tumble into anti-Judaism. Let the sermon address instead our own sense of holy times and places.

MORE CONFLICTS OVER HEALING ON THE SABBATH

Luke 13:10–17

[10]He was teaching in one of the synagogues on the Sabbath. [11]Look, there was a woman who had been sickened by a spirit for eighteen years. She was bent over and couldn't stand up straight. [12]Catching sight of her, Jesus called her over, saying, "Woman, you're free from your illness." [13]He put his hands on her and, immediately, she straightened up and was glorifying God.

[14]But the leader of the synagogue was incensed that Jesus had healed on the Sabbath. He was addressing the crowd, "There are six working days to come and be healed, but not on the Sabbath day." [15]The Lord answered him, saying, "You're phonies. Every one of you, won't you untie your ox or your donkey from a stall on the Sabbath and lead him to drink? But this daughter of Abraham, bound by Satan for eighteen years, wasn't it as necessary to untie her on the Sabbath day?"

[17]So speaking he shamed his opposition, and the crowd rejoiced over all the glories being done.

Luke 14:1–6

[1]Jesus happened to go into the house of a leading Pharisee to dinner on the Sabbath day. They were watching him closely. [2]Look, in front of him was a man who was suffering from dropsy. [3]Jesus addressed the lawyers and Pharisees asking, "Is it legal to heal on the Sabbath or not?" [4]They were silent. So Jesus took hold of the man, healed him, and sent him on his way. [5]To them, he said, "If any of you have a [son] or an ox who falls into a well on the Sabbath day, won't you get him out quickly?" [6]And they were unable to answer him.

These two stories are found in Luke and are written in Luke's distinctive style. The first story, though set in a synagogue as is Mark 3:1–6, is quite distinctive. The second story, about the man with dropsy, is not set in a synagogue but otherwise is much like the story in Mark. Jesus asks a question about what is permitted on the Sabbath. His critics are silent. Then Jesus acts decisively to heal.

In the first story, a leader of the synagogue addresses the crowd, reminding them of Sabbath regulation. Instead of addressing the dignitary, Jesus speaks to the whole assembly. Any Galilean, he argues, would untie thirsty animals and lead them to drink on the Sabbath. Jesus uses the same verb, "untie," to describe healing the woman long bound by Satan.

In the second story, "if any of you have a son or an ox" is a bit jarring. In some manuscripts "son" has been replaced by "ass," because the logic or the argument seems to require another animal. Nevertheless, most manuscripts have "son." If "son" is correct, then there are no grounds for conflict; life-saving would override all Sabbath regulations according to the law. However, at the time of Christ, the Qumran community would not have relaxed Sabbath law at all.

The argument in both stories is essentially the same: If you have an animal who needs help, you respond, although it may be the Sabbath day. How much more important is it to rescue a human child of God. Though the stories reflect conflict over the Sabbath, and though there is dialogue in both, there is no final memorable saying in either of them. Again, the healing is a decisive action replacing the usual saying.

The arguments in Luke's stories are more developed than in Mark so that, all in all, the Matthean rewrite or the Lukan stories are preferable to the somewhat blunt, overdramatic Mark, particularly with Mark 3:6.

Chapter 5

Two by Two

Further Controversy over Jesus:
  Conflict over Jesus' Healings (3:20–30)
  Conflict over Jesus' Family (3:20, 31–35)
Further Controversy over the Disciples:
  Conflict over Washing before Eating (7:1–23)
  Conflict over a Syrophoenician Woman (7:24–30)
An Aborted Controversy:
  The Pharisees Ask for a Sign (8:11–13)

*F*ollowing the five conflict stories in Mark 2:1–3:6, there are two additional stories in the third chapter that seem to swirl around Jesus himself, his unauthorized exorcisms, and his family life. Then in chapter 7, there are two more conflict stories that may relate to the character of early Christian communities, their break from Jewish purity ritual, and their turn toward a Gentile ministry. Finally, in chapter 8, Pharisees come demanding a sign to authorize Jesus' actions.

CONFLICT OVER JESUS' HEALINGS

Mark 3:20–30 (also Matthew 12:22–37 and Luke 11:14–23)
  [20]Jesus went into a house. Again he drew a crowd, so there wasn't any way for them to eat a meal. [21]When his family heard about it, they went to corral him, for people were saying, "He's out of his mind!"
  [22]Scribes down from Jerusalem came, and were saying, "He has Beelzebul, for he drives out demons by the ruler of demons!" [23]Calling them over, [Jesus] spoke parables to them: "How can Satan drive out Satan? [24]If a realm is divided against itself, the realm cannot survive. [25]And if a household is divided against itself, the household cannot survive. [26]If Satan stands up against himself, divided, he cannot possibly survive; he's finished.
  [27]"No one can get into a strong man's house to steal his things unless he first ties up the strong man. Only then can he ransack the house.

[28]"Amen, I tell you, every sin and blasphemy humans can commit will be forgiven, [29]but whoever blasphemes against the Holy Spirit will never be forgiven, but is guilty of an eternal sin." [30](Remember, they were saying, "He has an evil [lit., unclean] spirit.")

[31]His mother with his brothers arrived and, standing outside, they sent word to him, calling him out. [32]A crowd was sitting around him, and they were telling him, "Look, your mother and your brothers and your sisters are outside wanting you." [33]Answering them, he said, "Who are my mother and my brothers?" [34]And looking at those who were gathered in a circle around him, he said, "See, here are my mother and my brothers. [35]Whoever does the will of God is my brother, sister, and mother."

Other Versions

While all of the Synoptic Gospels tell of the Beelzebul controversy, Matthew and Luke seem to be drawing on their common Q source as well as Mark. Both skip Mark's first two verses, dropping the reference to Jesus' family, and instead tell of Jesus' exorcizing a mute demoniac. The crowd is amazed when the man speaks, but others ("Pharisees" in Matthew) accuse Jesus of wielding the power of Beelzebul, "the ruler of demons." Matthew and Luke then parallel Mark but with two significant additions no doubt drawn from Q. Right after Mark 7:26, they add:

> Now if I drive out demons by Beelzebul, by whom do your people drive them out? So let them be your judges. If I, by the Spirit of God [Luke: "finger of God"] cast out demons, then God's new order has come among you.

Immediately after repeating Mark 7:27, Matthew and Luke also add, "Whoever is not with me is against me, and whoever doesn't gather with me scatters." Matthew also replaces Mark's verse 29 with the following: "Whoever speaks a word against the son of humanity will be forgiven, but whoever speaks against the Holy Spirit will not be forgiven, in this age or in the age to come." These additions and alterations seem to have come from versions of Q.

Mark's Story

Mark begins with a transitional verse that again mentions the crowds around Jesus. Then he drops in a verse referring to Jesus' family. His mother and brothers, thinking he is out of his mind, have come to corral him. Mark frequently designs such literary "sandwiches." He will begin a story, divert to another story, and then return to his original narrative. Here he introduces Jesus' family, diverts to discuss the Beelzebul controversy, and then, with verse 31, returns to the story of Jesus and his family. Using the device, Mark allows the two stories to interact.

The Beelzebul story features scribes, "down" from the heights of Jerusalem, who accuse Jesus of doing exorcisms with the power of Satan. In turn, Jesus asks, "How can Satan drive out Satan?" a question he backs up with a triad of metaphors on divided government, divided households, and finally a divided Satan. Though Jesus asks a question about Satan, giving the name credence, his comments indicate that Satan is either inevitably doomed (v. 26) or at least completely bound and thus impotent (v. 27).

Then Jesus adds a different metaphor: No one can rob a strong man unless the strong man is tied up by someone stronger. Then the strong man's house can be ransacked. Scholars are divided: Is the saying from Jesus or a product of early Christianity? Early Christianity believed Satan had been curtailed, if not outright defeated by Christ. But the saying is well attested, showing up in both Mark and Q as well as in the *Gospel of Thomas*, and may well go back to Jesus. The idea is that Satan may be strong, but if Jesus can drive out demons, then Satan has been bound.

The idea of binding Satan shows up in Revelation 20:1–3. There Satan is chained and locked up for a thousand years. The idea is a reversal, for usually it is Satan who binds victims, chaining them in illness or madness. In the story of the woman crippled for eighteen years whom Jesus frees (Luke 13:16), Jesus labels her condition bondage: "This daughter of Abraham, bound by Satan for eighteen years, wasn't it necessary to untie her on the Sabbath day?" Here the idea is that Jesus, stronger than evil, has bound Satan so that he can do damage no longer.

The passage concludes with a difficult saying about sin against the Holy Spirit that is probably not an original Jesus saying. Mark seems to believe that inasmuch as Jesus expels demons by the power of the Spirit, his accusers who claim he has an evil spirit have blasphemed the Spirit of God.

The Controversy

Once again we have an accusation and a counterquestion. Is the saying about the strong man a pronouncement? Probably, although such a wordy saying may not seem epigrammatic enough to qualify. Translation may be cumbersome; something as crisp as "You can't steal from a strong man's house unless he's tied up" might do. The implication: If demons are being driven out by Jesus' command, then Satan has been bound. Trevor Ling, a British scholar, has argued that Satan is being diminished, indeed demythologized, by early Christianity.[1] He believes that the status of Satan can be seen to lessen as Christian documents proceed from the early to later writings. Perhaps so, for Christians were quite sure that the devil had been defeated; as our passage says, "He's finished."

Dualistic apocalyptic Christianity, such as that portrayed in Revelation, tends to posit a potent Satan with demons in battle with God and God's angels. But we must be cautious about crediting the devil with too much power. If the devil is accorded too much power, God's sovereignty may be undercut and human moral responsibility may be reduced. Systemic evil can seem sinister indeed, but nevertheless must be dealt with as a human social product. Having so argued, I will balance my position with words from Denis de Rougemont: "The Devil's cleverest wile is to convince us he does not exist."[2]

The name "Beelzebul" is obscure. The name appears nowhere in the Hebrew Bible and nowhere in Christian writings other than here in Mark and in Q. Not only is the name obscure, but it is uncertain as well. Some manuscripts have "Beelzebul," or sometimes "Beelzeboul," perhaps deriving from an old Canaanite god and meaning, "Baal the Prince." But other manuscripts have "Baalzebub," meaning "Lord of the Flies," a satiric name that appears in 2 Kings 1:3 and 6. Mark's scribes use "Beelzebul," meaning that Jesus is said to be possessed by a chief of demons.

Mention of an "unforgivable sin" has caused all sorts of unhealthy speculation. But in Mark 3:20–30 the meaning is specific: Jesus' opponents are calling the power of God evil. Why? Because they already have decided to condemn Jesus and are no longer open-minded. Therefore, they must call a good thing—namely, healing—evil to confirm their own position. They are unassailably fixed in mind and thus cannot recognize a good work of the Spirit. Matthew and Luke have a peculiar version from the Q source: "Whoever speaks a word against the son of humanity will be forgiven, but whoever speaks against the Holy Spirit will not be forgiven, in this age or in the age to come." The distinction is not entirely clear or theologically helpful. Through the years the idea of an unforgivable sin has led to all sorts of unfortunate nonsense. Think of dear Christian people tormenting themselves because they suspect they have somehow managed to commit an unforgivable sin. But Mark's version is part of Mark's story and probably should not be extended as an accusation into other human occasions.

Homiletic Theology

Underlying the controversy is a way of thinking. First, all good things are from God. Second, we, the religious establishment, are officially approved "God people." Third, anyone functioning apart from us must not be of God. Ergo, though Jesus has some sort of power, it cannot be God's power. He is an unauthorized, unlicensed healer.[3] Moreover, because this chap Jesus has drawn together a movement that is to some extent challenging us, he must represent an anti-God power. As long as there can be something like an approved religious establishment, even a Christian religious establishment, such thinking can occur.

All such premises must be questioned: In a Graham Greene novel, an agnostic architect upbraids a parish priest: "You try to draw all the virtues into your net of faith," he says, "but you can't steal all the virtues. Gentleness isn't Christian, self-sacrifice isn't Christian."[4] While all good things may well come from God, virtuous, humanistic pagans can display worthy human virtues. We might want to insist that, ultimately, God is the generator of such virtues, but we should not expect the pagan to so affirm. The other assumption, "We are officially approved 'God people,'" is the problem. The statement implies that there are no other approved God people, a supposition repeatedly contradicted by biblical faith. God's free and gracious Spirit can work through all sorts of people, many of whom may be morally dubious. Protestants came into being by protesting absolute claims of the Catholic Church. But of late, Protestants have tumbled into the same claims. If we claim to be a redemptive community, we must also admit that God alone is the one who redeems us; the community does not save. The forming of redemptive life is achieved in the freedom of God, a God who is not required to work singularly through the church—a fairly tedious restriction. There is a story about a con-artist evangelist who set up fake healings to bring more cash at revivals. But, to his surprise, some people were healed. The question: How could God work through an outright fraud? The answer: Why not? The scribes, down from headquarters in Jerusalem, should have seen that God was doing a miracle by the power of the Spirit. They could not see, however, because of their blinding commitment to official religion. No wonder Jesus grieved over their hardness of heart.

The text mentions the unfortunate possibility of an unforgivable sin. If the verse means that God cannot forgive some particular sin, it is false. God is God, and God is The Mercy. Either the words refer to some structure of the human self that adamantly refuses to acknowledge forgiveness, or, theologically, they are nonsense. But even if the text refers to a free choice (I, John Doe, reject God's mercy), it cannot mean that God has not forgiven the person. Instead, awareness of mercy has been blocked. Such persons are forgiven but may be miserable; in denial, they refuse to be forgiven. But the text has provoked speculation—What kind of sin could not be pardoned by God? Answer: None.

The issue for Mark is obvious. Jesus is healing by the power of God's Spirit. The scribes label his power "evil." Thus, whatever they may be saying of Jesus, they are smearing God's own Spirit in action. They are blaspheming

God, for they are calling God's active power satanic. Whatever Mark may have meant, verses 28–29 are not useful texts for any preacher's preaching.

Preaching the Conflict

The big problem in preaching the passage is Satan. Though early Christianity gradually de-emphasized the whole notion of Satan, lately odd forms of contemporary Christianity have reanimated the symbol and run wild. Our age is apocalyptic and, therefore, people seem to be grooving on the book of Revelation. The Second Letter to Timothy has a phrase for our current American scene: "itching ears" (2 Tim. 4:3). Americans may not be much interested in anything like traditional Christianity, but they will chase down clues in *The Da Vinci Code* and will digest volume after volume of the appalling *Left Behind* series. We have "itching ears," but no ear for the gospel! So these days esoteric nonsense about Satan is once more fascinating many, perhaps fanned by "Axis of Evil" political rhetoric. But political rhetoric and apocalyptic religious rhetoric have much the same structure: There is evil and there is good. Our world is a battleground between the two forces. Happily, we are the good! There are no gray shades, no nuances, no room for any modifying ethics. Within such a model, a blundering self-righteous America cannot understand itself or the surrounding human world.

If we preach the passage, we will have to demythologize "Beelzebul," defining systemic evil as a social product and personal evil as a personal product. Moreover, we may have to demonstrate that evil is within all our "goods"— democracy, patriotism, religion. Evil is not easily isolated and name-tagged, but is hidden in every human ambiguity. Thus, we humans cannot single-handedly triumph over our own evil. Attempts to squash evil in our own lives inevitably turn to self-destruction. Indeed, as with the Iraq war, our warfare to destroy a social evil, such as terrorism, itself becomes an unjustifiable evil. We cannot exorcize ourselves!

Jesus' exorcisms were not overdramatic wrestling matches with evil. His healings were modest but effective. We possess some texts used by religious exorcists in the first century. They are long, elaborate formulas designed "to cast out demons." By contrast, Jesus simply commands the demons to go, "Shoo!" and a healing happens. But as Morton Smith has argued, Jesus was an unauthorized healer; he was not healing under the authority of the Temple or as a representative of acknowledged religious leadership. Therefore, he was suspect, a "magician," performing with evil power, a practitioner animated by Beelzebul.

Jesus' reply, "How can Satan drive out Satan?" exposes his opponents' accusation. If liberation is a good, how can it be labeled evil? We church types often tumble into the same trap as the scribes. If a healing isn't Christian or connected with our affirmed faith, we are apt to denigrate it. Thus, we claim a franchise on God's power. But God's Spirit can choose to act where and when God wills, and frequently does so quite beyond churchly purview.

Finally, we need to deal with the "strong man" theme. Early Christianity seemed to believe that the powers of Satan had been either destroyed or straightjacketed by the power of God through Jesus. So why have eager Christians rehabilitated Satan? In Christ Jesus, we should demythologize the figure. Though Satan is not, evil is. And God alone can overcome human evil. Confident in God's power, we can acknowledge the reality of evil tucked into all human enterprise but then turn to God begging grace.

Given our evasion of evil and our current openness to "Ghoulies and Ghosties and long-leggity beasties and all things that go bump in the night," any sermon on the passage will be difficult.[5] We must help people to banish Satan, while at the same time they own up to the hard fact of human evil. We dodge ownership. Nowadays it's fashionable to explain evil as pathology. We don't do evil. Instead we are dysfunctional victims of our psychological past. We were not loved enough in infancy. We were deprived. We were scarred by sibling rivalries. Our parents were inept. Actually, we are good people, but psychologically helpless, committing inadvertent blunders. Who does evil when everyone is a misunderstood victim? But, sooner or later, most of us are forced to admit, we are what we do. Evil has a human trademark. Though our eyes are slowly beginning to widen, we still blink away the systemic evils that seem to be thriving within American corporate economic activity,[6] not to mention national policy; as for example, our recent willingness to authorize torture in violation of the Geneva accords. In any sermon on this passage, we will have to own up to evil in the patterns of our common life and then turn to call upon the power of God, the same power that, through Jesus, reached out to those ostracized by illness.

CONFLICT OVER JESUS' FAMILY

Mark 3:20, 31–35 (also Matthew 12:46–50 and Luke 8:19–21)

[20]Jesus went into a house. Again he drew a crowd, so there wasn't any way for them to eat a meal. [21]When his family heard about it, they went to corral him, for people were saying, "He's out of his mind!"

[Here Mark inserted the Beelzebul controversy.]

[31]His mother with his brothers arrived and, standing outside, they sent word to him, calling him out. [32]A crowd was sitting around him, and they

were telling him, "Look, your mother and your brothers and your sisters are outside wanting you." [33]Answering them, he said, "Who are my mother and my brothers?" [34]And looking at those who were gathered in a circle around him, he said, "See, here are my mother and my brothers. [35]Whoever does the will of God is my brother, sister, and mother."

Other Versions

Both Matthew and Luke skip verse 21, which suggests Jesus' family members consider him deranged. They do not mention Jesus' sisters. Though the word "sisters" is omitted in many manuscripts, it appears in some. ("Sisters" also appears in Mark 6:3.) In Matthew and Luke, verses 34–35 become a general teaching. Luke reduces the story to a minimum: The family wants to see Jesus but cannot reach him because of the crowd. Someone tells Jesus his family is outside, and he responds with a final verse: "My mother and my brothers are those who hear the word of God and do it."

Mark's Story

In Mark's version, Jesus' family is troubled by his notoriety; they suppose he is beside himself. Evidently they have shown up to haul him home. Mark, the earliest Gospel, is no doubt historically correct. Any family living in Nazareth may have been quite conservative religiously, as was Jesus' brother James. Surely Jesus was an embarrassment to the whole clan. As a result, Mark deliberately associates the family's concern with scribes in the Beelzebul controversy. Both groups were critical of Jesus' activity.

Early Christians often found themselves ostracized by their families. Elsewhere, Matthew has Jesus paraphrase the prophet Micah (7:5–6):

> Don't think that I've come to bring peace on earth. I didn't come to bring peace but a sword. See, I have come to set a man against his father, a daughter against her mother, and a daughter-in-law against her mother-in-law. A person's enemies are members of the same household. (Matt. 10:34–36)

The words were spoken to Matthew's embattled Jewish Christian community, a "Jesus synagogue" surrounded by families from traditional synagogues. But surely the words would have made sense to any early Christian community. If Christians went on the road with the gospel message, they were no doubt blamed for neglect of their families. Devout Jewish families may have viewed those who became Christian as mentally disturbed or flat-out traitors to the faith. So Jesus adds, "Whoever loves father or mother more than me is not worthy of me; whoever loves son or daughter more than me is not worthy of me" (Matt. 10:37). The cost of discipleship may have been dear indeed.

Mark is also the Gospel that mentions Jesus' "brothers and sisters." Subsequently, his younger brothers are named in Mark 6:3 as "James and Joses and Judas and Simon," and "sisters" is in the plural. Both Luke 2:7 and Matthew 1:25 single out Jesus as "firstborn," but they allow the possibility of other children. Because the Roman Catholic Church affirms the perpetual virginity of Mary, Catholic theologians (as well as Reformers Luther and Calvin) usually have argued that these brothers and sisters were either cousins or the children of Joseph by a previous marriage. But the word for "cousin" is *anepsios* (as in Col. 4:10), whereas here and in Mark 6:3 it is clearly *adelphoi*, "brothers." If they were half-brothers, presumably the split-familial relationships would have been signaled somewhere, because *adelphoi* normally designates full brothers. The perpetual virginity of Mary may well be a useful theological symbol in Christian tradition, but historically it does not seem likely, at least according to the Gospel of Mark.

The Controversy

The controversy includes a statement: "Look, your mother and your brothers and your sisters are outside wanting you." Then Jesus replies with a question: "Who are my mother and my brothers?" Finally, we get a pronouncement: "Whoever does the will of God is my brother, sister, and mother."

Jesus' counterquestion exposes a mind-set. The crowd, like any crowd nowadays, is convinced that immediate familial relationships—mother, brothers, sisters—have priority over other relationships. In effect, they were sure that blood is thicker than water. Of course, if honest, most of us will have to admit that, as we grow older and our families scatter, we have friendships that are more intimate than sibling bonds. Nevertheless, for good or ill, family life is the soil in which we were formed and from which we have grown; thus, family members tend to be a priority with us. We speak of family life as the core of the social order. How could Jesus denigrate family? His question is as troubling now as then.[7]

But, looking back, can we admit that we may romanticize family life? Almost all families are dysfunctional in some respects. Sibling rivalries and alignments are often less than helpful. And in spite of courses on "parenting" these days, most parents flunk parental responsibilities when measured by the self-giving love of God; after all, we are sinners. Maybe we are lucky to survive aspects of familial interaction, lucky to come away knowing we are all forgiven and justified. Maybe we come to realize that family is not an ultimate!

For early Christians, many of whom may have been run out of their own families, the church was a new family of God. Many of us complain, saying we wish our church was more like an intimate family. Early Christianity reversed the whole notion; leaders urged members to make family life a small-scale *ecclesia*—a church! Jesus' pronouncement says as much; his family members are those who, with him, seek to obey God's will. His well-known words from the cross affirm the new interrelating of the people of God: to his mother, "Woman, here is your son," and to the beloved disciple, "Here is your mother." Though the passage is usually preached as the pathos of mother-son love, the passage affirms the new "family" of Christian community. For Christians, family is not *the* priority. Instead, in Christian community, water is thicker than blood—namely, the water of baptism. In Christian community, we belong to one another.

No wonder that Jesus' pronouncement "Whoever does the will of God is my brother, sister, and mother" resonated with early Christians. He is endorsing the new family of the Christian community: those who have been gathered by his word.

Homiletic Theology

The issue of family affection jars most American readers. Doesn't Jesus love his mother? We are all supposed to love our mothers. As for siblings, isn't blood thicker than water? Are they not always our brothers and sisters and, therefore, bound to us more immediately than others? Of late the family has taken on unusual importance in our nation as other institutions have declined. "Democracy" has been corrupted by lobbying cash—"the greatest little congress money can buy." With the high cost of litigation, our courts no longer seem to be open to the poor as they should be. Our churches, trivialized by competitive denominationalism, limp along losing members. The church-going population is now estimated as less than 20 percent. Therefore, we have tended to overinvest in the idea of the family. The family, we suppose, undergirds the land. So Toys "R" Us has become big time. And churches have been building expensive "family life centers." Political candidates are all fervent supporters of the family. On television, advertising firms flash pictures of happy families at us *ad nauseam*. What on earth is Jesus doing knocking family life?

Family life is not shunted aside by the Scriptures, particularly the Hebrew Scriptures. Concern for the family is built into the Ten Commandments: We should not covet a neighbor's spouse. We should honor our parents.[8] The Bible approves constancy in marriage, care in raising children, and fine, festive family pleasures such as partying together. Biblical images are scarcely stuffy: Psalms celebrates the joys of marriage (Pss. 127 and 128), and even Ecclesiastes, filled with dour ironies, urges us to enjoy life in marriage (Eccl. 9:9). Moreover, the Bible pictures (instruction can be so tedious) profound patterns of family love again and again, involving parents and children as well as children and children. All in all, though the family is not an ultimate in Scripture, it is celebrated as a good gift of God's creation.

Moreover, the Bible uses family images to bring out our true relationship with God. God is a husband to Israel (Hos. 1–3), and Israel is God's chosen bride (Isa. 50:1; 54:4–6; 62:5). God is a mother cleaving to her young (Isa. 49:15; 66:13). God is a parent, indeed *the* parent of earth's human children. Such metaphors cut both ways; they illumine the character of God but also call us to godly love in family life. Implicitly, the Bible urges familial devotion, saying in effect, "You must be parents as God is a parent"—no small responsibility. Every parent serves under the true parentage of God.

The idea of God as the true Parent of us all is worth further consideration. If God is the ultimate Parent of our children, we are called to both freedom and trust. We can regard our kids as "charges" under God's ultimate parentage: Our children are not *our* children—the possessive pronoun is always inappropriate. They are God's children though under our temporary care. But if children are ultimately God's children, we are relieved of a terrifying burden: our children need not worship us, thank God, much less regard our word as law, truth, or perfect wisdom. We are sinners and, as parents, enmeshed in ambiguity. But together with our children we may seek God's will and, happily, rely on God's good mercy which, fortunately, is both wonderful and generously wide. So, again, how come Jesus seems to be down on the family?

Here's an answer: With us, family life may have become idolatrous. But with Christians, the family is emphatically *not* an ultimate. From the start, newborn Christian faith strained patterns of ancient family life.[9] Family securities were shaken when early apostles left home to go "on the road" with the gospel message; clearly, preaching the gospel took priority over familial responsibilities. Likewise, family hostilities were enlarged when converts left traditional patterns of Jewish family practice for life in upstart Christian communities. Were early Christians castigated for family neglect? Probably, for there are a number of snarly texts in our Christian Scriptures that pit faith against family.

In Luke, young Jesus seems quite unconcerned for family cohesion when he remains in the Temple "to be about my Father's business" (Luke 2:41–50). Later, in the Mark passage, when Jesus' family members come chasing after him, he asks bluntly, "Who are my mother and my brothers?" and casts his lot with his bedraggled audience, crowding around to hear him speak (Mark 3:31–35). There is also Jesus' sharp retort, "Let the dead bury the dead," aimed at a man who pleaded for time to observe his father's funeral, a rejoinder that subverted the sacred notion of family ties (Matt. 8:21–22).

Early Christian communities were regarded as new families that superseded all previous family loyalties. Were they not designated "households of God"? Did not Christians address one another affectionately as "Sister" and "Brother"?[10] They saw themselves as children of God, a new family on earth, adopted by God through the saving love of Jesus the Christ. Though nowadays we complain that the church ought to be like a family, first-century Christians reversed the logic: every family was called to be a mini-church—with Christian instruction like cheerful preaching and Christian family meals like small-scale Eucharists. In other words, family life took its clues from the character and the calling of the church, and not vice versa. For Christians, the community of faith is the primary family in which we find our true brothers and sisters, mothers and fathers.[11]

Sermon

Here is another sermon from 1960, preached on "Christian Family Sunday" in the Presbyterian Church of Fredonia, New York.

Introduction   If we were to compile a list of words least likely to be printed on a Mother's Day card, these words of Christ could top the list. Said Jesus: "Who are my mother and my brothers?" The words have disturbed devout Christians ever since they were uttered. The French scholar Ernest Renan read them and exploded in anger: "This Jesus," he wrote, "tramples underfoot everything that is human—love and blood and home."[12] Admittedly, when it comes to the family, Jesus' words are hard to understand. Yes, he did tell his disciples that they must forsake father, mother, sister, and brother to follow him. And he did say that he had come to bring division in the home instead of peace. But for downright callousness the words of today's text take the prize. One day when his mother and brothers came to see him, he turned to the crowd and asked: "Who are my mother and my brothers?" The words are scarcely the kind of thing you'd find on a Mother's Day card but, nevertheless, he said it, and we must seek to understand.

I

1 Said Jesus: "Who are my mother and my brothers?" *What kind of a son was he?* Had he no fine family feelings? Or was he a bachelor, aloof, alone, and utterly indifferent? Richard Rogers recalls a time when he would walk right past his parents because he did not wish to admit that they were his. Was this the way with Jesus? No, Jesus loved his life at home. Read through the parables and see for yourself: they are filled with homey references. And, at the last, did he not look down from the cross with concern for his mother? And when he sought some image for God, it was the story of a loving father that came to his lips. One thing for sure, Jesus loved his family.

2 "Who are my mother and my brothers?" said Jesus. *Jesus may have loved his home, but he left it.* The Bible does not hide the fact that he was separated from his family. They had turned against him, but who can blame them? He was a disgrace. Instead of settling down to work at an honest trade, off he went, wandering the wide land preaching to a little band of unwashed peasants. He was out of sight, and as far as they could see he was out of his mind as well. They could not, would not, understand. Christ did not leave his family because he hated them, or because he loved his family less than friends. No, he simply owed a higher obedience to God. For months, John Bunyan was imprisoned in a Bedford jail because of his faith. His letters are poignant. "The parting from my wife and children," he wrote, "hath been as a pulling of the flesh from the bone"—particularly from a blind child, his youngest. "Nevertheless," said Bunyan, "I must obey God."[13] Christ served the will of God even though it meant turning his back on home. Said Jesus with yearning: "Who are my mother and my brothers?"

II

3 Jesus answered his own question: "Whoever does the will of God," he said, "Whoever does the will of God is brother, sister, mother!" *For Jesus saw the family as under God's will.* The family exists to serve God, praise God, and seek God's will in all things. Families that live for themselves cease to be families; they become a form of organized selfishness, which is exactly what has happened in our generation. We live for the sake of our own. If ancient Chinese could be accused of worshiping ancestors, modern Americans are not much better; they worship their home life. Today, John Bunyan would never find himself in jail; he'd be too busy building a family room in the basement. The symbol of our faith is not the lonely cross but the cozy, family-filled Cape Cod cottage. God, if we have room for God at all, is a sort of spiritual appliance that no home should be without. No wonder the words of Christ offend us; he served God first and last. A few years ago there was a musical comedy on Broadway in which a mother and daughter sang together, "We belong to a mutual admiration society."[14] No, Christ defined the family in a different way—as a holy adoration society serving the Lord.

4 "Whoever does the will of my Father . . . ," said Jesus, defining family life. *For Jesus saw the family under the judgment of God.* His words jar us, for

we have grown sentimental, if not silly, over family life. Nostalgically we croon, "There's no place like home." But if psychiatrists can be believed, nostalgia always covers up a hard truth. Christ was not blinded by sentiment. He saw the family as a small-scale world with the same loves and hates, goods and evils as the wider world. Yes, home life was indeed the school of faith, but it was as much the school of doubt as well. We learn to share in family life, but also to be defensively selfish. And while we develop cooperation in the family circle, competition is there as well. Just as most manufactured goods in this country bear a trademark, so personality wears a trademark that reads, "Made at home!" God confronts every home, every heart, asking only, "Do you love one another?" And we must answer.

5 But, wait, *Jesus saw family life under the mercy of God as well.* In one of Alan Paton's novels, on the night of his son's execution for murder, a father goes off alone to pray saying, "Oh God forgive me."[15] The fact is that every parent and every child lives in need of the mercy of God simply because we cannot truly forgive each other. No father is good enough to forgive a son. No son is worthy enough to pardon a parent. Forgiveness is given by God; it's not manufactured at home. Only as a family lives in the mercy of God can forgiveness become the pattern of family life. Lewis Sherrill tells of how one day, after a rush of anger, he and his son climbed to the top of a near mountain together and there on the windy height felt close again, each humble and at one. Thereafter, whenever there were words between them one would say: "Remember the mountain," and they were reconciled.[16] So the Christian home remembers a high hill and a cross where God and humanity met in mercy and in the memory finds reconciliation. God forgives, and we forgive one another—one family living in The Mercy.

III

6 Said Jesus: "Who are my mother and my brothers?" Looking out at the crowd around him, he spoke sharply: "These are my mother and my brothers." *The family exists to be dissolved.* Does that sound strange? Listen again: The family circle is created in order to be broken. The closeness of home must be crucified in order that a new, larger family be found. How hard it is for parents to let go of their children. How hard it is for children to let go of parents. In Arthur Miller's drama *All My Sons,* a grasping father learns of his son's death in the South Pacific. He speaks haltingly: "Sure, he was my son, but I think, they were all my sons, and I guess they were. . . . I guess they are."[17] We may learn to love each other in a family, so we may learn to love all our human relatives as we love our own.

7 "These are my mother and my brothers," said Jesus to the crowd that gathered around him. *If God is Father, then we are all one family.* All our early roles—wife, parent, child—are no more than trivial distinctions. In God's sight we are all the children of his love. God sent Christ the son among us to recall our prodigal hearts to everyone's true parent. No wonder life is so temporary. Children grow up and leave home so that we may claim all children as our children. Our parents grow old and pass from our sight so we may claim all our elders as parents. Our family is the whole human earth— every color, every creed—under the father-love of God. You know, I never cease to be startled when visiting a Pentecostal congregation where I find myself addressed as "Brother Buttrick." I never know how to reply: "Thank you, Mrs. Jones," or to get into the spirit of the thing and say, "Sister Jones." Actually, it's an old and lovely custom in churches. For in Christ we are all related one to another. Said Jesus, facing the crowd—a crowd like us— "These are my mother and my brothers."

Conclusion   One day when Jesus was with his friends, someone came to him saying, "Your mother and your brothers are outside." And Jesus answered strangely saying: "Who are my mother and my brothers?" It is a question we need to ask ourselves. Who do we call our own? Who are members of our family? We are not related by blood or marriage. Actually, we are related by love—the power of God in our lives. And as your love grows large, your family grows until you're a brother or sister to every soul on earth—until you can say with Christ, waving a hand to the far horizons, "These, all these, are my mother and my own."

Discussion

Actually the sermon has held up pretty well considering it was written in the 1960s. But there are still problems.

Introduction   The introduction is too wordy. I had not learned how to toughen them by reducing the adjectival. The quote from Renan is unnecessary; I could have said the same sort of thing without introducing an additional speaker. Now I limit introductions to around eight sentences at most.

I   I was still outlining sermons using the 1, 2, 3, a, b, c format. Section I has two subsections. The first, "What kind of a son was he?" is okay, if brief. The second, "Jesus may have loved his home, but he left it," also works pretty well.

II   Here the structural design of the sermon creaks. Within the section, there is a rather interesting first paragraph: "Jesus saw the family as under God's will" is the key sentence. Though the move is filled with edgy stuff, it is designed badly because it gives most of its space to the family as a "mutual admiration society" and contains very little on the paragraph's supposed subject, that is, the family under God's will. Then there is a pair of sub-paragraphs: (a) "family under the judgment of God"; (b) "family under the mercy of God." Both moves are brief, perhaps too brief. The second is a problem because it splits, with each section illustrated by a father figure.

III The final section has two parts: (1) "The family exists to be dissolved," and (2) "If God is Father, then we are all one family." The first move is underdeveloped and too brief to form. The second is stronger, but, unfortunately, has an illustration that focuses on the preacher. Personal reference illustrations are always wrong, because they split focus.

Conclusion   The conclusion is adequate, if a bit wordy.

The problem with the sermons from the 1960s I have included is design. Homiletics in the first half of the twentieth century taught a semitopical system of I, II, III; 1, 2, 3; a, b, c—outlining, creating subject matter paragraphs and subparagraphs. As a result, the movement of the sermon is plodding and the conflict story logic—question, counterquestion, pronouncement—is obscured. As we have seen, categorical sections—1, 2, 3 under a single topic heading—are intrinsically tedious; they are static points made under a topic and about as exciting as a series of mailboxes. Moreover, they trivialize, because they put a profound gospel message into a list. We use lists for groceries, for errands, for sorted laundry, and the like, but scarcely for the most significant moments in our lives.

CONFLICT OVER WASHING BEFORE EATING

Mark 7:1–23 (also Matthew 15:1–20)

[1]When the Pharisees, along with some scribes from Jerusalem, were gathered around Jesus, [2]they noticed that some of the disciples were eating bread with impure hands, that is, unwashed hands. [3](For the Pharisees and all Jews, holding to the tradition of the elders, do not eat unless first they scrub up their hands; and when they come from the market, [4]they won't eat until they have washed thoroughly. There are many traditions they observe, washing cups and pitchers and kettles [and beds].) [5]The Pharisees and scribes questioned him, "Why don't your disciples walk in the tradition of the elders instead of eating bread with impure hands?" [6]He said to them, "Isaiah did well prophesying about you phonies! It's written:

This people honors me with the lips
> but their heart is far from me.

They worship me in emptiness,
> teaching as doctrine human-made commandments.

[8]Abandoning the commandment of God, you cling to human traditions!"

[9]Then he said to them, "How neatly you skipped over the commandment of God so as to establish your own traditions. [10]For Moses said, 'Honor your father and mother' and 'Those who curse father and mother, let them be executed,' [11]but you say, 'If people say to their father or mother, "Whatever support you may have expected from me is *Korban* (that is, *consecrated*)," [12]then you won't allow them to continue doing anything for their father or mother.' [13]With your hand-me-down tradition, you cancel out the word of God! You do lots of such things."

[14]Calling the crowd together again, he said to them, "Listen to me, every one of you, and understand: [15]There is nothing outside a person that, entering, can defile; but things coming from inside a person are things that defile. [[16]Anyone with ears, listen!]

[17]Leaving the crowd, he went into a house where his disciples began asking him about his saying. [18]He said to them, "Are you still dumb? Can't you understand? Nothing outside can defile by getting into a person, [19]because it cannot reach the heart, but goes to the stomach and out to the outhouse. So much for cleansing food!" [20]But he continued, "What comes out of a person can defile; [21]for out of the human heart come evil thoughts, sexual immorality, thefts, murders, [22]adulteries, greed, wickedness, deceptions, promiscuity, envy, blasphemy, arrogance, and utter foolishness. [23]All these things come inside-out to defile a person."

Other Versions

The only other version is in Matthew. But Matthew rearranges the passage, replacing Mark's lengthy introductory section with a quick question, placing the *Korban* example before the quote from Isaiah 29:13 rather than after, adding material from Q (vv. 12–14) about the blind leading the blind, and abbreviating the list of vices by removing dispositions, for example, "evil thoughts," so the list includes only legal offenses that come "out of the heart" (v. 19).

Though Luke does not have Mark's story, he does deal with similar issues in 11:37–41. In Luke's story Jesus himself fails to wash up before eating. When Pharisees react, he lashes out, "You Pharisees clean the outside of the cup, but inside you're full of greed and evilness." Then in 11:42–44, Jesus launches into a tirade that begins, "Woe to you, Pharisees . . ."

Mark's Story

Mark has created a rather choppy, patched-together story that includes (a) a controversy over disciples who, by not washing their hands, are accused of violating "the tradition of the elders"; (b) a reply by Jesus, who observes that Pharisees are overthrowing God's commands with their own traditions; (c) an example of such, involving parental support; (d) a saying of Jesus about inner and outer defilement; and (e) a private review of the saying with his disciples. The story is cumbersome.

The story begins with a somewhat lengthy description of the situation. Mark has Gentile readers and, therefore, in a sketchy way, he has to explain why hand washing is a matter of concern. The issue is not personal cleanliness but ritual defilement. Hands could be defiled in many ways. A section of the Mishnah entitled *Yadayim* ("Hands") covers the several forms of defilement as well as specific instructions for washing: "A quarter-*log* of water do they pour for hands for one, also for two. A half-*log* for three or four. A *log* for five and for ten and for a hundred." A *log* equals the volume of six eggs.[18]

The scene seems somewhat contrived. Notice the disciples are accused, but not Jesus. Thus, the passage probably reflects an accusation leveled against the practices of early Christian communities who appeared lax to scrupulous Jews. The criticism is parried by a modified quote from Isaiah 29:13 and then sharp words from Jesus: "Abandoning the commandment of God, you cling to human traditions!" Traditions are oral regulations passed down from teacher to teacher. The *Korban* example is particularly vivid. Though the fifth commandment is specific—"Honor your father and mother"—according to the tradition, persons could pledge an advanced contribution to the Temple; such monies were then vowed *Korban* and thus reserved as a sacred untouchable gift. The result was that mothers and fathers would be shortchanged. In the example, oral tradition seems to nullify one of the Ten Commandments of God. Says Jesus to the critics, "You do lots of such things."

Then abruptly, Mark has Jesus "calling the crowd together again," though there has been no previous mention of a crowd. Jesus then hands out a pronouncement: "There is nothing outside a person that, entering, can defile; but things coming from inside a person are things that defile." Though a few ancient manuscripts add, "Anyone with ears, listen!" most modern translations omit the verse.

According to Mark, Jesus then holds a private seminar with his disciples. Previously, Jesus gave private instruction following the parable of the Sower (4:11–12), which Mark remarks was customary: "He explained everything in private to his disciples" (4:34). Here again disciples ask for further instruction. "Are you still dumb?" replies Jesus, and then he goes on to repeat what he said previously. But he now adds a long list of corruptions that come out of a person: "evil thoughts, sexual immorality, thefts, murders, adulteries, greed, wickedness, deceptions, promiscuity, envy [lit., 'evil eye'], blasphemy, arrogance, and utter foolishness." Almost all the private seminars with disciples are products of Mark. Here he offers a list of vices, a convention found in intertestamental Jewish literature and in the Pauline letters (Rom. 1:29–31; Gal. 5:19–21; 1 Cor. 6:9–10).

The Controversy

The controversy pattern is not easily discerned. Prompted by the careless behavior of Jesus' disciples, the Pharisees and scribes ask, "Why don't your disciples walk in the tradition of the elders instead of eating bread with impure hands?" A leader could be blamed for the laxity of his disciples. But Jesus picks up on the phrase "tradition of the elders" and observes, "Abandoning the commandment of God, you cling to human traditions!"

The final pronouncement appears to be, "Nothing outside can defile by getting into a person . . . [but] what comes out of a person can defile." But the crisp movement of a conflict story is somewhat broken up by additional material: an explanation of purity laws pertaining to hands, a paraphrased and somewhat inaccurate quote from Isaiah, a digression on *Korban*, and, finally, a private seminar for disciples.

Mark is essentially right with regard to purity laws governing washing up before eating. These laws, though of particular Pharisaic concern, were generally practiced by most pious Jews. The laws are based on Leviticus 19:2: "You shall be holy, for I the Lord your God am holy"—an injunction that has motivated Christians as well. The rest of Leviticus 19 expands on how we are to live honorably with one another as a people of God, namely, by loving our neighbors as our own (19:18). But Leviticus 11–22, the "Holiness Code," is quite specific, spelling out in no uncertain terms what it means to be holy. Purity regulations are found in chapters 11 and 15. These regulations were profoundly wise in earlier times when disease was prevalent. What they did was to specify unclean things that could contaminate or spread disease. A corpse could contaminate, and blood and semen could contaminate. But natural water, given by God, could wash away contamination. Therefore Israel was to be clean, have clean cooking implements, eat clean foods, and maintain personal cleanliness. In general, purity was a concern among all faithful Jews.

But Christianity, originally a Jewish sectarian movement, was gradually becoming Gentile. Thus, there were questions raised not only by scandalized

Jewish observers but by Gentiles, who would not readily accept circumcision and, what seemed to them, overscrupulous purity regulations as well. The tearing away of Christian communities from Jewish tradition was exceedingly difficult and has scarred relationships between Christians and Jews for centuries. But did Jesus himself flaunt carelessness toward purity laws, as in Luke 11:37–41? Probably not. But his disciples might have seemed lax to the overscrupulous Pharisees. Jesus turns "cup" into a metaphor and remarks that Pharisees are concerned with the outside of the cup but overlook the human "inside." From within, says Jesus—namely, the human will—come all kinds of immorality.

The example of *Korban* is not quite fair. No dedicated scribe or Pharisee would permit a personal vow to overturn Israel's primary obligation to obey the commandments of God. But in the first century there may have been some confusion between primary oaths and secondary personal vows. Numbers 30 contains an elaborate discussion of primary oaths and secondary personal vows. Could these distinctions have been mixed, indeed corrupted, by scribes as Jesus suggested? Perhaps. But the later rabbis would have been appalled. How could any personal vow supersede obedience to the Ten Commandments? In all likelihood, the example has been added to the story. Almost certainly, it does not go back to Jesus.

The basic teaching Jesus offers is that external cleanliness is not the primary problem, because from the inner self—human desire, impulse, and willfulness—come all sorts of corrupting behavior. The list of human sins—"evil thoughts, sexual immorality, thefts, murders, adulteries, greed, wickedness, deceptions, promiscuity, envy, blasphemy, arrogance, and utter foolishness"—is possibly a later addition to the story, matching similar sorts of lists found in the Pauline letters (e.g., 1 Cor. 6:9–10).

The passage is overloaded with issues: purity codes, external cleanliness and internal motivations, conflict between moral responsibility and religious vows. In addition, and perhaps underlying all the issues, is one basic accusation against scribal critics: "Abandoning the commandment of God, you cling to human traditions!" In Jewish thought there are two Torahs, one written and the other oral. Both Torahs go back to Moses in the presence of God on Mount Sinai. The one Torah is written and is foundational; the other Torah is transmitted orally from sage to sage from memory. The one is written law, the other is living tradition, but they are equally necessary for the life of Israel.[19] Jesus is clearly concerned that traditional oral law, scribal law, not overrule the force of the basic commandments. Evidently, as the scribes and Pharisees addressed human situations, oral law might have superseded the written Torah. Flavius Josephus admits as much: "The Pharisees have imposed on the people many laws from the tradition of the fathers not written in the laws of Moses."[20] Jesus' position matches his ethic of the Sermon on the Mount: he asks Christians not to ignore the law but to exceed the law in their living.

A Sermon

Here is another sermon I preached in the 1960s at the Presbyterian Church of Fredonia, New York. The sermon is based on the passage in Luke 11:37–41, where Jesus himself does not wash before eating. As with all the 1960s sermons, it is designed as a series of sections containing point-making subordinate paragraphs, a method I would now want to reconsider.

Introduction   There is an Episcopal priest in our state who takes great delight in disturbing his clerical friends. Whenever the Episcopal clergy meet to eat at a Friday noon luncheon, when all the others order fish, he loudly asks for beef steak. "You should see their eyebrows wiggle when I do," he chuckles. Jesus raised his share of eyebrows. When he sat down to dine without scrupulously washing his hands, the Pharisees were outraged. Who was he to instruct people when he behaved so irreligiously? He healed on the Sabbath, dallied with drunkards, and ate profanely like a common pagan. They were astonished to see that he did not first wash before dinner.

I

1 *Why did Jesus break the law? Why did he deliberately offend the Pharisees*? They were a decent sort. We are so used to labeling Pharisees as the villains of the Bible story that we forget how worthy they really were. We are like the little boy in Sunday school who said, "Pharisees were bad people who used to wash." The definition leaves much to be desired. They were not bad people—they were good. They supported their nation, they were progressive, generous, tolerant, honest, true-blue. In Fredonia, you would find Pharisees in well-mannered homes with well-mannered children. They'd be working for the United Fund, contributing to schools and churches. They'd be members of the Kiwanis and probably the Presbyterian Church. Pharisees weren't narrow. They weren't painfully pious. No, they were the kind of people you'd want for friends. So you wonder what prompted Jesus to taunt them.

2 *Why did Jesus break the law?* He seemed to do so with carefree and deliberate gusto. Why? Was Christ a crank, a Palestinian "beatnik," a nonconformist impatient with tradition? When he was young, the poet A. E. Housman turned away from trite custom proudly:

> The Laws of God, the laws of man,
> He may keep them that will and can;
> Not I; let God and man decree
> Laws for themselves and not for me;
> And if my ways are not as theirs
> Let them mind their own affairs.[21]

Christ was not an overgrown adolescent flaunting freedom in the face of tradition. He kept the Passover and the holy days, and worshiped as his fathers had. Nor was he being deliberately different in order to call attention to himself. There was a recent cartoon in the *New Yorker* which showed a bearded, bedraggled artist being chided by his wife, "Why do you have to be a nonconformist like everybody else?" Jesus was not a nonconformist, and yet he did seem to break some of the holy laws. "The Pharisees were astonished to see that he did not first wash before dinner." Why did Christ break the law?

II

3 *The trouble with the law was that it made people artificial. It divorced them from their true selves.* The Pharisees were so busy disciplining themselves that they had no time to be themselves. A biographer of Queen Victoria has a nice description: "When the Queen was crowned she took as her motto, 'I will be good!' and followed her motto through a long and tedious life."[22] Well, the Pharisees were so busy trying to be good, they became tedious. They lacked spontaneity. No tears spilled down their faces, no sudden laughter shook them. They were always under pious control. Never were they carried away with joy, despair, or devotion. Franz Kafka has a short story titled "A Hunger Artist" about a man who worked in a sideshow. His stunt? He didn't eat, and people came to see him, all skin and bones—the man who hadn't eaten for forty days. On exhibit next to him was a panther pacing back and forth, alive and roaring. Kafka points to the contrast between the animal's vitality and the hunger artist's apathy.[23] The Pharisees fasted and followed the law and, in the process, may have been losing their lives.

4 *Jesus opposed the law if laws separated people from their neighbors.* The Pharisees were an exclusive class who kept themselves aloof and apart from the world—like that small college in Kentucky that boasted it was located geographically "seven miles from any form of sin." The Pharisees kept their distance from sin and sinners. Carefully they chose their friends from among a pious few, uncontaminated by the common herd. Such an attitude is still a present danger. See it in the temperance groups that set themselves apart from drinkers. See it in the cultured class that will not mingle with lowbrows. See it in our own church, which would just as soon sidestep Puerto Ricans' moving into town. The penalty of exclusiveness is spiritual loneliness. Did you read about that woman who was found dead in a Brooklyn apartment? She was so afraid of public germs that she refused to venture out for food and died of starvation. So the Pharisees were locked in their own clique, dying from a form of spiritual elitism.

5 *Actually, the real danger of the law was that it kept people from God!* The Pharisees would stand in the Temple reciting "O how I love thy law," but seldom said, "I love thee." They were concerned with religion rather than God. A magazine asked C. S. Lewis to comment on what they called "the growing interest in religion." "I suppose," answered Lewis, "there is a widespread interest in religion. . . . It's too bad there isn't a widespread interest in God!"[24] It's true that in America we talk about religion but seldom speak of God. We boast of our churches, our membership, our circles and societies, but we seldom talk of God to one another. So in Jesus' day, the Pharisees followed the law, but did they seek the will of God? When will we realize that religion can stand in the way of God? When will we see that concern for "right and wrong" can replace concern for the real mystery of God? No wonder Jesus repudiated trivial laws.

III

6 *"The Pharisees were astonished that he did not first wash up before dinner." They were astonished by his freedom.* Was there ever anyone more free than Jesus from common cant and conformity? He lived his life in liberty. Freely he expressed his feelings, wept and laughed without restraint, spoke his fears, and admitted his doubts even on the cross. When he was angry, he was openly angry. There was nothing inhibited about him, was there? He who ate and drank with sinners, common crooks and plain prostitutes, Pharisees and publicans. And he was as free in his life with God, for his prayers were not carefully prepared, but carefree words poured out in the most intimate way. Even the disciples were embarrassed by his freedom. In a recent autobiography, Moss Hart describes his collaborator, George S. Kaufman: "He was not driven by the savage necessity to be liked. He cared little for the good opinion of the world. He adhered to his own standards."[25] So Christ lived. He cared little for the good opinion of religious leaders. He cared little whether he was liked or disliked. He lived by his own standard, which happened to be the mighty will of God. Was there ever a man as free as he?

7 *Christ lived not by law but by love.* Neighbor love was the source of his freedom, for, with him, it was not a matter of dos and don'ts, of rigid formulas.

Love adapts itself to every different situation. Christ picked grain on the Sabbath because he loved creation. He healed the sick on the Sabbath because he loved people. He drove moneychangers from the Temple because he loved God. There was nothing stereotypical about his behavior because it was based on the love of God. One of Graham Greene's heroines chides a high school girl: "Milly, dear Milly, beware of formulas. If there's a God, he's not a God of formulas."[26] God isn't a God of laws and commandments: God is a God of love, and love writes its own commandments—each moment new, each moment true. Christ was free in love.

8 Yet *Christ was constrained by love as well.* Love governed every action, every impulse, every word he spoke. His freedom was not simply a rush of rash assertion but the working out of love in every situation. Listen! There are two ways of dealing with the impulses of the soul. One way is the way of law—to check the impulse, to curb desire, to squash self-will whenever it arises. This is the way of the Pharisees. But there's another way—the way of love. If you love God dearly and deeply, love will control your impulses. You will offer your anger to him and your fears to him—all that you are to him—in love. The result is not repression but worthy expression called forth by the Holy Spirit of love. Wrote Boris Pasternak, "I think that if the beast that sleeps in man could be held down by threats, then the highest emblem of humanity would be the lion tamer in the circus with his whip, not the Christ who sacrificed himself."[27] The Christian does not live under the whip of moral law but within the love of Christ as a free soul.

Conclusion   "The Pharisees were astonished to see that he did not first wash before dinner." Jesus raised his share of eyebrows, didn't he? I suppose that people who truly follow Christ will do the same; they will raise a share of eyebrows! They will not cower in the face of public custom. They will not follow slavishly any rule from either church or culture. They will love. And love may lead them into lonely paths, absurd courtesies, and foolish expressions. But Christians will never be a minority of one. They will be at least a minority of two, themselves and the Spirit—the same Spirit who is with Christ.

Discussion

No seminary, even a very good seminary, can prepare students for their ministry, particularly their pulpit ministry, in three years' time. At first, preachers simply do not know enough. Ministers are trapped into too much busywork that lay people can handle as well or better. Ministers need time to read—at least a book a week—and think. Though I did have enough sense to respect the Pharisees (in fact, more than Luke), I tended to turn Jesus into something of a 1960s' free spirit. Though I kept hedging the claim, the sermon was something of a problem.

Introduction   The introduction seems a little silly now, but more than forty years ago fish and Friday were a norm. But the introduction was lean and less than ten sentences.

1 The first two paragraphs introduce the characters in Luke's story: Pharisees and Jesus. In the first move I defend the Pharisees against popular labeling. I make them "progressive, generous, tolerant, honest" as well as community leaders. And, as I was then preaching in a Presbyterian Church, I made sure to put Pharisee and Presbyterian together.

2 In the second move, I ask if Jesus was a nonconformist. The Housman poem could be cut down by a few lines, but it works pretty well. I wanted to counter the antinomian and anti-Jewish tendencies with "He kept the Passover and the holy days, and worshiped as his fathers had."

3 Moves 3, 4, and 5 are part of a second section. Now I am critical of legalism, arguing that the overscrupulous can become both tedious, like the young Queen Victoria, and inauthentic. The illustration from Kafka's "A Hunger Artist" contrasts overdiscipline with natural vitality.

4 Another criticism: Legalism separates us one from another. Notice I tie the problem in with temperance groups; the town where I was speaking was the birthplace of the Women's Christian Temperance Union. I also chase my own congregation for not welcoming an influx of Puerto Rican migrants. Again I link Pharisees and Presbyterians.

5 The move seems to be based on a distinction then being made by Karl Barth, a distinction I would not now want to defend—namely, that Christianity is a faith and not a religion like other world religions. Another problem: obviously Pharisees did seek to obey God's will as revealed in Torah. But can morality become a closed system that isolates us from a certain immediate awe before the mystery of God? Maybe.

6 Moves 6, 7, and 8 are a final set. In move 6, I argue that Jesus in his freedom is free from social conformities. He is free to be himself. But the move is foggy and not well defined.

7 Here I suggest that Jesus is motivated not by legislation but by love of God and neighbor. But I make an error: in a positive move, the brief quote from Graham Greene rejects the alternative, namely, behavioral formulas. Plus, three moves in a row feature quotes from male authors. Thus, all three moves may sound much the same.

8 Now look what I have gone and done—a move with no more than a quote by Pasternak that functions much as did the Graham Greene quote in rejecting an opposite of the move's stated subject. Though the sermon starts out pretty well, its final section, which should be powerful, is clearly weak without strong imagery. The conclusion works nicely.

The sermon, delivered by a preacher less than a decade out of seminary, shows some imagination, but it also has technical problems, above all, a degree of thoughtlessness with regard to what the controversy stories were doing with the Jewish-Christian "law" theme.

CONFLICT OVER THE SYROPHOENICIAN WOMAN

Mark 7:24–30 (also Matthew 15:21–28)

²⁴From there, he got up and went off to the region of Tyre. He went into a house, hoping to stay without anyone knowing, but he couldn't avoid notice. ²⁵Immediately, a woman whose daughter had an unclean spirit, hearing of him, came and fell at his feet. ²⁶The woman was a Greek, by race a Syrophoenician, and she started begging him to drive out her daughter's demon.

²⁷Jesus answered her: "First, let the children be fed. It's not right to take the children's bread and throw it to dogs!" ²⁸But in reply, she said to him, "But sir, even the puppies under the table get the children's scraps." ²⁹And he said to her, "For that answer, go, the demon has left your daughter." ³⁰After she went home, she found her child lying on the bed with the demon gone.

Other Versions

There is another version of the story in Matthew, but it is quite different. Has Matthew added to Mark's account? Not likely. Normally Matthew abbreviates material from Mark. But here, though parallel, Matthew 15:21–28 is so different that it probably has come from some other source:

²¹Jesus left there and went off to the district of Tyre and Sidon. ²²And, look, a Canaanite woman from the area came crying out, "Have mercy on me, sir, you Son of David, my daughter is severely possessed." ²³He said nothing to her. The disciples came up to him complaining, "Send her away; she's nagging us." ²⁴Answering, Jesus said, "I was sent only to the lost sheep of the house of Israel." ²⁵But she knelt down before him, saying, "Lord, help me." ²⁶He replied, "It's not right to take the children's bread and throw it to dogs." ²⁷She said, "Yes, Lord, but even the puppies eat

scraps that fall from their master's table." ²⁸Jesus then said, "O woman, great is your faith. Let your wish come true." And her daughter was healed from that moment on.

Mark pictures Jesus alone; Matthew has him with disciples. In Mark, the woman is a Syrophoenician; in Matthew, she is a Canaanite. The woman addresses Jesus as "Son of David" in Matthew. The dialogue is slightly different, and Jesus' final words are quite different: "Woman, great is your faith. Let your wish come true." The addition of the disciples in the Matthean account makes a more dramatic story that is much better for preaching.

Mark's Story

The story may be prompted by the tale of Elijah and the foreign widow in 1 Kings 17. Jesus is in the same general area as Elijah. According to Mark, Jesus has gone north from Galilee to the region of Tyre. Mark's Jesus is peripatetic, moving rapidly from one setting to another. Many scholars suppose that Mark's geography is symbolic, for frequently it is bizarre. After Jesus' encounter with the Syrophoenician woman, Mark says that he "left the area of Tyre and traveled through Sidon to the sea of Galilee, via the middle region known as Decapolis" (v. 31), which is a little like saying someone went from Pittsburgh to Cleveland via the short cut through Cincinnati. But, for the story, Jesus' trip to the area around Tyre puts him in Gentile territory. Residents of Tyre had long been bad-mouthed by people from Galilee. Much of Galilee's agricultural produce was shipped to Tyre, while peasants living in Galilee went hungry.

Though Jesus seems to want to be alone, a Greek woman who has heard of him comes begging for him to drive a demon from her daughter. Jesus answers rather offensively, "First, let the children be fed. It's not right to take the children's bread and throw it to dogs!" Scholars have often argued that if Jesus says something in Scripture that seems offensive to us, it is probably authentic. But here we seem to have words so starkly prejudicial that they run counter to everything else Jesus reputedly said. Thus, I suspect that here we have a popular expression of prejudice Jesus is deliberately quoting: "It's not right to take the children's bread and throw it to the dogs!" The area near Tyre and close to Galilee was a border area that involved some mingling of Jews and Gentiles. The saying Jesus quotes might well have been common in the region. No doubt Gentiles had been labeled "dogs" by Jews, and vice versa. Dogs were not family pets in Israel. Wild dogs roamed around villages and were regarded as filthy; they fed on the flesh of the dead. "Dog" is a nasty slur.

In any event, the woman answers with wit and modesty, "But sir, even the puppies under the table get the children's scraps." "Sir" is a tricky word; in other settings it is often translated "Lord," or in parables "Master" or even "Boss." After the racial slur, the deferential expression "sir" can be either an expression of calculated self-control or irony. Jesus hears her reply and, apparently, is delighted. He approves, which demonstrates that his earlier, "It's not right to take the children's bread and throw it to the dogs!" is almost certainly the quoting of a popular racial slur. Then Jesus sends the woman home to find her daughter restored.

Most scholars think the story functioned in the early debate over a Gentile mission, perhaps between the Peter and Paul factions within Christian communities. Is the gospel message for the children of Israel alone, or should the reach of evangelism extend to the Gentile world? Mark seems to be writing for a predominantly Gentile community. Thus, it is possible that the racial slur has been put on Jesus' lips to represent an argument animating some early Christian communities.

The Controversy

Is the story of the Syrophoenician woman a conflict story? Does it have a question, a counterquestion, and a pronouncement? Not really. There is dialogue between Jesus and the woman: she asks for help, Jesus replies offensively, she counters with considerable wit, and then Jesus heals her child. There is dialogue, but the passage does not display the usual controversy form. Matthew's version of the story is much more like a controversy because the disciples want Jesus to dismiss the shouting woman. He attempts to do so by defining his mission: "I was sent only to the lost sheep of the house of Israel." The additional dialogue shows us the issue and the mind-set involved. The disciples understand Jesus in terms of a mission to the Jewish world. The Gentile woman, who in Matthew kneels before Jesus and says, "Lord, help me," articulates the claim of the Gentile world.

The controversy agitated early Christian communities. Was Christianity a Jewish religious movement? Probably the historical Jesus so envisioned his own mission. But postresurrection Christianity, under critical attack from the Jewish community, moved out toward the Gentile population. Passages from Christian writings can be lined up to show the gradually changing positions. Mark has a different pattern than Matthew. In Mark, Jesus says, "First, let the children be fed," which is quite different from Matthew's exclusive, "I was sent only to the lost sheep of the house of Israel." Mark assumes there will be a Gentile mission, but only after the Jewish mission. Mark seems to agree with

Paul: first Jews, then Greeks (Rom. 1:16; 2:9–10). In Mark, the puppies are already feeding on scraps. In Matthew, the woman's speech seems to earn the opening of a Gentile mission.[28]

Homiletic Theology

Again and again, the church has struggled between the impulse to hold on to itself protectively and the call to reach out to a wider community. The conflict can be seen in the United States when areas change their ethnic population and, often, an older white congregation is not willing to open doors to the neighborhood. The same disinclination shows up when conservative Christian groups refuse to accommodate a changing social ethos but demand that new members become as doctrinally defined as the majority. How do we protect the essential character of Christian faith and yet move into very different cultural worlds? With Vatican II, the Catholic community resolved to adjust to a more modern world. The wonderful Italian term for such adaptation is *aggiornamento*, literally, "bringing up to date." Times and spaces change, so *aggiornamento* is a chronic Christian responsibility.

Many Christians fear that essential Christianity will be lost in the midst of translation. Answer: Of course it will. Christianity has repeatedly changed. Why else would theological libraries have huge volumes with titles like *The History of Christian Thought*? In the nineteenth century, Adolf von Harnack wrote a five-volume history tracing such changes. In the twentieth century, Jaroslav Pelikan matched Harnack's output with a similar five volumes. Christianity, under the urging of the Spirit, has changed and will change. Is there an essential Christianity? Perhaps, but in spite of many attempts, no one yet has successfully defined an "essence of Christianity." The only obvious constants are preaching and the breaking of bread. Christian faith seems to embody itself in different languages and in different cultures. Perhaps we are called to reach out by speaking faith in every land and era, then to see what kind of Christianity will develop. After all, God is a great innovator!

A Sermon

The sermon was preached in the Evangelical Lutheran Church of East Jordan, Michigan, in September 2001. The church follows the Common Lectionary, so the passage was assigned.

Introduction   There was a book published a few years ago with an odd title: *Things We Wish Jesus Had Never Said*. Guess what? The story of the

Syrophoenician woman topped the list. The woman comes stumbling up to Jesus pleading for help. Her little daughter is seriously sick. And what does Jesus say? "No," he says. "It's not right to give the children's bread to dogs!" It's not right to give what belongs to the children of Israel to Gentile "dogs." The words are outright, outrageous prejudice. Here is Jesus calling a Gentile woman a dog, and what's more, saying so to her face. Things we wish Jesus had never said—what are we going to do with the story of the Syrophoenician woman?

1 Begin by picturing the scene. Jesus has traveled out of Galilee to the borderlands of Tyre and Sidon. Back in the old days, borders were not well defined. There was no chain-link fence, no painted line across the highways, no sign reading, "Welcome to Phoenicia. Drive safely." No, borderlands were wide areas, "demilitarized zones," where Jews and Gentiles lived together uneasily. Was there name calling? Of course. Did the people shun one another? They did indeed. The border territories were nothing but trouble. A few weeks ago President Clinton tried to urge a peace treaty between Israel and the PLO, but the talks broke down. Why? Because of borderland areas. Yet when Jesus, a Jew, shows up on the border, a Gentile woman comes begging for help. And what does Jesus do? He slaps her down with a harsh word: "It's not right to give the children's bread to dogs." We can picture the scene, but it doesn't help any. Prejudice is prejudice, period.

2 You hear the words and you wonder. Has the Bible got the story straight? Did Jesus actually say such harsh words? You ask, because nowhere else in the Gospel record does Jesus show any signs of such blatant racial prejudice. His circle of friends is huge and, yes, a mix. There are the sons of Zebedee; they own a fishery. Among the disciples is also Simon the zealot, an Israel love-it-or-leave-it type, a superpatriot. Then there is Mary Magdalene, who may have been an ex-prostitute, and Zacchaeus, a notorious racketeer. As for Gentiles, did not Jesus praise a centurion for faith and then heal his sick slave? Oh, sometimes Jesus did have harsh words for scribes and Pharisees, but with actual people he was always affirming: Nicodemus was a scribe Jesus loved, and Simon the leper, a Pharisee, threw a dinner party for Jesus. William Lyon Phelps once said that Jesus was the only man he ever heard of who looked like God, acted like God, talked like God.[29] Why? Why because, according to Phelps, his love was unlimited and inclusive. Jesus welcomed everyone. So how could Jesus snarl prejudice at a Gentile woman? Could the Bible have gotten the story wrong?

3 Maybe there's an answer. Just maybe Jesus is quoting a cruel slogan—one of those awful phrases we've all heard that are full of prejudice. Maybe he is confronting all of us with our prejudice. Look, America was settled by white-skinned European people, and from the earliest days there has been prejudice among us. Foreigners, Jews, Asians, blacks—there's always been a "them" for us to label and blame—us and them. How many forms of prejudice have there been? Among Protestants there has been prejudice toward Catholics. Among workers there has been prejudice against bosses and "scabs." Among white folk there has been prejudice against people of color. In Charlevoix County there's been a longtime prejudice against native "Indians." Us and them. Some years ago a Chinese laundry in New York City put a big sign in their window: "We're two hundred percent American," the sign read. "We hate everybody!" So was Jesus quoting a familiar Jewish slogan, as if to say, "Listen, here's what your prejudice sounds like"? Maybe there's the answer.

4 So what about the Syrophoenician woman? What does she say? She has a comeback! "Yes sir," she says with laughter, "but under the table puppies can eat the children's crumbs." She answers prejudice with laughter. How do you answer prejudice? Anger simply breeds more anger and drives the prejudice deeper. So the woman laughs and turns the harsh word "dogs" into playful puppies under the table. You can almost hear the woman and Jesus laughing together over her words. Almost twenty years ago, the Ku Klux Klan put on their bedsheet uniforms to parade through the streets of Nashville. There was a tense, angry crowd lined up watching. But all of a sudden a little girl turned to her mother and exclaimed, "Do they think it's Halloween?" The crowd began to laugh, and the remark passed along with a wave of spreading laughter until the parade was chased away by gales of laughter. So the woman, because she cared for her daughter, turned prejudice into laughter: "The puppies eat the children's crumbs," she said, and laughed the cruel slogan away.

5 Then what happens? *In the midst of Jews and Gentiles, Jesus speaks: "Go," he says. "Your daughter is cured."* The woman goes home and, sure enough, her daughter is sleeping peacefully, completely cured. What does the story say to us? God is great, greater than our we's and they's. We say "our God," as if God could be limited to our land or our purposes or our beliefs or, yes, our color. But no, God's love is larger than the limits of our minds. We are all the children of God—underline the word *all.* Yes, God loves ELCA Lutherans, but God loves the children who worship at St. Joseph's just as much. And God loves Christians but also loves those who pray to God as "Allah." Yes, God loves those who believe but also those who do not and will not believe. God loves the loveless. God loves our enemies. There is no limit to the astonishing love of God. Jesus announced the healing of a child so that everyone in the borderland, Jews and Gentiles, would know the great, gracious love of God. Did you read about the huge conference of world religious leaders held at the UN three weeks ago? There were Muslims, Shintoists, Buddhists, Catholics, Protestants, African tribal shamans. An American evangelist got up and condemned all the other religions: there was only one God, his name was Jesus, and they would have to convert or perish. But the next speaker was a gentle priest from Sri Lanka. "There are many rivers flowing into the sea," he said, "the great mysterious sea of God!"—neither Jew nor Gentile, but a God whose love knows no borders. "Go, your child is well," said Jesus, and for everyone, yes, including us, he made God very great.

Conclusion   What an embarrassing story! How did it get into our Bible? Maybe the early Christians struggling to leave their Jewish roots and spread across the Gentile world treasured the story. We can too. We can spread news of God's love beyond ourselves with laughter and, of course, with love.

Discussion

Introduction   The introduction is compact. All it does is raise the question about Jesus' awful remark: "It's not right to give the children's bread to dogs!" Did Jesus call a Gentile woman "dog"?

1 The move locates us in a border area where Jews and Gentiles would have mingled warily. By using contemporary images—"demilitarized zones" and likening the biblical situation to President Clinton's negotiations between Israel and the PLO—we can locate the story into contemporary consciousness.

2 Now I raise the question: How could Jesus say such words? I then describe Jesus' inclusive relationships—with Jews, Gentiles, businessmen, zealots, a tax collector and possibly an ex-prostitute, scribes and Pharisees. So the prejudicial words don't match the character of Jesus.

3 Finally, I suggest an answer: Jesus is confronting us with our prejudice by using a familiar hate phrase. I list common antagonisms—foreigners, Jews, Asians, blacks! Then mention a particular prejudice in the local area against Native Americans, who have been slurred for years.

4 Here I present the woman's witty reply. The illustration of the KKK parade broken up by a child's funny remark fits pretty well. How do you deal with outright prejudice? If you're a victim, you've learned to parry it with humor. Anger intensifies, while laughter chases away.

5 Jesus heals the woman's child, a demonstration of the inclusive love of God that reaches out compassionately to all people—Protestants and Catholics, Christians and Muslims, believers and nonbelievers. We are all the children of God. The idea is illustrated in the contrast between the fundamentalist evangelist at the UN conference and the priest from Sri Lanka.

Conclusion   The conclusion that follows is brief but useful.

The sermon moves along much like the plot of a story, which, of course, is what we are given in the passage.

CONFLICT OVER A SIGN

Mark 8:11–13 (also Matthew 16:1–4)

[11]The Pharisees showed up and began to argue with him. To test him, they were demanding a sign from heaven. [12]He groaned inwardly, and asked, "Why does this generation seek a sign? Amen. I tell you, no way will this generation be given a sign." [13]Leaving them behind, he went off to the other side again.

Other Versions

Matthew follows Mark rather closely but alters Jesus' words in the following way: "*You know how to interpret the appearance of the sky, but you can't discern the signs of the times. An evil, immoral* generation asks for a sign, but in no way will this generation be given a sign *except the sign of the prophet Jonah.*" A few manuscripts of Matthew also add a preface to his answer: "In evening you say, 'It'll be fair weather, for the sky is red,' and in the morning, 'It'll be stormy today, for the sky is overcast.'" But Matthew, drawing on Q, has still another entirely different version of the demand for a sign (see 12:38–42), and Luke has scattered the same Q material in 11:29 and 12:54–56.

Mark's Story

Mark locates this brief encounter with the Pharisees after the spectacular healing of a deaf man and the miraculous feeding of the four thousand. Though they should have been awed, the Pharisees show up still wanting a sign from the sky! The sequence is typical Markan irony.

The start of the story is similar to the controversy over authority in Mark 11. The Pharisees show up demanding that Jesus display some sign of God's power to certify his message. From their point of view, Jesus' teaching is divergent and contrary to Torah and thus requires some spectacular sign of God's endorsement. Jesus groans and asks plaintively, "Why does this generation seek a sign?" His response calls to mind Psalm 95:9–10:

> When your fathers put Me to the test,
>> Tried Me, though they had seen my deeds.
> Forty years I was provoked by that generation
> I thought, "They are a senseless people;
>> they would not know My ways."

The psalm recalls the Israelites, who were fed by miraculous manna and sustained in their wilderness wandering by the hand of God; though given such signs, they were unbelieving (Num. 14:1–11). They are called "this evil generation" in Deuteronomy 1:35 for the same unbelief and for testing the Lord their God.

No wonder Jesus ends the discussion abruptly: "Amen. I tell you, no way will this generation be given a sign." To compound Jesus' dismay, the disciples show up shortly thereafter complaining that they have no bread, though they have recently witnessed Jesus feeding four thousand hungry people.

Is the brief passage a conflict story? No, the question-counterquestion-pronouncement pattern is not present.

Preaching the Passage

Though not a conflict story, the passage speaks to our age. We have been called "a nation of seekers," and maybe we are. But lately, what have we been seeking? Either we chase esoterica—"lost books of the Bible," "new visions from Fatima"—or we chase down the paradoxical musings of the gnostic *Gospel of Thomas*. Maybe we are seeking inner experiences, dreams, and some immediacy of God's felt personal presence. The distorted "gospel" of the *Left Behind* series grabs our attention, while the audience for a gospel message from local pulpits dwindles. Our ears are bruised by the daily traumas we hear broadcast on the news and by the deceits of White House news "spins." Will nothing be spectacular enough to catch our attention? Will nothing convince our jaded minds of truth?

Maybe we already possess a hint of truth, for most of us have a vague familiarity with Scripture, however fragmentary, and most of us have heard, however ineptly, the gospel of God's love spoken to us. Most of us struggle to hold on to faith but then search for more meaning by asking and studying and, yes, listening. But for many people nowadays, that's not enough. Uncertainty riddles them. They demand some tailor-made, big-time, God-shaped personal experience to guarantee their faith. Listen to the voice of Jesus: "Amen. I tell you, no way will this generation be given a sign!"

Chapter 6

On Discipleship

Conflict over Divorce (10:2–12)
Conflict over Children (10:13–16)
Conflict over Wealth (10:17–31)
Conflict over Power (10:35–45)

*T*he conflict stories in Mark 10 all seem to swirl around the question of life in Christian community. If we are divorced, can we still be disciples? Are children full members of the community? Can we be rich members without sharing? Can we seek power and yet be members of an egalitarian servant community? All these queries are still very much with us.

CONFLICT OVER DIVORCE

Mark 10:2–12 (also Matthew 19:1–12)

[2]And they came to test him, asking, "Is it legal for a husband to dismiss a wife?" [3]Answering, he asked them, [4]"What did Moses command you?" And they said, "Moses allowed the writing of a Certificate of Divorce and the dismissal." [5]And Jesus said to them, "He wrote you the commandment because of your hard-heartedness. [6]But from the beginning of creation, 'God made them male and female.'[7]'For this reason a man shall leave his father and mother [and be joined to his wife], [8]and they shall become one flesh.' Thus they are no longer two, but one flesh. [9]So what God has joined together, don't let anyone tear apart."

[10]In the house, the disciples again asked him about this. [11]And he said to them, "Whoever divorces his wife and marries another commits adultery with her. [12]And if she marries another after divorcing her husband, she commits adultery."

Other Versions

Matthew provides a modified version. He adds "for any cause" to the question being asked. Then Matthew reverses the order of the passage; he has Jesus cite Scripture and then has the Pharisees ask, "Then why did Moses command us to give a Certificate of Divorce and dismiss her?" Jesus replies, "Because you were so hardhearted, Moses let you divorce your wives, but it wasn't that way originally. Now I tell you whoever divorces his wife except for infidelity commits adultery." Matthew has added specific grounds for divorce with the phrase "except for infidelity." Thereafter, in response to another question— "Isn't it better not to marry?"—Matthew adds a saying from another source on the subject of eunuchs.

Mark's Story

In translating the story, I have decided to translate the Greek *apoluein* as "dismiss." Many translations have "divorce," which is probably intended.[1] In Galilee, at the time of Christ, no one would have asked, "Is divorce legal?" Husbands were allowed to divorce wives; the only question was over the grounds for divorce. Laws governing divorce were specific. People were married after drawing up a betrothal contract specifying a dowry that would revert to the wife in the case of divorce. A written certificate (I have translated it a "Certificate of Divorce") basically canceled the marriage contract, permitting a husband to get rid of a wife. The law is specified in Deuteronomy 24:1: "A man takes a wife and possesses her. She fails to please him because he finds something obnoxious about her, and he writes her a bill of divorcement, hands it to her, and sends her away from his house." The debated issue: What exactly is "something obnoxious"?

Two rabbinic schools, Shammai and Hillel, argued over the phrase. Shammai insisted that only outright infidelity was a proper ground for divorce, whereas Hillel allowed more liberal grounds. Women themselves had no official rights of divorce. Here, however, Jesus' questioners ("Pharisees" in some manuscripts) are not debating grounds for divorce; they are asking about divorce per se. Probably the question comes from some subsequent Christian community. At the time of Christ a question of divorce per se would not have been asked. But in Christian communities after the resurrection, apocalyptic urgency or a more-than-the-law ethic might have prompted such a question.

We have seen Mark add an "in-house" private conversation between Jesus and the disciples (7:17–19). Here we can see more clearly how such addenda may function. Though Jesus offers nothing more than an epigrammatic saying, Mark is now laying down specific laws for a local congregation: "Whoever divorces his wife and marries another commits adultery with her. And if she marries another after divorcing her husband, she commits adultery." There are variant readings for the law applied to women, one of which begins, "If a woman leaves her husband, . . ." perhaps reflecting Jewish custom. But any mention of women "divorcing" their husbands is clearly a product of the Gentile world. In Israel at the time of Jesus, a woman could leave her husband, but she could not divorce him. Only husbands could divorce. If a woman wanted to divorce a husband and remarry, she would have to get her husband to do the divorcing. Divorce in Jesus' time was clearly a male prerogative. Thus, Mark's legal addition referring to a woman "after divorcing her husband" must have been determined by a different Gentile context. In Matthew's congregation, Jesus' saying evokes a somewhat different policy, recognizing a specific ground for divorce. But, above all, recognize that Jesus' pronouncement is deliberately *not law*. Both Mark and Matthew have added legal verses to the original conflict story to legislate for their own communities.

The Controversy

The controversy includes a question, "Is it legal for a husband to dismiss a wife?" and a counterquestion, "What did Moses command you?" The counterquestion shows us the mind of the questioners; they are asking for a legal answer allowing divorce. Instead, Jesus announces, "He wrote you the commandment because of your hard-heartedness." "Hard-hearted" is a metaphor for unteachable, stubborn rigidity. Jesus then goes on to quote from Genesis 1:27 and 2:24. Many early manuscripts only have the initial phrase from Genesis 2:24, "For this reason a man shall leave his father and mother," but the rest of the verse is surely implied. Jesus then adds a pronouncement: "What God has joined together, don't let anyone tear apart." Though I have used "anyone" in the translation, the text has "a man," no doubt reflecting original male rights.

The controversy seems to include Scripture quoted against Scripture. Though the Pharisees cite Deuteronomy 24:1, Jesus goes back to God's purpose in creation, citing two verses from Genesis. Thus, by quoting from Genesis, the law in Deuteronomy is portrayed as a secondary divine concession to human sinfulness. But here's an insight: While Deuteronomy 24 hands a husband rights of divorce, the text from Genesis 1 refers to the creation of male *and* female, so Deuteronomy is shown to reflect patriarchy and Genesis 1 God's creating purpose, namely, a world designed for both men and women.[2]

The final pronouncement, like most of the pronouncements, is not law but a wave toward the purposes of God. While Christian groups may propound laws interpreting Jesus' words to guide members, the pronouncement itself is decidedly nonlegal. Indeed, laws are made to appear as divine concessions at best. Though there is clear precedent for churchly law giving—both Mark and

Matthew do so and, what's more, attribute their laws to Jesus—nonetheless, the controversy moves toward the purposes of God in creation. In other words, there is a shift from law to theology!

Homiletic Theology

Obviously a theology of marriage must begin not with liturgy but with sex.[3] Men and women have been coupling with or without benefit of ritual long before anyone devised a marriage service. If we intend monogamy, then all that is necessary is some sort of social acknowledgment—"Look, John and Mary have become coupled." Calvin recognized the ordinary nature of marriage. "Marriage," he wrote, "is a good and holy ordinance of God; and farming, building, cobbling, and barbering are also lawful ordinances of God."[4] However, Calvin did go on to observe that marriage may be seen as a covenant analogy, as between YHWH and Israel, and/or Christ and church. The strange mix of secular and sacred is a feature of all theologies of marriage. Male and female are a gift of creation, but marriage ritual is based on analogy.

Let's begin at the beginning. To suggest that from the start of things God instituted marriage is a bit silly. Customs surrounding human coupling are varied, sometimes multiple, and always astonishing.[5] Instead, let's begin where Scripture does, namely, with the creation of sexual difference: "And God said, 'Let us make human being in our image, after our likeness. . . . And God created human being in His image, the image of God He created him; male and female He created them" (Gen. 1:26–27). Each of the creation narratives in Genesis suggests that God created male and female, different in gender yet designed for relating. Without unpacking the complicated idea of an *imago Dei,* we can observe that "earthling" (*'adama* = "earth" and, therefore, *'adam* = "earthling") was created male and female. But then the second chapter of Genesis concludes with verse 24, in which male and female in Hebrew are suddenly referred to as *ish* and *isha,* indicating some sort of wedded status. There may be a hint here of the profound notion that sexuality is ultimately fulfilled in covenant.

Now, a second step: In sexual coupling we "know" one another. Again and again, the Hebrew Scriptures use the word "know" for sexual intercourse, as for example in Genesis 4:1. The word is apt, for in coitus there is self-disclosing, an expression of personality both complex and profound. Perhaps the reason for the primal fear of sexuality that lives in most human beings is precisely because sex does expose. But we must be cautious: intercourse does not offer "another" way of knowing, a transcendent suprahuman knowing such as German romantics were wont to suppose. We have quite enough sexual Gnosticism in our culture without adding more! No, sex involves a communication of all the senses, but it offers no extraordinary mode of intuition. In coitus there is an intimate, remarkably concentrated expression of self. Thus, in sexual coming together, we do "know" one another.

Of course, the self that is known sexually is not exempt from sin. Contra D. H. Lawrence, in sexual coupling we do not meet an Edenic other, sans fig leaf, restored to primal purity. While sex is good, a gift of God, and any Christian tradition that assigns demerit for sexual friskiness is clearly less than Christian, nevertheless, sexual participants are no better or worse than they are otherwise. Yes, insofar as we may seek to relate to another human with passion, courtesy, and affection, we may be "at our best," but "our best" scarcely cancels our common sinfulness. Sex is *eros* and, therefore, ever an admixture of grace and self-seeking. So we cannot exempt coitus from the human condition. The self displayed in sexual intercourse is a sinner—a broken self with quirks, idolatries, fears, brute insensitivities, and blatant hang-ups, all caught up in a brief gracefulness of flesh. Surely the account of the fall in Genesis makes it clear that the naturalness of sexuality is lost and that rivalry, blame, shame, and suspicion now disfigure our relating. Let us admit blunt truth: the self known in sexual coupling is self-as-sinner.

Now, a third shift in thought, the knowing of self via intercourse calls for acceptance, for some sort of justification by grace. In coitus, we know and are known, and insofar as we possess self-awareness we may confront ourselves—our truly ambiguous selves. What mercy will cover such self-disclosure? The damage of "one-night stands" is that they are designed to abandon a disclosed self (there is, after all, a difference between an accepting grace and "So long, kid!"). Casual dalliance can be demonic, for while it involves self-exposure, at the same time it excludes covenant making, except in an often uneasy, if fading, friendship. We might remark that the act of coupling in and of itself can be the affirmation of another's flesh and recognize some validity in the romantic tradition. Nevertheless, we must also allow that transient coupling can lead to despair of the unjustified. Justification of flesh ultimately requires the constancy of covenant love. In covenant, we are assured that our self-as-sinner once disclosed will not be abandoned but will be sustained, affirmed, and kept in the splendid covenant rites of sex.

We began with the fact of sexual difference, which, at minimum, may imply a coming together (Gen. 2:24). We end by calling for a mutual justification of our flesh through covenant love, a love analogous to God's faithful love for Israel, or, among Christians, to Christ's love for Christian communities. Christian marriage offers a redemptive analogy to sexual exiles from Eden and, more, a redemptive community in which the Spirit of Christ is present through

Word and sacrament. The strange mix of "social" and "religious" we notice in most marriage ceremonies is not strange at all but is grounded in the revelation of a God who created male and female and who redeems male and female. Because the fact of male and female is being used these days to disallow other kinds of covenanting, I should be more specific and say that the fact of sexuality per se ultimately calls for human covenants. Whenever people appeal to orders of creation to disallow social change, the notion of creation is being misapplied. We are to celebrate creation as a gift of God and not as a theological straightjacket (with stress on the word "straight").

We have scarcely exhausted the meaning of marriage. Theological doodling is always incomplete. How many themes have we neglected? Certainly we should pick up Origen's famous idea that married families should be "little churches" in which forgiveness is a cheerful habit, where a knowledge of God is learned and grace abounds, and where lives are turned inside out in common service toward common neighbors. Marriage should create something more than a mutual admiration society. We also should explore the role of Christian communities in sustaining marriage at a time when social pressures seem to be threatening all bonds of covenant.

What about divorce? Divorce is tragic. It always leaves two selves separated and with ragged edges. Something has been torn. Realism acknowledges that the marital conflict can harden, preventing any return to love. During such a crisis, Christian communities are called to surround couples with tender understanding quite beyond ethical rules and, above all, with a shared declaration of pardon for all broken people. We all live in The Mercy—married, unmarried, or remarried. In The Mercy, we must accept and exchange forgiveness as gracefully as we can.

Preaching the Passage

I don't think I have ever heard a sermon on the passage. Ministers realize there are members of the congregation who have struggled through divorce. They may suppose that, lest they trouble those persons, the subject is better unspoken. As a result, divorce is consigned to "pastoral care" or silence. Perhaps we should reconsider, for nationally the number of marriages broken by divorce edges toward 50 percent. Most divorced members of the congregation know divorce was a troubled last resort. And they know divorce has left them with scars. Most would admit that while divorce is legal, and often necessary, properly marriages ought to be glad and lasting. What matters is how the subject is preached. In the distant past, many mainline Protestant denominations had the equivalent of Catholic marriage tribunals, councils that encouraged stability in marriage and helped persons sort through the moral issues involved. But now marriages and their problems are relegated to a minister's counseling practice, for which only some clergy are adequately prepared. The result is that Protestant communities do not support the newly married well, and struggling midlife marriages often not at all.

The conflict story itself will design a sermon. An introduction could begin by facing a national problem such as the high percentage of failed marriages. We can ask what word we have from Jesus on the subject. Then a first move can begin by admitting, "Well it's legal, isn't it?" A second move can explore Jesus' comment about "hardness of heart." Marriages sometimes do "harden" into fixed positions for which there may be no solution short of divorce. Jesus was realistic. But a third move can turn to the question of moral purpose. We know that marriage is meant to be a good partnership, a mutuality of love. Such is God's purpose. The creation of male and female seems to call for covenant like God's own faithful covenant with humanity. Finally, we need to be honest about the mercy of God. Those of us who have struggled through divorce are surrounded by God's special grace. And those of us who are well married had better acknowledge the grace that has endlessly forgiven us. We all live in The Mercy. The conflict story suggests a sermon that will declare the gospel message.

CONFLICT OVER CHILDREN

Mark 10:13–16 (also Matthew 19:13–15 and Luke 18:15–17)

[13]They wanted to bring children to him so he could lay hands on them, but the disciples scolded them. [14]Seeing this, Jesus was furious and said, "Don't stop them. Let them come to me. For of such is God's new order. [16]Amen. I tell you whoever doesn't accept God's rule like a child can't get into the new order." [6]And taking them into his arms he put his hands on them to bless them.

Other Versions

As usual, Matthew and Luke reduce references to Jesus' human emotions. They drop mention of Jesus' anger, and skip the verse in which he hugs the children. Matthew does retain a formal "He laid his hands on them and went on his way." The *Gospel of Thomas* has a somewhat different version: Jesus sees a nursing baby and announces, "These infants being suckled are like those who enter the kingdom." But thereafter, the passage drifts into some rather murky gnostic imagery.

Mark's Story

Mark has two passages in which children are highly regarded and even held up as exemplars of the new order. The other one is Mark 9:36–37, in which the disciples are arguing over "who was greater":

> Having sat down, [Jesus] called the twelve together and said to them, "If someone wants to be first, he will be last and the servant of all." Then he took a child and set him among them. Taking [the child] in his arms, he said to them, "Whoever accepts a child like this, accepts me. And whoever accepts me, doesn't accept me so much as the one who sent me."

These remarks about children follow Jesus' demand that disciples "be last and a servant of all." The two images relate. Disciples should give up striving for social status and become like children, who have no social status. In the social hierarchy of first-century Israel, they were least of the least.

In chapter 10, the conflict story (if that's what it is) hasn't much of a story line. People wanted to bring their children to Jesus. Probably mothers came with children wanting a protective blessing from Jesus. In the ancient world, children needed all the protection they could get. The infant mortality rate may have been as high as 30 percent. Because people themselves did not live for too many years, often parents would perish before children were full grown. Children were vulnerable. Eventually they could become useful workers. They would perpetuate the clan and perhaps provide care for aging parents. But until they matured, they had no status within clan or wider society. They were marginal. In a way, little children were "nobodies."

When some parents try to bring their children for a blessing, the disciples scold them and try to block their path. But Jesus is irate and tells them not to stop the children, for God's new order is composed of folk such as children. A second saying is added that unless we accept God's rule like children, we cannot enter the new order.

Do the sayings go back to Jesus? Verse 14 certainly fits in with Jesus' welcome of the socially excluded, for children in the ancient world had no rights. Again and again, Jesus' image of God's social order is inclusive and egalitarian—"a kingdom of nuisances and nobodies," says John Dominic Crossan.[6] Verse 16 reverses the disciples' action: Jesus takes children into his arms and blesses them. Some scholars suppose the verse may have an indirect reference to baptism, but I doubt that infant baptism was an early practice.[7]

The Controversy

The story lacks usual conflict-story form. We could argue that those who wanted to bring children to Jesus were enacting a request, thus a question—Will you bless our children? The disciples try to shoo them away, but Jesus' sharp command to them—"Don't stop them. Let them come to me"—while not exactly a counterquestion, certainly exposes the disciples' view of children. To the disciples, children are no more than a nuisance. Finally, there is a pronouncement: "Amen. I tell you whoever doesn't accept God's rule like a child can't get into the new order."

Whatever the form, I think we can sense that we are dealing with a controversial issue, not so much in Jesus' lifetime but in subsequent Christian communities. What exactly is the status of our children? The issue has been with us for centuries. Are young children "believers," or mere family baggage? Do children share in the eucharistic mystery, as in Eastern Christianity, or should they be held back, as is the practice in Western Christianity? An early document recommends that mothers not offer infants eucharistic bread lest they choke. Instead, mothers are advised to dip a finger in the cup of wine for babies to suck and thus receive "medicine of immortality." But sensible advice does not make a theological argument. What is the status of Christian children? Are they "members" or "learners"? Do they have rights and privileges within Christian community? In biblical times, children under seven were considered infants and were to be reared by women. After seven, they were to be trained until maturity for their determined social roles as men and women. Other than custom, there was little awareness of what we label developmental stages.

Homiletic Theology

A famous theologian who migrated from Germany to America confessed to a class, "In the old country, the parent rules the child. In this country, the child rules the parent." He shook his head pathetically, adding, " I lose both ways!" How can Americans, who find it hard to refuse their children anything, understand ancient cultures? If we want to understand, we must enlarge the word "family." In our nation, the word is applied to the nuclear family—a mother, a father, and a modest number of children. But in biblical times, "family" was often a clan in which a number of young children might be raised. Parental lives could be brief; the average life span was barely beyond the twenties. And given the risks of childbirth, women were particularly vulnerable; thus, there was need for a wider family to raise children. In those days it still took two to produce a child, but they relied on a wider clan, often a village, to raise the child.

Our primary focus on the nuclear family tends to undercut a Christian claim: In baptism, the church is meant to be a new-order family, replacing blood relationships. Thus, in Christian Scriptures, it is not the nuclear family that is basic to the social order, but Christian community. Nowadays the shape of Christian community shows up sometimes at "family night suppers" where the kids seem to be children of the whole congregation. Again, in times of tragedy, the Christian family appears when the community as a whole rallies to care for those ailing or grieving. Maybe church as an advance-guard family of God's new order was more apparent in the first century when many Christians were alienated from their blood relatives.

We tend to think of young children as bundles of potential. Thus, we are apt to view family life as a field for the growth of a child's personal potential. But Leviticus 19:18 is a helpful corrective: "You shall love your neighbor as your own," that is, your own kinfolk.[8] The purpose of our lives, therefore, is to widen the circle of neighbor love. The family is meant to be a school for neighbor love and, therefore, a training ground for life in God's new order. The notion of the kingdom, God's new order, redefines family life as well as the nurturing of children.

Preaching the Passage

Two problems attend our preaching of the passage. First, we romanticize our infants. We view them as innocent creatures packed with wonderful potential. They trust; we do not. They love so readily, and we do not. We reject the horrid notion of "original sin." But actually, little children are bundles of self-interest. Their peripheral vision is decidedly limited. They have needs, which prompt strident demands. How hard it is for infants to acknowledge anyone else's needs. Simply put, little children can be fairly offensive. Think, for example, of those unpleasant children on television singing of how they want to be Oscar Mayer wieners! Almost all children in TV advertising are painful. Our children are easily corrupted by us, if ever they were innocent. After all, they were not born in Eden. Wasn't it one of Ignazio Silone's characters who announced: "We all lose our innocence, it's the usual thing."[9] How can we sinners breed innocence? We can't.

The second problem has to do with our attempts to find a reason for Jesus' approval of children—it's their freedom, their imagination, their creativity, their playfulness, and the like. Congregations love such sermons. But whatever our sermons may claim, they are not supported by the two passages in Mark, nor by Christian theology. In Mark, when Jesus refers to children as models for life in God's new order, it is not because of their innate potential;

after all, we are saved by grace through faith and not by inborn abilities. If anything, Jesus' welcome includes children along with other socially excluded persons. The nonstatus of children is unacceptable in God's new order and therefore in our churches. Children are a trust given us temporarily by the God of creation. We are temporary tutors, if you will, but only for a few years. Children are meant to grow beyond us, but, we pray, not beyond the people of God. In the first of Mark's passages, disciples are vying for position—to be the "greatest." Jesus then singles out a child as an exemplar of life in the kingdom. Why? Because the child is dependent and does not have social position. In the second of Mark's texts, children are welcomed as persons in the sight of God for no reason except for God's astonishing love.

Church policy should be corrected by the conflict story. In baptism, children are named and recognized by God as members of God's covenant people. The old baptismal formula, "John Doe, child of the covenant," is splendid. As children in covenant, they inherit all the promises of God. The idea that such promises are to be actualized by subsequent "confirmation" is a dubious ecclesial invention. No wonder both Luther and Calvin rejected the rite. "Monkey business," said Luther. Calvin, untypically, was cruder (see *Institutes* 2:1459). But Reformers did set up Christian education systems, designed with rigor so the young could become lay theologians. Today churches promote courses on "parenting." But to be truthful, most of us inevitably flunk parenting; after all, we are sinners. About all we can hope to do is to equip children with a knowledge of God and devotion enough to see their unfolding lives within such knowledge. Worldly success is not a criterion for Christians; neighbor love is.

CONFLICT OVER WEALTH

Mark 10:17–31 (also Matthew 19:16–30 and Luke 18:18–30)

[17]As he was going along, someone ran up and, kneeling before him, asked him, "Good Teacher, what must I do to inherit eternal life?" [18]Jesus said to him, "Why do you call me good? No one is good but God alone. [19]You know the commandments: Do not kill. Do not commit adultery. Do not steal. Do not give false testimony. Do not defraud. Honor your father and your mother." [20]He said, "Teacher, I have done all these things since I was young." [21]But Jesus, looking at him with love, said to him, "You lack one thing; go, sell everything you have, and give to the poor—you will have 'treasure in heaven.' Then, come, follow me." [22]Shaken by the words he heard, he went away sad because he had many properties.

[23]Then, looking around, Jesus said to his disciples, "How hard it is for monied people to get into God's new order!" [24]The disciples were puzzled

by his words. So Jesus spoke to them again, "Children, how hard it is to get into God's social order! [25]Easier for a camel to squeeze through the eye of a needle than for a rich person to get into God's social order!" [26]They were absolutely confused, saying among themselves, "Who can be saved?" [27] Jesus looked at them and said, "With humans impossible, but not for God; everything is possible for God!"

[28]Peter began to speak to him: "Look, we've left everything to follow you." [29]Jesus answered, "Amen. I tell you there's no one who has left house or brothers or sisters or mother or father or children or fields for my sake and the sake of the gospel [30]who won't get back a hundred times—houses, brothers and sisters and mothers and children and fields, [with persecutions] now in the present, and in the age to come, eternal life. [31]Many of the first will be last, and the last first."

Other Versions

Matthew has difficulty with Jesus questioning his own virtue, so the address is changed from "Good Teacher" to "Teacher," and Jesus' reply from "Why do you call me good?" to "Why do you ask me about the good?" Matthew and Luke both correct the list of commandments, deleting "Do not defraud," thus losing what might be an important Markan subtlety. Matthew adds to the list "You shall love your neighbor as yourself." Both Matthew and Luke remove the reference to Jesus "looking at him with love." In addition, both Matthew and Luke change Jesus' reply to Peter's question in verse 28. Matthew adds, "when the son of humanity sits on his glory throne, you also will sit on twelve thrones judging the tribes of Israel," a saying that appears in Luke 22:28–30. Luke simply reduces Mark's verse 30 to "will not get back many times more in this age and, in the age to come, eternal life."

Mark's Story

Here again we seem to have a narrative along with extra conversations between Jesus and his disciples. There is the dialogue with the rich man (vv. 17–22); a comment by Jesus that stirs up a reaction from the disciples (vv. 23–27); and Peter's question and Jesus' reply, ending with a tag line in verse 31—"Many of the first will be last, and the last first"—an odd, unconnected saying that appears also in Matthew 20:16 and Luke 13:30, as well as in *Gospel of Thomas* 4:2.

The dialogue begins when a man runs up and kneels in front of Jesus. Somewhat unctuously, he addresses Jesus, "Good Teacher." Normally, in patterns of Middle Eastern courtesy, a bit of flattery earns a bit of flattery in return. But Jesus interrupts with a sudden question: "Why do you call me good? No one is good but God alone!" Then, abruptly, Jesus hands the man a list of commandments: "You know the commandments: Do not kill. Do not commit adultery. Do not steal. Do not give false testimony. Do not defraud. Honor your father and your mother." The order is casual, but notice that an extra command, not from the Ten Commandments, has been slipped into the list: "Do not defraud." Some scholars suppose that Mark is summarizing Exodus 20:17. But Ched Myers argues persuasively that this extra commandment is sneaked into the list because the man's wealth may have come through sharp dealing. The Greek word *apostereses*, "defraud," means to profit by holding back wages or refusing to return held properties.[10] The man, who probably is neither young (Matthew) nor a ruler (Luke), says blandly, "Teacher, I have done all these things since I was young." Then Jesus tells him to sell off his properties and give to the poor so he will have "treasure in heaven." The phrase "treasure in heaven" is a traditional way of affirming the meritorious worth of almsgiving. Finally Jesus says, "Follow me!" The man drifts away shaken because he has many properties.

Then we have still another private discussion with Jesus and his disciples. Jesus remarks, "How hard it is for monied people to get into God's new order!" When the disciples—in Mark they are obtuse, if not positively bone-headed—appear baffled, Jesus reiterates his statement, adding what was probably a folk saying: "Easier for a camel to squeeze through the eye of a needle than for a rich person to get into God's social order!" The saying has troubled Christians, particularly affluent ones. Thus, some manuscripts substitute "rope" (*kamilon*) for "camel" (*kamelon*), supposing that the camel metaphor is too extreme. Some commentators have even proposed that there was a camel gate in Jerusalem called "the Needle," but there is no basis for the claim. Jesus' extravagant saying stands, as appalling to affluent Americans as it was to the disciples, who bluntly ask, "Who can be saved?" Jesus' answer, "With humans impossible, but not for God; everything is possible for God!" is not a cop-out. He is not saying that those who are wealthy need not worry because God will permit them an exception to the rule. Rather, Jesus is underscoring a theological truth: eternal life is God's gift and not a merit badge to be earned or deserved.

Then, as spokesperson for the disciples, Peter, who fares badly in Mark, as usual begins with the wrong question: "Look, we've left everything to follow you." The unspoken query is "What's in it for us?" The disciples, in contrast to the wealthy man who went away glum, have left everything in order to follow Jesus. Is there no reward? Jesus responds:

Amen. I tell you there's no one who has left house or brothers or sisters or mother or father or children or fields for my sake and the sake of the gospel who won't get back a hundred times—houses, brothers and sisters and mothers and children and fields, [with persecutions] now in the present, and in the age to come, eternal life.

The reply, almost certainly the product of a later Christian community, is a bit peculiar. Though it repeats a sequence—house, brothers, sisters, mother, father, children, fields—the word "father" is omitted in the repetition, perhaps because for the Christian community there is only one true Father. Also, the phrase "with persecutions" appears to have been added clumsily. Has Mark added to a source here because of his own situation? Finally, the last saying, "Many of the first will be last, and the last first," seems somewhat inappropriate here. Evidently the phrase is a detached saying, a "floating *logia*" of Jesus that has come to us without a specific context, for it shows up elsewhere in the Synoptic Gospels.

The Controversy

There is no doubt that Jesus was profoundly concerned over money. "You can't serve God and Mammon" ("Mammon" could be rendered neatly by "the Almighty Dollar") is a saying that almost certainly goes back to Jesus. Though reportedly he dropped in on rich Zacchaeus and dined with wealthy Simon the leper, his message was good news for the poor and at times harshly critical of the rich. The Bible itself seems split on the subject; sometimes wealth is regarded as a sign of God's approval, but at other times it is treated as a violation of corporate responsibility and neighbor love. Early Christianity seems to have been worried over money. Obviously, if someone gets rich, others will get poorer. We belong to one another, and therefore unshared wealth is *always* an offense. Christian community benefited from affluent supporters, but, as a movement, it mostly spread among the urban poor. The book of Acts describes with approval a kind of early "communism" in which money and property were held in common and private wealth was thought to violate membership in "the family of God." But the issue was complicated in early Christianity, as the conflict story with the rich man so testifies.

The controversy begins with a question: "Good Teacher, what must I do to inherit eternal life?" Generally in the Christian Scriptures, "eternal life" refers to a quality of life in the here and now. Thus, in effect, the man might be asking, "How can I live a full life now?" But obviously, he is interested in his personal future. Nowadays we might imagine him saying, "What have I got to do to get me into heaven?" After all, the book of Daniel puts it bluntly: "Many of those that sleep in the dust of the earth shall awake, some to eternal life, others to reproaches, to everlasting abhorrence" (Dan. 12:2).

Suddenly, Jesus snaps back, "Why do you call me good? No one is good but God alone." I have suggested that Jesus' counterquestions expose the minds of his questioners. The man comes with flattery, but his unctuousness is not the issue. Rather, the man is a self-reliant moralist. He supposes that he can be good, do good deeds, and thereby get a gate pass to forever-after. Jesus' reply acknowledges inevitable human ambiguity: "No one is good but God alone." The statement has troubled Christians down through the ages (as has also the idea of Jesus repenting in waters of baptism). Isn't Jesus supposed to be sinless? Here Jesus is saying that no one is good enough to deserve God's new order; every entrance pass is stamped "free grace."

Then Jesus lines out the commandments as if to say, "You've had the answer to your question all along." (The same sort of reply shows up in the parable of the Rich Man and Lazarus, the beggar. When the rich man [he has no other name] asks Father Abraham to send Lazarus back from the dead to warn his brothers, Abraham's answer is blunt: "They have Moses and the prophets; let them hear them" [Luke 16:29].) But in listing the commandments, Mark's Jesus slips in the specific, "Do not defraud." Incredibly, the man answers rather glibly, "I've done all these things," establishing two points: he wants to be earnest and, at the same time, he is astonishingly naive. He simply doesn't understand the deep meaning of God's commandments. Does Jesus look on him with love because, however naively, at least he wants to be good? Who knows?

Abruptly, Jesus tells him he must sell his holdings and give the cash to the poor. Then Jesus invites the man to follow him. John R. Donahue says that in the biblical world, a rich man was expected to prosper and then become a Benefactor for those in need (see Job 1:1–5; 29:1–25), earning gratitude from the poor and a good social reputation. Because Jesus has the man divesting himself of all his goods and properties, he is depriving him of living the admired role of Benefactor.[11]

The follow-up discussion with disciples has Jesus announcing, "How hard it is for monied people to get into God's social order!" and then, throwing in a little hyperbole, for good measure he adds, "Easier for a camel to squeeze through the eye of a needle than for a rich person to get into God's social order!" Together they comprise a somewhat negative pronouncement to conclude the controversy.

Homiletic Theology

The subject of money is not preached much in America's mainline churches. Our bourgeois mainline churches have failed, clearly because they have not reached out to the poor. We do not tell our congregations that the poor will be welcomed in God's new order. We seldom, if ever, tell them that money and property are morally dangerous in the sight of God. The problem is capitalist ideology. Capitalism is a competitive system that encourages personal profit, whereas the image of God's new order is a cooperative system calling for neighbor love. A trickle-down economy, which by now we should know doesn't work, is actually a violation of neighbor love. John Calvin justified government-controlled capitalism as a concession to human sinfulness, to our normal, if regrettable, greed and power lust. We are sinners; thus, we need a system that recognizes inevitable greed, but the system needs government control because free, unlimited pursuit of greed is a huge social danger. Calvin may have influenced Puritan culture, but these days Calvin's realism is definitely out of favor. Instead, we cheer Adam Smith, who argued for laissez-faire free-market economics. Smith's thesis was supported by two notions. The first is from his *Theory of Moral Sentiments* (1759), which holds that human beings have an innate, built-in sympathy toward other human beings; the second is from *An Inquiry into the Nature and Causes of the Wealth of Nations* (1776), which contends that a benevolent God watches over human commerce, balancing things out to provide general happiness for the human world. Thus, even though we exercise greedy self-interest competitively, God's "invisible hand" will shape our uncontrolled profit-making into benefit for our whole society. Following Adam Smith, we Americans have despised regulation and have espoused free, ungoverned economic competition. Appropriately, our coins are stamped, "In God we trust." But John Calvin would raise a skeptical eyebrow over the idea that human beings have a built-in disposition to care for others. Malefactors of great wealth seldom seem to want to share, which is why trickle-down economics never works. John Calvin would also be distressed by the notion that we sinners should presume on the graceful, benevolent, invisible hand of God to guarantee economic prosperity for all. Of course, these days the notion of an "invisible hand" is no longer backed by Smith's Scottish Presbyterian belief in divine providence. Capitalism itself is regarded as the automatic invisible hand, which is, of course, idolatry. Preachers should be questioning the capitalism of multinational corporations in America today. But if churches have become part of the system, what then? We could do with a little more Calvin and less positive-thinking economics from the social descendants of Adam Smith.

Why were the early Christians so very disturbed over wealth? After all, in the Hebrew Scriptures there are many passages in which accumulated wealth is viewed as a sign of God's favor or as a reward for righteousness (e.g., Job 42:10–17). Proverbs 10:15 states boldly, "The wealth of a rich man is his fortress; the poverty of the poor is his ruin." But at the same time, there are harsh words aimed by the prophets at the rich, such as Amos 6:4–6, which describes the indolent wealthy: "Lolling on their couches, Feasting on lambs from the flock." According to Amos, the Lord declares, "They shall lead the column of exiles, They shall loll no more at festive meals." Amos continues: "Listen, you who devour the needy, annihilating the poor of the land, saying . . . We will buy the poor for silver, the needy for a pair of sandals" (8:4–7). Isaiah 10:1–2 goes after the slick dealers:

> Those who write out evil writs,
> And compose iniquitous documents,
> To subvert the cause of the poor,
> To rob the rights of the needy My people;
> That widows may be their spoil,
> And fatherless children their booty.

As many scholars have noted, the biblical God seems to have a preferential option for the poor.[12]

The Christian Scriptures are no more favorable toward the rich. According to Acts, Christians shared what they had—food, clothing, money, property—so no one was hungry and no one was in need (Acts 4:32–37). When Mr. Ananias and his wife, Sapphira, tried to hold back proceeds from a land sale as "private property," they were rather abruptly disciplined by the Holy Spirit (Acts 5:1–11). As for Jesus, he may have had wealthy friends, but he himself, along with his disciples, evidently had no possessions. Certainly, the witty phrase, "Easier for a camel to squeeze through the eye of a needle than for a rich person to get into God's social order!" sums up Christian experience. Sharing is essential behavior in God's new order. Therefore "rich Christian" is an impossible contradiction in terms. If you are rich and become Christian, soon you will divest your wealth in sweet charity! The description of America by many overpartisan supporters as "a Christian nation" is inappropriate, for in a world where billions live day to day in hunger and impossible poverty, frequently homeless or ravaged by disease, America doles out only a bit more than 1 percent of the national budget to help, a percentage substantially less than that given by most other nations. In the Bible, rulers are judged by what they do for the poor, a criterion that would shame our political leaders.

The underlying theological issue is simple: We belong to one another as children of God. We are not separated by nationality, race, religious affiliation, or any other artificial limit. God has chosen us all. Therefore, we are to "love our neighbors as our own"—as our own kin, as sisters, brothers, parents, children, all. Neighbors have a claim on us under our common parent, God.

In Matthew, Jesus is blunt: "You can't serve God and cash" (*mammon* is aptly rendered "cash"). The accumulation of cash—to have something, get somewhere, or be somebody—prevents free charitable concern. The same blunt warning is articulated throughout the Christian Scriptures, though seldom heard in sermons.

Preaching the Passage

Though clergy are often paid less than their parishioners and usually contribute to the church and other charities at a higher rate, they will have to ignore such realities. Preachers must speak of "us" and of "us Americans." Moreover, they must set "us" in a world where statistically most human beings are poor, while "we" by contrast are inordinately wealthy. Sermons are not to push local church support, or denominational support alone. Need must supersede any other loyalties. The Hebrew Scriptures express a strong sense of kinship among Jews, yet listen to Leviticus 19:33–34:

> When a stranger resides with you in your land, you shall not wrong him. The stranger who resides with you shall be to you as one of your citizens; you shall love him as [your own], for you were strangers in the land of Egypt: I the LORD am your God.

There should be no limits set on the term "neighbor." Thus, the publication of Christian business directories, along with the admonition to "buy Christian," is always emphatically unchristian. We must love beyond what we may consider our own. That song refrain "They will know we are Christians by our love" is pernicious if it means people will look at how church people love one another. Others should notice our love precisely because it reaches beyond our own, even including, if you recall Jesus' teaching, enemies. These days, many mainline churches are financially hard pressed, but if they only spend on their own buildings and program, they cease to be Christian churches. The criterion by which we assess our churches must be neighbor love, far-reaching neighbor love.

What about the saying "Easier for a camel to squeeze through the eye of a needle than for a rich person to get into God's social order"? We must not modulate the words but must face the truth, not only in our personal budgeting and spending but in our nation's economic policy. Our corporate culture, stock-market driven, may be an out-of-control corporate wickedness. To live in God's kingdom is to live out our days in a series of exchanges, realizing that we depend on neighbors, often unseen neighbors from all over the world, and that we too must be self-givers who live in the same glad system of exchanges. The late poet, novelist, and theologian Charles Williams called such mutual giving, "the Way of Exchange."[13]

Why are the Christian Scriptures so worried over wealth? Many Americans see cash as nothing more than a medium of exchange and, hence, as morally neutral. But Jesus believed that money could easily become an idolatrous Almighty Dollar. Looking around our land, Jesus seems prescient. Money is always a danger because it is not neutral, not a mere medium of exchange. Instead, money comes with social meanings attached, meanings that cannot be deleted. Money in our culture can mean superiority, success, security, social status, power, and the like. Ad agencies know exactly what money means. Can money corrupt us? Sure. Can money be ordered by self-absorption rather than by neighbor love? Yes, obviously. In Christian circles, money is meant to be an instrument of neighbor love—a message we can preach from any pulpit.[14]

CONFLICT OVER POWER

Mark 10:35–45 (also Matthew 20:20–28 and Luke 22:24–27)

[35]James and John, the sons of Zebedee, came up to him saying, "Teacher, whatever we ask, we want you to do for us." [36]He said to them, "What do you want me to do for you?" [37]They answered him, "Let us sit, one on your right hand and the other on your left, when you're in your glory." [38]Jesus said to them, "You don't know what you're asking! Can you drink the cup I drink? Or be baptized in the baptism with which I'll be baptized?" [39]They said to him, "Sure we can." And Jesus answered them, "The cup I drink, you will drink, and the baptism I'll be baptized with will be your baptism [40][but to sit at my right and left is not mine to award, but is given to those for whom it's been reserved]."

[41]Listening in, the ten [other disciples] were furious with James and John. [42]So, calling them together, Jesus said, "You know that those who supposedly rule nations lord it over them, and their VIPs dominate them. [43]But it's not to be that way with you. [44]Whoever wants to be great among you must be your servant; and whoever wants to be 'number one' first must be everyone's slave. [45]Even as the son of humanity didn't come to be served but to serve, and to give his life as a ransom for many."

Other Versions

Matthew cannot allow apostles to be interested in a power grab, so he adds a mother to the story. The ploy is clumsy, for she disappears as soon as her question is asked. Matthew, who generally removes whatever he considers unnecessary from Mark's verbiage, drops the allusion to baptism but nevertheless adds "by my Father" to verse 40. Luke omits the story of the sons of Zebedee entirely, but immediately after the Last Supper (22:24–27) he has sayings that parallel Mark's verses 42–44, which evidently come from some different source.

Mark's Story

Immediately before the two sons of Zebedee come forward, Jesus announces a third passion prediction:

> Look, we're going up to Jerusalem, and the son of humanity will be handed over to the chief priests and scribes, who will condemn him to death and turn him over to foreigners. They'll make fun of him, spit on him, lash him, and put him to death. But, after three days, he will rise again. (10:33–34)

Counting on the resurrection, the two disciples come up to Jesus and try to get in on the glory: "Let us sit, one on your right hand and the other on your left, when you're in your glory." Jesus replies with a sharp question: "Can you drink the cup I drink? Or be baptized in the baptism with which I'll be baptized?" Yes, James and John will be pleased to get in on the glory, but are they willing to undergo the abuse, pain, and death? Their rather glib answer is appalling: "Sure we can." Whereupon, Jesus hands out a grim prophecy: Yes, indeed, you will drink the same cup I must drink.

The addendum—"to sit at my right and left is not mine to award, but is given to those for whom it's been reserved"—is most peculiar. In both style and content it doesn't fit with anything else in the passage. Jesus deflects the disciples' request with "You don't know what you're asking." Apparently, they expect Jesus to be enthroned as a messianic king, even though he has spoken of rejection, ridicule, and terrifying death. They are eager for political power. Instead of opening their eyes to a different notion of kingship, an idea Mark has been busy setting up, verse 40 seems to support the disciples' power-grab fantasy. In previous passion announcements (Mark 8:31–33; 9:30–32), Jesus has predicted his death and then sharply corrected any hint of triumphalism ("Get out of my way, you Satan!"), so why now would he suddenly buy into the disciples' fantasy? I have bracketed verse 40; it is suspect and can be labeled secondary.

If verse 40 does not mesh with verses 35–39, it is even less consistent with the discourse that follows:

> You know that those who supposedly rule nations lord it over them, and their VIPs dominate them. But it's not to be that way with you. Whoever wants to be great among you must be your servant; and whoever wants to be "number one," first must be everyone's slave.

Mark's final verse is a two-part statement: "The son of humanity didn't come to be served but to serve, and to give his life as a ransom for many." While Luke 22:25–26 matches Mark's content in verses 42–44, Luke's parallel does not have "and give his life as a ransom for many." Mark may have put an early Christian dogmatic statement on Jesus' lips. Nowhere else in the Synoptic Gospels does Jesus discuss the saving benefits of his own death. But the first part of the sentence, "The son of humanity didn't come to be served, but to serve," seems consistent with Jesus' teaching.

The Controversy

James and John come up to Jesus with a rather crass demand: "Teacher, whatever we ask, we want you to do for us." One of the problems interpreters face when reading the Gospel of Mark is the portrayal of the disciples. They are stubbornly stupid and power hungry. They don't understand what Jesus is all about and, as for his message, not only do they not get it, they frequently don't want it! Some years ago Theodore Weeden argued that Mark's picture of the disciples is deliberate, an attempt to discredit a powerful Petrine party within the early church.[15] Maybe. The dialogue is damning, for when Jesus asks bluntly, "What do you want?" they eagerly spill out their big dream. What the sons of Zebedee want is a guaranteed promise of political advantage ahead of their ten colleagues. Not only do they misunderstand Jesus' egalitarian gospel, they are after raw personal power: "Let us sit, one on your right hand and the other on your left, when you're in your glory."

Jesus' answer is to ask, "Can you drink the cup I drink? Or be baptized in the baptism with which I'll be baptized?" The "cup" and the "baptism" are metaphors drawn from Christian ritual practice, but here they allude to his predicted suffering and death. The two disciples answer too easily, "Sure we can!" Do they misread Jesus' question as referring to early Christian rituals? In any event, Jesus counters with a terrible promise: "The cup I drink, you will drink, and the baptism I'll be baptized with will be your baptism." He predicts their eventual apostolic sufferings and death. We have here a complicated dialogue, but so far without a final pronouncement.

The pronouncement occurs in the second half of the passage. "Whoever wants to be great among you must be your servant; and whoever wants to be 'number one' first must be everyone's slave," says Jesus, and then he adds, "The son of humanity didn't come to be served but to serve, and to give his life as a ransom for many." Here we have a saying followed by a "son of humanity" saying, a pattern we have seen before in Mark 2:9–10 and 2:27–28. Does this "son of humanity" saying attach to the "son of humanity" passion pronouncement (10:33), or is it much like the sayings in Mark's second chapter? The paradoxical "Whoever wants to be 'number one' first must be everyone's slave" is backed up by "The son of humanity didn't come to be served but to serve." The sayings call a new humanity to serve neighbors without concern for personal position or achievement.

"Give his life as a ransom for many" may be authentic words of Jesus, or they may reflect a forming theological understanding within early Christian communities. In any case, I am quite certain that a theological reading of Isaiah 53 was early.[16] Moreover, notions of sacrificial life and death were part of Jewish thought since Maccabean times (2 Macc. 7:37–38; 4 Macc. 17:21–22). Thus, if they were not within the thought patterns of Jesus, they were certainly available to the earliest Christian apologists (see 1 Cor. 6:20 and 7:23). The idea of a substitutionary atonement is often written off as theological addenda to the simple gospel of Jesus, but frequent allusions to Isaiah 53 in the earliest Christian scriptures seem to stand against such an assertion. Thus, though I suspect Jesus may not have spoken the phrase himself, it is an early Christian understanding.

Homiletic Theology

During the Reformation, Luther was convinced that political power, while necessary in a worldly kingdom to restrain the wicked, was not appropriate for those who live by grace in God's kingdom. On the other hand, Calvin urged Christians to become useful magistrates even within systems that may be corrupted. Two-kingdom theology can turn into somewhat sticky pietism, a kingdom of the church contrasting with a kingdom of the world of which we must be wary. I will opt for Calvin, but not without caution. Lately, we have watched right-wing Christianity jockeying for political power, at times with obvious intent to take over the land in the name of Jesus. Calvin has something very different in mind. He argues that Christians can do all sorts of things because, with a few obvious exceptions, any occupation can be a Christian vocation. Our task is to be capable and, presumably, both moral and charitable within structures that, like all human structures, beg for redemption. But Christianity should never attempt to take over, as if Christians were exempt from human corruption. We are all always sinners, though forgiven sinners, and we all live in broken structures waiting for God's promised redemption.

The notion that because social systems are corrupt, Christians may as well employ dubious tactics but with ethical savvy and for good purposes is naive. We are sinners and probably couldn't spot a good purpose if we stumbled over one. "Power corrupts" is not a foolish adage. We live for the Lord God, and as best we can, guided by the Word and the Spirit, manage the complicated trade-offs of the modern-day *polis*. In the merciful grace of God, we "sin bravely."

A Sermon

Introduction   Have you noticed how devious children can be? How down-right tricky kids are? They'll get you to promise without knowing what you're promising. "Daddy, Daddy, will you do anything we ask you to do?" Well, if Daddy's smart, he'll back off and see what's at stake. One day, two disciples, James and John, came hustling up to Jesus. "Teacher, Teacher," they cried, "We want you to do whatever we ask you!" Jesus was cautious. "What do you want?" he asked. Then they blurted out their wild dream: "Allow us to sit at your right hand and your left when you come into glory." Did ever ambition reach so high? "Grant us to sit at your right hand in glory."

I

1   *We overhear the conversation and, like the other disciples, we're outraged.* Is there anything more embarrassing than an obvious lust for power? Particularly among Christians? After all, haven't we been taught that the meek are blessed, that the lowly in heart are God's special friends? Oh yes, according to Alfred Adler the lust for power is in us all, a drive as insatiable as sex or hunger, but surely Christians understand that the drive has got to be controlled. Yet here are two of the original twelve disciples, men who've lived their lives close to Jesus, and what are they after? Nothing less than raw power. Have you read John Dean's autobiography, *Blind Ambition*? He was brought up in a Sunday school and educated in a church college, but was driven by ambition. He wanted to see himself standing in the Oval Office at the right hand of the President.[17] Allow us to sit at your right hand in glory, sang out the disciples. Blind ambition. We listen in and, like the other disciples, we're outraged. Is there anything more embarrassing than a Christian lust for power?

2   *Of course, to be honest, the same impulse is among us.* The church is always trying to get in on Christ's glory. You see it in denominations, you see it in every congregation: We all want to trade on the power of Christ. After all,

if Christ has been raised, if he rules the world enthroned by God, well then we ought to make out alright! Aren't we the body of Christ right here in the world? Success ought to be ours. As old Horace Bushnell used to say from his pulpit, "God has reserved the world for us!"[18] His mind still lives in the church, for down deep most of us feel that the church ought to be number one in American life, a power in politics, an influence in the community—that it ought to grow and prosper. Heard about a minister who was building a new church building. He had surveyors measure all the other buildings for ten blocks around, so his church tower could be taller. "The cross," he explained, "ought to stand on top of the world." If Christ has triumphed, then surely his church ought to make it big as well. "Teacher, Teacher, grant us to sit at your right hand in glory!" Fact is, if we're honest, we'll have to admit the lust for power lives among us too.

II

3 *So what does Jesus say to us?* Jesus says what he said to the first disciples: *"Can you drink the cup I drink?"* Can you follow me? Jesus seemed to have the odd idea that wherever he went, his disciples would be. And there's the rub. Leaf through the Bible and see where he went. He didn't sit in church and get a stained-glass suntan; he was out in the world, the messy world. See him hobnobbing with scaley lepers, or hoisting a few with Mafia types, or rubbing shoulders with B-girls in the Jerusalem streets. Follow him and guess where you'll be! On the wrong, wrong side of life, hanging out with all those disreputable people you've been trying to move away from all your life, people you've been trying to protect your kids from, morally disreputable people. Follow him and you'll never make any real money or get anywhere. To the socially in-group you'll be an out. There was a wonderful letter in a church magazine the other day by an American Christian in South Africa: "I've been trying to follow Jesus," he wrote, "but I never thought I'd end in jail." Then he added a punch line: "How exhilarating! Well it does sound more exciting than this little job, and this little house, and this little IRA account for the rest of your days. Can you drink the cup I drink?" Jesus asked his disciples, "Can you follow me?"

4 *Well do you know what the disciples said? They said, "Sure we can!"* Yes, Lord, we're able, good heavens we are. We've been baptized—right here in church. And we take the cup at your table in monthly Communion. Little churchiness! But what does it mean to be a Christian? Well, you get to church once in a while, and fill out a pledge card, and presto, you've got it made; you belong to Jesus Christ. Saw a travel folder advertising a tour of the Holy Land. It pictured a bunch of affluent people filing into a jet plane.

Inside the pamphlet was a schedule: a day in Rome, two in Athens, a week in Jerusalem, then ten days on the Mediterranean with a "happy hour" every afternoon. The title: "Walking in the Steps of Jesus." How do we become Christians? We join an organization. The first disciples had nothing on us when it comes to glibness. "Can you drink the cup I drink?" And we answer "Sure, Lord, we're able." Scaling down the cost of discipleship to a little churchiness!

5 *Well, we could get away with it if it weren't for the cross.* Somehow or other we can't get the cross out of our minds. Oh, we can take down the ugly pictures of Jesus from our church school rooms and turn Jesus into a song and dance *Godspell*, but once a year Holy Week rolls round again, and there's the story of the garden and the cross and the tomb. "Father," cried Jesus, "if it be your will, take the cup from me!" But God didn't, and Christ walked the way to Golgotha. What was his baptism? Soldier spit. What was his cup? Vinegar on a stick stabbed in his mouth. Oh "the Son of man, the Son of man must suffer many things and die." There is a story about a man walking down a Boston alley when the stone crucifix on top of a church tower cracked in the wind and came wheeling down to smash in the street. Broken Jesus smashed to bits, and all the man could say later was, "I have seen the Lord!" Well, we have seen him.. Ever since childhood we've seen the broken Jesus hung on a cross. "Let this cup pass," but it didn't. He was baptized by his suffering. He drank the cup of dying for our sake. A vision of Christ on the cross is clawed into our minds. We can't forget, for it's Holy Week again.

III

6 *Then, Jesus turned to his disciples and spoke the most terrible words in the Bible. "You will drink the cup I drink,"* he said. *"You will be baptized with my baptism."* Listen, do you understand what he is saying? You don't just belong to a church; you belong to him. And Christ doesn't hand out gold certificates of church membership; he hands out a cross. "You will drink the cup I drink." Does Jesus mean that his church may not succeed? Can he be saying that if we speak his word we're going to get what he got? Yes, dear friends, that's exactly what he means. After all, we are the body of Christ, and in this world his body gets broken. In one of Frederick Buechner's novels an old evangelist and his daughter talk together. The daughter says, "What is it makes people want to dump on you, Bip? Your whole life they've been dumping on you." His answer is wonderful: "Jesus never let on it was going to be any different," he says. "It goes with the territory."[19] Well, it does. Our territory is world, and as the world hated him, if we are faithful, the world will hate us. Does that mean that our churches may not grow, that

we'll lose members? Maybe. Could it mean that the United Methodist Church may die? Perhaps. Listen, as the man said, "It goes with the territory." If, if, if we are faithful. "You will drink the cup I drink. You will be baptized with my baptism." Dear friends, let us hear the word of the Lord.

Hard, isn't it, to give up our golden dreams of triumph? Success has always been an American virtue—even in churches. Lord, we want to make it big with you! But every year about this time there's the story of the cross, and no matter how you read it, it doesn't sound much like success. Can't get rid of the cross, can we? Like it or not, we can't get rid of our cross either—if we are faithful. If, if we are faithful.

Discussion

This sermon was preached in the late 1980s on Palm Sunday in the chapel of Duke University, a chapel under the auspices of the United Methodist Church. The sermon turned out to be shockingly inappropriate. Palm Sunday is an ambiguous day, because it is also Passion Sunday, and the sermon was designed for Passion Sunday. Instead, the Duke Chapel chose to replicate the supposed, if unlikely, triumph of Palm Sunday, with palm branches, massed choirs, and what could only be described as a "coronation liturgy." My, oh my! What a "downer" my sermon was going to be! But should I have preached a triumphant sermon? Nope.

Introduction   The introduction is a two-part analogy. (Introductions should have few moving parts. They are simple focused systems. No more than two shifts is a good rule.) The introduction sets up the image of avid, demanding children and then picks up the situation of the passage. Probably the introduction expresses the mood of the passage, and does so in around ten sentences.

1 I begin by inviting the congregation to join the other disciples in outrage: "Haven't we been taught that the meek are blessed, that the lowly in heart are God's special friends?" Yes, we have. The illustration mentions John Dean's best-selling book, in which he admits that his ambition to be "at the right hand of the President" led him into trouble. Notice the deliberate repetition of the second sentence as a framing conclusion. The move works pretty well.

2 The second move forces us to admit our own triumphalist ambitions, not as individuals but as Christians! The Bushnell quote sets a rhetorical tone. Then the illustration of the minister measuring the neighborhood so the church tower would be taller gives a visual expression to our Christian ambition. Note that the second move ends with a line from the introduction, a rhetorical way of closing the two-move set.

3 The third move lets Jesus address us as he addressed disciples in the passage: "Can you drink the cup I drink?" which I turn into "Can you follow me?" Then we look at where we'll be if we follow Jesus, namely, on the wrong side of life. The true illustration of the young man in South Africa (at that time under apartheid) pictures both the dangers of following Jesus but also the exhilaration compared with the drag of "normalcy."

4 Here I try to represent the glibness of "Sure we can!" Rather too quickly I grabbed the example of a travel folder I had seen that spring. Yes, the illustration fit. But there was a problem: the congregation laughed and laughed. Humor, ever a danger, simply overwhelmed the move. Oops! I should have rewritten the move to reduce the level of congregational reaction.

5 Here's a move that took some careful writing. The rather violent clipped images were carefully designed: "Soldier spit," "a stick stabbed in his mouth," followed by a doubled start to "Oh, the son of man, the son of man, must suffer many things and die." The design sequence of the move and the power of the illustration "I have seen the Lord" counter the easy glibness of the previous move.

6 Here I address the longing for church triumph encountered in move 2. To be powerful, sermons designed with plotted "movement" should be as interactive as the biblical passages. The move is rough: "Does Jesus mean that his church may not succeed?" and later, "Does that mean that our churches may not grow, that we'll lose members?" and then, "Could it mean that the United Methodist Church may die?" In between, there's the wonderful quote from an early Buechner novel. After the triumphalist pageantry of Palm Sunday, the move was a huge reversal.

Conclusion The conclusion does two things: it recapitulates the basic shift in the sermon, but it does so with a hard, rhythmic, conditional conclusion.

Compare the way the sermon moves to the earlier categorical "point making" sermons. There is more power in a sermon with plotted movement, as well as more homiletic excitement in designing the moves.

Chapter 7

Final Conflicts

Conflict over Authority (11:27–33)
Conflict over Taxes (12:13–17)
Conflict over Resurrection (12:18–27)
Conflict over the Great Commandment (12:28–34)
Conflict over the Son of David (12:35–37)
Conflict over the Anointing of Jesus (14:1–9)

All these controversies occur in Jerusalem. The four conflict stories over taxes, resurrection, the Great Commandment, and the Son of David may all be from a single source. David Daube has argued that they are designed to match traditional questions asked during a Passover eve service. Bracketing the four questions, there is a prior question on Jesus' "authority," no doubt prompted by his prophetic action in the Temple. Then, in chapter 14, there is a final conflict story, telling of a tribute given Jesus by an anonymous woman that, at the same time, raises the question of the cost of devotion. All these conflict stories relate to the passion narrative that follows them.

CONFLICT OVER AUTHORITY

Mark 11:27–33 (also Matthew 21:23–27 and Luke 20:1–8)
27bAs Jesus was walking in the Temple, the chief priests, scribes, and elders came up to him, 28saying, "By what right do you do what you do? Who gave you authority for your actions?" 29Jesus said to them, "I've got one question for you. If you answer me, I'll tell you by what authority I act. 30Tell me, was John's baptism heaven-sent or of human origin?" 31They debated among themselves, saying, "If we say 'heaven' then he'll say, 'Why didn't you believe him?' 31but if we say 'human' . . ." They were afraid of the crowd, for everyone considered John to be a genuine prophet. So they answered Jesus saying, "We cannot say." 32Jesus spoke, "Then I won't tell you where my authority is either!"

Other Versions

For the most part Matthew and Luke follow Mark, with only minor shifts in style. Luke makes the priests' fear of the crowd physical: "all the people will stone us." Luke also makes a more significant change by writing a somewhat casual first sentence: "One day, when he was teaching people in the Temple and preaching good news . . ." The question of authority was connected with the cleansing of the Temple in Mark, but Luke has severed the specific connection, so the authority question is aimed at Jesus' whole ministry.

Mark's Story

The question over authority in Mark follows directly on the cleansing of the Temple and the fig tree metaphor that sandwiches Jesus' prophetic action. Presumably Jesus likens the temple cult to a fig tree that produces no fruit.

The cleansing of the Temple is much debated. What is going on? Mark suggests that the Temple may be involved in commercial profiteering and that because money changing is taking place in the court of the Gentiles there is a prejudicial desecration of holy space as well. Mark's Jesus quotes Isaiah 56:7, "My house shall be called a house of prayer for all peoples," adding a phrase from Jeremiah 7:11, "But you have made it 'a den of thieves'" (Matthew and Luke drop "for all peoples"). Other scholars suggest that Jesus' action is an apocalyptic statement: a corrupted Temple will be replaced in the coming new order by a new Temple.[1] After all, Jesus apparently predicted the destruction of the Temple. In either case, the cleansing of the Temple dramatically raises the question of Jesus' prophetic authority.

Jesus' action in the Temple provokes sharp opposition from "the chief priests, scribes, and elders," guardians of the temple cult. They corner Jesus in the temple precincts and ask point blank, "By what right do you do what you do? Who gave you authority for your actions?" Jesus replies to their question by asking another question: "I've got one question for you," he says, and then brings up John the Baptist. "Tell me, was John's baptism heaven-sent or of human origin?" Suddenly the whole issue of authority is moved beyond a legal authorization over to God's involvement in human affairs. The priests, scribes, and elders are now on the spot.

When Jesus asks about "John's baptism" he cites an action, but he intends more—he includes John's preaching, the enthusiastic crowds that came to hear him, the number of people repenting in the waters of the Jordan, and his martyred death. Jesus brings up the whole event of John the Baptist. Was the event of John the Baptist heaven-sent? Was God involved? The priests sense the trap: If they acknowledge God's presence in John's ministry, then Jesus could ask them, "Why didn't you believe him and repent?" But the alternative is equally impossible. If they deny God's involvement the people will turn on them, for popular opinion regarded John as a certifiable prophet, perhaps even *the* prophet promised in Malachi 4:5–6. How to answer Jesus' question? Their reply is simply evasive: "We can't say." Jesus counters blandly, "Then I won't tell you where my authority is either!"

The Controversy

The controversy begins in a usual way with a question and a counterquestion. But when the priests and scholars refuse to answer the counterquestion, then there can be no final pronouncement. Here we have a conflict story but one deliberately aborted and designed without a final pronouncement.

The question being asked is legitimate. Jesus has walked into the temple precincts and disrupted the commercial support for sacrifice. The passage is often preached as Jesus' dismay over the commercialization of religion, but the protest is not simple. Worshipers in the Temple would not view the sale of doves for sacrifice as a commercial venture. The doves were a necessary provision for worship. Money changing was also a necessity, for how could a pious Jew pay the temple tax (Exod. 30:11–16) with pagan Roman coins? The temple authorities were providing the means of worship. Therefore, why would Jesus tip over the money changers' tables and protest people passing through the Temple's "court of the Gentiles" carrying stuff connected with temple activity? No wonder priests asked Jesus to justify his prophetic actions.

By asking a question about John the Baptist, Jesus shifts concern from temple practice to theology. Did John preach God's Word? John the Baptist spoke out boldly. The Gospel of Matthew depicts his preaching in this way:

> You sons of snakes! Who warned you to run away from the fury to come? Bear fruit of repentance. Don't suppose you can say, "We have Abraham as our ancestor!" I tell you God could raise up children of Abraham from stones. Even now the axe is at the root of the trees; every tree that does not bear fruit will be hacked down and thrown into the fire. (Matt. 3:7–10)

John announced the coming judgment and an inauguration of God's new order. His baptism was a sign of repentance—Israel's repentance. Probably John was put to death for being outspoken about Herod's indiscretions as well as for drawing a huge, potentially dangerous, popular following. But Jesus is asking, Was John one of God's prophets? Was his baptism an act of God? By implication, he was asking about his own prophetic actions.

Jesus' counterquestion exposes the mind-set of the priests and scholars. They are devout religious people, but they are also members of a powerful religious establishment in the midst of a significant temple building program. Jesus' question is unnerving. If they say John the Baptist was a man of God, then Jesus will ask them why they didn't respond to his word, a word that called Israel to repent. If, on the other hand, they deny John's godly credentials, they will lose popular support, for John the Baptist was generally revered. They are obviously stymied, so they admit, "We cannot say." And the controversy ends abruptly without a pronouncement.

Homiletic Theology

In Mark, Jesus is twice asked about authority, here by "chief priests, scribes, and elders," and by Pharisees in 8:11–13. In chapter 8, Jesus answers, "Why does this generation seek a sign? Amen. I tell you, no way will this generation be given a sign." The term "this generation" seems to speak to a larger audience than just particular Pharisees. Is Jesus deliberately including Pharisees, who are proud to be separate, within a condemned cultural generation? Why are the Pharisees not given a sign? Perhaps because they wouldn't believe any kind of sign unless it meshed with their own religious agenda.

Here the demand for a sign is asked by "chief priests, scribes, and elders." "Elders" were not necessarily an official group, but by age, social position, and experience they were respected guardians of temple tradition. Jesus mentions them earlier in his initial passion prediction: "He began to teach them the son of humanity was destined to suffer greatly, be rejected by the elders, chief priests, and scribes, and be killed, then, after three days, rise" (8:31). These three groups comprised the Sanhedrin, which, in Mark 14:53–64, examines and condemns Jesus. Of course, they have every right to question Jesus, who has marched into Jerusalem drawing a crowd and who thereafter stages a prophetic disturbance in the temple courts. Their questions, though justified, are scarcely being asked with genial affection.

Questioning is nothing new. Prophets expect to be questioned. How else can we decide who is a true prophet chosen by God and who is not? Do we assess their spirituality, their moral history, their associates, or how? Again and again, we get crossed up because God doesn't seem to choose prophets on the basis of piety or even morality. God's prophets are frequently as ambiguous as any of us. In the early days of the civil rights movement, a sizeable number of white Americans (including J. Edgar Hoover), and even a few black churchmen, questioned Martin Luther King Jr.'s "authority." Was he speaking for God or not? Even more strident questions were asked about Malcolm X. But nowadays we seem to question almost anyone who advocates social change, because a reactionary, if blundering, America is desperately eager to hold on to itself.

How can we judge and certify the prophetic spirit? We can assess the message! The great Hebrew prophets spoke between memory and hope. They remembered God's covenant and, at the same time, they projected God's promises into the future. So we judge a prophet's message by precedents: First, is the message in accord with the liberating purposes of the covenant-making God, purposes that are set forth in the law and the prophets? If a speaker advocates murder, outright theft, or sexual humiliation, then we should question both the message and the messenger. How can the message be "Word of God" if the speaker is advocating violations of God's bottom-line Ten Commandments? Second, is the message in accord with the biblical vision of *shalom*, which, in fact, is the same as Jesus' vision of God's new order, an egalitarian society of people giving themselves to mutual serving? The Beatitudes offer a helpful definition of God's ultimate social purposes. Above all, we must ask, Is the message a word of God? Additionally, some of us suppose that the great social movements in human history have been led by nonviolent prophets.

I have stressed message rather than person here because God shapes the "word" on the lips of sinful men and women. We are all ambiguous people. If prophets had to accord with our conventional law-and-order moralities, there would be no prophets at all. (After all, the only champion of law and order in Scripture is "the Accuser"—Satan!) Living in the status quo is not a prophetic job description. Any good prophet calls for social change, which usually includes the changing of bad laws. Think of laws that were designed to support racial segregation; should they have been broken? Moreover, because we are ambiguous, prophets may well speak God's word and yet be morally weak. In South Africa, Allan Boesak was a great prophetic preacher who, subsequently, was accused of misappropriating some charitable gifts he received. Apparently there was a breakdown in moral judgment that may have discredited the word he was speaking. Nonetheless, judged by Scripture, his message was without doubt an authentic "word of God."[2] Good heavens, if our lives were publicly unpacked, we would all be discredited along with the gospel we affirm. Can broken sinners speak a "word of God," a word set on our stained human lips by God? The answer is yes. The Second Helvetic Confession announces, "We know that the voice of Christ is to be heard, though it be out of the mouths of evil ministers; because the Lord himself said: 'Practice and observe whatever they tell you, but not what they do' (Matt. 23:3)."[3] We don't check motives; all motives are mixed. We don't weigh morality against social norms; social norms are variable. And we certainly cannot approve or disapprove on the basis of patriotism; national loyalty almost always borders on idolatry. No, instead, we listen with the words of Hebrew prophets in mind, along with the voice of Jesus, who preached of God's new order. They will be our guides.

Preaching the Passage

In an introduction, we will probably need to justify Jesus' critics—the priests, scribes, and elders. After all, we would ask the same questions. Suppose someone marches into our town with a parade of hippies in tow, and then on Sunday morning shows up in church and disrupts our worship. What's more, suppose it happens on Easter Day? We'd be asking questions, hard questions, wouldn't we? Such a strategy will let us identify with the Jewish leaders and at the same time deal with the whole subject of God's social prophets.

We can then show why we will always question prophets. In God's name they criticize us. They use our religious beliefs, speak our religious language, stand in God's name, but criticize us! They bring our nation, our common values, our ways of doing business, our family life, and our religious practices before God and condemn us. No wonder that prophets have ended up as martyrs, from Amos to Jeremiah, all the way to Martin Luther King Jr. Prophets want social change. We don't. A sinful social order will always try to turn back time and prevent social change, so as to hold on to what we have—"Come weal or woe, our status is quo." Example number one in the world today is the USA. Not only are we resisting change self-righteously, but in foreign policy, we are trying to turn the wider world into us!

But God wants prophets. God doesn't hurl thunderbolts to get our attention. No, God calls prophets and sets a word on their lips—from Isaiah, to John the Baptist, to the prophetic voice of Jesus, to Lucretia Mott, Karl Marx, or Desmond Tutu. The big question we ask, Is the prophet speaking for God? Give us some sign! Jesus refused. If a people will not believe that God can speak through human voices, there is no proof that will satisfy. We can be open to the voice of God. We can listen to past prophets and learn to spot the distinctive style of God's prophetic word.

Nowadays, the church is called to speak Jesus Christ's word. The church must be prophet, priest, and king as Jesus was. We offer priestly services gladly, and we would be delighted to rule anyone who will let us rule—but prophesy? We would rather not be prophetic. Prophets are seldom popular in church or out. And these days, after losing members, mainline churches are busy as can be marketing themselves. But God has called us and God has commissioned both our priestly and our prophetic words. If we neglect the prophetic, our priestly words will turn unctuous. Bluntly, silence does not become us.

A Sermon

I have no sermon on the controversy from Mark 11:27–33. But discussion of the prophetic calling has prompted a concern. We ought to preach from the prophets regularly, but except for passages from Isaiah in Advent, my impression is that preachers have neglected the prophets. So here is an odd example. The lectionary listed only half a passage, Hosea 2:16–20, a sweet promise of fidelity from God. So I added a selection of verses from Hosea 2 preceding the lectionary's choice. I rallied my shaky Hebrew to translate the absolutely stunning passage. Here are two halves of the passage, side by side:

Accuse your mother! Accuse her!
  For she is not my wife
  and I am not her husband. . . .
Tell her to wipe the whoring from her
    face
  and the signs of adultery
  from between her breasts.
For she said: I will go after my lovers—
  They give me my bread, my wool,
    my flax, my oil, my drinks. . . .
She didn't know that I gave her the grain,
    the new wine, the olive oil,
  that I showered her with silver and
    gold, which they made into Baals.
So I will take back my grain when it's
    time.
  and the new wine when it's ready. . . .
I will uncover her sex in the presence of
    her lovers
  and no one will rescue her from my
    hand. . . .
I will bring an end to her pleasures;
  her feasts, her new moons,
  her Sabbath celebrations—
  all her partying. . . . When she would
    deck herself out with rings and
    jewels, chasing after her lovers.

So now, [again] I will woo her.
I will bring her into the wilderness
  and I will speak to her heart.
From there, then, I will give her vine-
    yards
  and the valley of Achor as a doorway
    of hope.
There she will respond
  as she did in the days of her youth,
  as she did when she came up from the
    land of Egypt.
On that day, says the Lord, then
  you will call me "My husband,"
  and no longer will you call me "My
    Baal!"
For I will remove the names of the
    Baals from her mouth.
They will be named by name no more.
On that day, I will make a covenant for
    you
  with the beasts of the field, the birds
    of the air,
  and creeping things on the ground;
  I will ban the bow, the sword, and war
    from the land;
I will marry you, my wife. in
    faithfulness,

So I will make you lie down in security.
I will marry you, my wife, forever.
I will marry you, my wife, in righteous-
      ness and justice,
   in sure love and in mercy.

and you will know the Lord.
And, on that day, then, I will answer,
   says the Lord.

Introduction   The United Church of Christ has a book of services. Worship services for all occasions. Guess what? In the book there are two marriage services. There's a regular marriage service, but then there's another—a Service for the Renewal of Marriage. Some couple gets together and says vows all over again. Well, in the Bible there's a renewal of marriage between God and Israel. Listen, for God is renewing vows with Israel: "I will marry you, my wife, in faithfulness. I will marry you, my wife, forever." God and humanity in covenant forever.

1 Can we be blunt? *God and Israel—the marriage sure needed renewal,* for God's marriage with Israel had ended up in the divorce courts. After all, it's mighty hard to hold a marriage together when your wife's walking the streets hot for other lovers—any lovers! Picture Israel all dolled up in a low-cut, bright red dress, rhinestone jewelry swinging between her breasts, singing "Hey, big money! You want to spend some cash on me?" Israel liked her bread on the table, oil to smooth her skin, wine for partying, and a wooly fur coat. Keep the good times coming! So she chased after Baal, believing Baal had provided it all. A little sex on the high hills, a little sex under the sheltering boughs, a little sex to make sure prosperity would continue. A book was published last week with a title something like *Dark Side of Love.* Evidently the book is all about how to manage a divorce: Take back the gifts. Get your spouse out of the house. Declare yourself free of your spouse's debts. So listen to the words of God: "I will take back the grain and the wine and the wool. I will strip her naked in the presence of her lovers. I will put a stop to her partying!" Wow. There's a dysfunctional marriage, a marriage on the rocks.

2 *Well, are you going to preach Hosea to America?* Are you going to preach judgment to our land? Oh, you'll have to change the imagery—no red dress, but instead a husband's pinstripe business suit, a suit you'd wear in corporate boardrooms or on the floor of the stock market. America seems to be on a prosperity tear. Did you read the business pages last month? Evidently the Christmas buying never stopped; Americans kept on buying big-ticket items, on credit cards of course. A little sex to keep the market going up—will it top 12,000 again? A little high-tech love for the sake of Nasdaq. "Hey, big money! You want to spend some cash?" We've been chasing corporate lovers one after another. In Nashville, there's the Adelphia Coliseum, the Gaylord Entertainment Center, AmSouth Amphitheater—keep the good times coming! Are you going to stand up in the pulpit and tell America the truth? America, Nashville: You have chased prosperity while the rest of the world is hungry. You traded up your real estate values while the homeless multiplied. Listen. God will strip you of your prosperity. America, you are adulterous. Hosea fits our time.

3 But wait. *Hold on. For suddenly, inexplicably, God's words turn sweet*—oh, how sweet! Listen to God speak: "I will woo her all over again," God says. "I will speak love to her heart." God is sure Israel will respond the way she did when she came up out of Egypt. She will say, "Ish, my husband." No longer will she say, "My Baal." Behind every hard judgment in the Bible, there is God the lover, whose love will not let us go. A faithful, utterly, unaccountably faithful God. A God who rung round with betrayal, heard us crying, "Crucify, crucify," in risen glory showed up to renew the covenant all over again. The God who will not stop loving us faithless, foolish people. You can read *People* magazine in any doctor's office—that is, as long as you don't mind back issues. Well, this week in a back issue there was the story of a Hollywood couple whose marriage ended up in outright, angry divorce. Well, they just announced they have decided to get married all over again. What's more, it will be a big church wedding. "We'd like to do it right this time," said the bride. "I will marry you in faithfulness, I will marry you forever." God always makes the first move, the first gesture of love. So you will call your congregations to faithfulness. Perhaps they'll turn to the God of glory and now and do it right.

4 Guess what, *as preachers in the new century, you will woo the world on God's behalf.* You will speak love to the land in a new way. You're even allowed to hand out promises, if they'll bring us around to God again. Sanibel Island, Florida, has a terrific second honeymoon package: "Come together again." With pictures of you and someone you love skipping through the waves. "Together again." Listen to God paint the future: "I will ban the bomb, the missile, the landmine. I will tame the wild animal and let the birds fly free." Look, do you expect Exxon to clean up all the oil spills? Do you expect General Dynamics to step out of the arms race? The only hope for our redemption is to draw America to God once more. You will speak with the vows echoing in your mind: "I will marry you, my spouse, in faithfulness. I will marry you, my land, forever!"

Conclusion How hard to preach in the USA! You're called by God not to manage churches, but to speak. How to speak to an adulterous America? Oh, you tell the truth and then, before they can throw you out, you start courting your people. You tell people of the God, the passionate God, who is the faithful lover of their lives.

Discussion

The sermon was preached to divinity school students in the spring of 2000. It was later published as "A Case of Adultery" in *Pulpit Digest* (October–December 2000). The sermon simply follows the movement of the expanded passage, but it involves some tricky homiletic footwork, including transforming a red-dressed unfaithful wife into a pin-striped all-American executive.

Introduction   The introduction establishes the crucial, underlying metaphor of the passage: a renewal of marriage. Then it draws the analogy of God and Israel, quoting God's pledge from the end of the lection.

1 The first move picks up the metaphor of a marriage in need of renewal. Then it explains the problem: Israel was an unfaithful wife. The imagery is pretty much drawn from the passage but set in contemporary language, including a pop phrase, "Hey, big money!" Then with the mention of a book on terminating marriage, I switch to the result of the infidelity, namely, God's response. I end up calling the marriage dysfunctional.

2 All of a sudden, I turn to address my audience of divinity students. Are they going to preach Hosea to America? Then I switch the images from an unfaithful wife, Israel, to an unfaithful husband, America, but retain some of the same images ("Hey, big money!"). Instead of Baal, I have us courting corporations, and I list a few in Nashville, where the sermon was preached. I end with "America, you are adulterous."

3 In the third move, I swing over to the second half of the passage. I speak about God the lover who will not let us go. God is faithful, though we rebel. With "Crucify, crucify," I slip in an image of crucifixion and then link marriage renewal with resurrection. The illustration from *People* magazine (a symptom of much that's wrong with our culture) has a couple remarrying and vowing to "do it right." The illustration fits the ruling image of the passage.

4 Here's a tricky move that may or may not have worked. I swing over to my audience again, who must "woo" America. In order to pick up the "wooing" from the passage, I use the honeymoon image. But then I have God woo us in a contemporary way—"I will ban the bomb, the missile, the land-mine. I will tame the wild animal and let the birds fly free"—with a remark that corporate America will not do so. Maybe it worked. I conclude with God's last words from the introduction: "I will marry you, my spouse, in faithfulness. I will marry you, my land, forever!"

Conclusion   Once more I am with the audience: How will students speak to adulterous America? They will tell the truth, but then woo with news of God, the lover.

The sermon has little to do with a conflict story on authority. But it may suggest ways for preachers to address the society in which they must preach with at least some prophetic concern.

CONFLICT OVER TAXES

Mark 12:13–17 (also Matthew 22:15–22 and Luke 20:20–26)

[13]They sent some Pharisees and Herodians to [Jesus] so they could trap him with his own words. [14]Coming up, they said to him, "Teacher, we know that you're honest, impartial, and not swayed by appearances but boldly teach the true way of God. Is it lawful to pay taxes to Caesar or not? Should we pay or not pay?" [15]But he saw through their phoniness and said to them, "Why are you testing me? Hand me a denarius; let me look it over." [16]They handed him one. Then he said to them, "Whose image is here and whose inscription?" They answered, "Caesar's." [17][Jesus] said to them, "Give to Caesar Caesar's, but give to God, God's." They were dumbfounded by him.

Other Versions

Matthew pretty much follows Mark, but Luke, a Gentile author, has made a few changes. Luke has secret agents representing the scribes and chief priests pose the question, hoping to turn him over to "the jurisdiction and authority of the governor." Subsequently, Luke (23:2) lists the taxation issue as one of the charges against Jesus in his trial.

Mark's Story

David Daube has argued that the four controversies in Mark 12 appear to follow the pattern of four questions asked on Passover eve: (1) a question of law, (2) a question with ridicule, (3) a question asked by "a son of pure piety," and (4) a question by the head of the family.[4] Here we have a question of law.

We can begin by acknowledging the huge burden of taxation, particularly in Galilee. Roman tribute was substantial. Herod Antipas, a city builder, levied huge taxes to support his construction programs. He erected public buildings, Roman style, in the provincial capital, Sepphoris, and subsequently in a new capital, Tiberias. On top of these taxes, there was a required temple tax, enlarged to support a temple building program as well. And then there were tolls charged on major transportation routes. Because of taxation, many peasants lost their property. Often they became sharecroppers on what had been their own land, land they believed God had given to their forefathers. Jesus preached in peasant places, so, in effect, he preached to the poor who were getting poorer. About 7 percent of the people in Galilee controlled more than 90 percent of the wealth. For the most part, those who were wealthy were also religious, connected either with the Temple or political power. Taxation was a hot topic, particularly Roman taxation. Nationalistic Jews resented paying hard-earned money to a foreign power currently occupying the "promised land" of Israel.

Jesus' questioners were "some Pharisees and Herodians." Pharisees were frequently wealthy. Herodians were supporters of current Jewish political power, namely the appointed sons of old King Herod, who were definitely playing ball with Rome. Herodians also were doing well. So their question was a trap. If Jesus said pay up, he would alienate many of his peasant followers. But if he urged people to refuse paying taxes to Rome, he could be arrested.

Many church people hear the story as advocating a split world, a church-state compromise, in which we give Caesar what Caesar requires and give God tithes and talents that God (i.e., churches) should have. They read the passage with a "two-kingdom" mind-set. They may even flip their Bibles to Romans 13, where Paul urges his listeners to obey governing authorities, because they have been appointed by God. Paul also tosses in a sentence or two on the subject of taxation: "Pay your taxes to public servants of God, who manage such matters regularly. Pay them all that's due them—taxes to whom taxes are due, revenue to whom revenue is due" (Rom. 13:6–7). Happily, to counterbalance Romans 13, there is the grand one-liner in Acts 5:29: "We must obey God rather than human beings!" But, contrary to popular understanding, Mark's story is not easily turned into a two-realm, God-and-country split.

The Controversy

The Pharisees and Herodians come up to Jesus and unctuously ask their question: "Teacher, we know that you're honest, impartial, and not swayed by appearances but boldly teach the true way of God. Is it lawful to pay taxes to Caesar or not?" The question is a hopeless trap, and they expect Jesus to tumble into trouble.

Jesus demonstrates that he has seen through their flattery. "Why are you testing me?" he asks, and then adds, "Hand me a denarius; let me look it over." His request sounds innocent, but it is not. At the time, there were two different coins, both commonly called "denarius." The silver coin was offensive to Jews because it had a picture of Caesar enthroned as a God—"The Divine Caesar." As a result, a bronze coin was struck with religious symbols so people could pay the temple tax without using a sacrilegious Roman coin. Many pious Jews would not carry the silver coin. Jesus cleverly asks his testers to produce a denarius, and they are exposed: "Whose image is here and whose inscription?" Jesus asks, probably with a sweet, innocent smile. They are forced to own up, admitting they are in on and profiting from Caesar's economy.

Then Jesus hands out an epigram, "Give to Caesar Caesar's, but give to God, God's." The first half of the saying is obviously true. A coin is the possession of the ruler who has had it minted. Thus, the coin is Caesar's; they got it from Caesar and they can give it back to Caesar. But the second half is not so easy. I have replaced "and" (Greek, *kai*) with "but," a permissible translation when interpreting parallel clauses: Caesar-Caesar's/God-God's. As soon as you ask what isn't God's, you realize that "but" is correct—Caesar's little coin versus God's created universe!

> The earth is the LORD's and all that it holds,
> the world and its inhabitants. (Ps. 24:1)

Homiletic Theology

Most citizens pay taxes without protest. Oh, we grumble as people have grumbled for centuries, but we pay. However dimly, we realize that a corporate whole must have common government and that such a government has legitimate costs. But for Christians, the issue can sometimes be ambiguous. As I write these pages, the United States is struggling in the aftermath of a dubious invasion of Iraq. As we were poised for war, the leadership of the Catholic Church in America as well as most mainline Protestant denominations petitioned the White House for an opportunity to voice concerns to the President. They were refused. Many Christian people believed the war was unjust and that our nation's policies were undercutting the status of the United Nations. So the issue of paying taxes for what seemed an immoral war was discussed by a number of congregations, particularly those familiar with the centuries-old "Just War" tradition. Though mainline Protestant churches have become remarkably middle-class Republican, questions were discussed. While war raises the issues for many Christian people, so does ecological policy, extravagant defense spending, capital punishment, and other governmental actions. If we turn to the Bible for guidance, we end up aiming different texts at one another—from Romans, from Acts, as well as the God and Caesar passage, variously interpreted. Though many churches have two flags up front, flags of nation and of church, issues don't often dovetail. There is certainly no biblical warrant for "My nation right or wrong." The Caesar/God passage is not simply about taxation but about Christian responsibility in a political world.

The American church *and* state solution is a matter of pragmatic convenience, and not necessarily a valid theological answer.[5] Indeed, the church and state solution has almost guaranteed there is seldom, if any, serious discussion of national obedience before God. Because we are determined to avoid partisan religion, we have lost anything resembling public theological concern. In the midst of deciding to launch an ambiguous war in Iraq, most local Protestant pulpits were silent, a scandalous fact. Does church *and* state mean that there are two separate provincial fields of concern? You stay out of our affairs and we will ignore yours. Or did clergy look out at their fairly conservative congregations, exclaim "Isn't pluralism wonderful?" and decide to say absolutely nothing? If God is God, then all things are in the province of God and those who speak for God must speak boldly. A number of theological ethicists have been asking for a "Public Theology." The public discussion of sociopolitical issues within a theological context is urgent and must begin within local churchly life. The assumption that any conversation about God is bound to be partisan must be questioned. There are angles of vision in all human conversation; do we therefore quit speaking and simply stroke one another? No, God must not be disallowed. Any "God discussions" are bound to include the issue of paying for programs that thoughtful religious people believe they cannot morally support.

When faced with the Caesar-God debate, Jesus did not simply flip a coin. His counterquestion exposes our idolatrous "military-industrial" involvements and, at the same time, does not shortchange the majesty of God!

A Sermon

The sermon was preached in the chapel of the Claremont School of Theology in the 1980s. The Scripture read was from Matthew's terse version of the story.

Introduction   Do you know that back in the 1940s there were two different one-cent coins? There were the usual copper pennies that collect on our bureau tops, but, to conserve copper, the government issued a zinc penny as well. If you dropped the zinc penny it didn't ring; it went "thunk." Well guess what, at the time of Christ there were also two coins: a silver denarius inscribed with a picture of the divine Caesar, and a bronze coin imprinted with temple symbols to appease scrupulous Jews. For how could a pious Jew carry around a picture of Caesar throned as if he were a God?

So here in the Bible there's a story about the two coins and a question. The Pharisees come hustling up to Jesus: "Is it lawful to pay taxes to Caesar?" they ask. There you are—two coins and one tough question!

I

1 *"Is it right to pay taxes to Caesar?"* The question is still a good question, particularly these days. Just how far can the church go in supporting the nation? Years ago, most congregations put two flags in their chancels, an emblem of the church and an American flag. Is it still possible to stand the flags side by side? After all, in recent years our nation has backed all sorts of strange causes, including General Noriega in Panama, Saddam Hussein in Iraq, and Papa Doc in Haiti. And what about our national budget? We spend 1 percent on education and about 300 billion dollars on the military, and that doesn't include veterans' benefits or past war debts. We spend more bucks on bombs than anyone else in the world. The Irish export fine lace and the French delicate wines. What do we export? Death—we are the biggest arms merchant in the world. Yet in our churches we preach Christ, "the Prince of Peace." So maybe Catholic Bishop Hunthausen was on-target when he refused to pay his taxes. The question was edgy in Jesus' day, but these days it's our question too: "Is it right to pay taxes to Caesar?"

2 Look, *the question isn't easy—not in our churches, not anywhere*. The question is contentious. In Jesus' day there were proto-zealots on the left and Herodians on the right, and any answer to the question was bound to be trouble. But in our churches these days divisions have multiplied. You've got the Eisenhower Christians who still lust for bigger church buildings, the 1960s Christians who want to be politically involved, the 1970s crowd keeping diaries of their faith journeys, and Christians from the 1980s doting on *Hee Haw* religion and Ronald Reagan (if there's a difference)! If there's a mere hint of civil disobedience in our sermons, we're in trouble—and, as we all know, bishops seldom applaud ministers in trouble. Did you see that wonderful cartoon with two ministers gazing ruefully into an all but empty collection plate—two buttons, a penny, and a "Win with Willkie" pin? Says one of the ministers, "Well, so much for prophecy!" For most ministers, it's much safer to dive headlong into a therapeutic gospel; we can avoid social issues and get a reputation for caring at the same time. "Is it right to pay taxes to Caesar?"—a tough question, now as then.

II

3 *What does Jesus say? Jesus says, "Show me a coin," and we are exposed.* Our church money has come from Caesar, no doubt about it at all. Listen, we can ask the question "Should the church play ball with the state?" but we cannot ask the question from innocence. We've already been co-opted. Denominations have invested funds in what John Kenneth Galbraith labeled "the military-industrial complex." So have most theological schools. There are chaplains in uniform, prayer breakfasts at the White House, and noted evangelists preaching at the Pentagon. As for local congregations, what on earth would we do without the wealthy? Or what about the tax breaks for clergy we so stoutly defend? Manses are tax-free, and ministers can get a double dip on housing allowances. Perhaps we've turned Christian faith into a Boy Scout "God and Country" competition. So here's a first for you: Jesus Christ sounding for all the world like Reinhold Niebuhr! We Christians hold out a coin, and he exposes our corruptions. Do you know that the dollar bills in your wallet don't belong to you? They are owned by the U.S. government and you merely use them. Now do you understand Jesus' words? Since we have played ball with Caesar, why "Give to Caesar what belongs to Caesar." There's an answer for you!

4 But hold on, *there's more to Christ than a trick answer to a trick question: See the man die!* He is judged by Pilate, a Roman governor, and strung up on a Roman cross. "Better for one man to die than for the nation to go down," said savvy old Caiaphas. Jesus tangled with the temple money changers and called the people to a new social order, God's new order, and so he was crucified. A few years ago there was an off-Broadway passion play in which the story of Christ's crucifixion was done up in modern dress. The high priest wore a pectoral cross and a miter. Pilate, Pilate became a cigar-chewing governor, backed up by an American flag. As for the crowd that traded Christ for Barabbas, some of them wore VFW hats, others Rotarian buttons, and most of them looked like us. A shocked reviewer summed it up: "My God," he wrote, "it all fits!" Listen, it's all very well to shrug our lives and admit, "We're all sold-out." We can learn to live with ourselves anyway. But, look, we are still stuck with Jesus Christ, who didn't sell out—Jesus Christ who was crucified outside a city's gates.

III

5 *So what is the other side of the equation? "Give to God the things of God!"* There you have it! Give to God what belongs to God. Well, with the separation of church and state, does that mean we toss God our prayers and hymns and spiritual feelings? Maybe divvying up works for a while, but sooner or later someone's bound to ask the question: "What isn't God's?" Then, the divvying up ends. "The earth is the Lord's and the fullness thereof," chants the Bible. Everything is from God! There's a fat-cat

Presbyterian Church—most of them are—outside of a northern city. They offer guided tours of their building and its precious furnishings. And they price tag everything: "This is our painting of the crucifixion, valued at a hundred twenty-five thousand. And this is our Celtic cross. And this is our hand-carved baptismal font." One day as a tour group walked into a cloister, one of the visitors asked, "How about your tree? How much did you pay for the tree?" The earth is a gift, a loan from God, and "the fullness thereof" is all from God. No, we'll never be pure, not even if we're striving Wesleyans, but in our brokenness we can still bear witness to the way of Jesus Christ. What else is a church for if not to witness? We hear the words "Give to God the things of God," and we are suddenly silent. "Love so amazing, so divine, / Demands my soul, my life, my all." Guess what, the old hymn is singing about politics too!

Conclusion Someone once suggested that Jesus took the coin and flipped it! "Give to Caesar Caesar's, but give to God God's," as if each individual must decide in a church-state society. Instead, we stare at the coins in our pockets and ask the terrible question: What isn't God's? What isn't God's? And we must live with the question before we can ever find an answer.

Discussion

Introduction The introduction does what it has to do, namely, focus on the two coins that soon will be crucial and, at the same time, pick up the issue of taxation. Rehearsing biblical background is always a risk, but the introduction begins in our world and hands out background in about eight sentences.

1 Immediately I move the question of taxes to our contemporary world. The structure of the move travels from chancel flags, to American military policy, to a respected bishop in Washington state who in 1990 refused to pay his taxes. The move travels too quickly over too many national issues.

2 Here I wanted to establish the controversial character of the issue, in biblical times and now. I seem to argue that in the 1990s there were more divisions and thus more controversy. The illustration picks up the risk in being prophetic. At the end of the move, I once more echo "Is it right to pay taxes to Caesar?" which returns to the passages, but with our contemporary meanings as well.

3 Having returned to the text at the end of the previous move, I can now have Jesus speak—"Show me a coin!"—which is followed by an unexpected "and we are exposed." I document the church's involvement in a military-industrial economy, showing that "we cannot ask the question from innocence. We've already been co-opted." I bring up the issue of manse

allowances to get at theological students. Did the allusion to Jesus sounding like Reinhold Niebuhr work? Probably not.

4 With a clumsy transition, I swing the whole sermon to the cross. A good
idea, but badly done. Notice that I developed Caiaphas but did not adequately show Roman power—not good at all! We need to see Christ's death
as a result of his political challenge to the economic status quo.

5 I see the last move as something of a disaster mostly because of the illustration, plus the final comments about witness. The move simply does not
do what it should do. The illustration needs to be replaced with something
more concerned with radical obedience to God. Instead it's all about price
tags and ecological wonder. The move, as it stands, is downright confusing.

Conclusion   The conclusion is fair, although it leads to a somewhat unclear
last sentence.

The sermon starts out powerfully but then flunks its final section. I don't
know if the idea got conveyed. Seminary students like to be amused, and the
sermon was not amusing. Plus, the sermon was more political than West Coast
Methodist piety might welcome.

ANOTHER STORY ON TAXATION

Matthew 17:24–27

²⁴After they arrived in Capernaum, those who were collecting the two-
drachma tax came up to Peter, asking, "Your teacher, doesn't he pay the
two-drachma tax?" ²⁵"Yes," he answered.

But when he went into the house, Jesus anticipated him, saying, "What
do you think, Simon? Who do the kings of the earth collect tolls or taxes
from, their own children or aliens?" ²⁶Answering, [Peter] replied, "From
aliens." "Then the children are exempt," said Jesus.

²⁷"But so we don't upset them, go to the lake and cast a line; the first
fish you catch, when you open its mouth you'll find a coin [lit., "stater"].
Take it, and pay them on behalf of both of us."

Matthew's Story

The peculiar story is found only in Matthew. The story looks as if it is prompted
by government toll collectors. A double-drachma tax was equivalent to a half
shekel and thus matched the temple offering required by Exodus 30:13. In the
first century such an annual tax was required of all male Jews to support the Temple in Jerusalem. Though the story features Jesus, would he have refused to pay

a temple tax during his lifetime? Not likely. Here again, the story fits the situation of early Christianity: Gentile Christians felt no obligation to pay a temple tax and, gradually, many Jewish Christians might suspect they could avoid the requirement as well. More broadly, if the story is aimed at public taxation, many Christians would not have wanted to support Rome's pagan civil religion.

What exactly is Jesus arguing? Is he opposing taxation per se? Certainly his analogy seems to suggest that as children of the king—that is, God—we should be free from imposed taxation. Nonetheless, whether a tax supports Temple or government, to avoid giving offense, we can choose to pay. Of course, at the end of the fish story, the magic fish with a stater in its mouth handles the required contribution for both Peter and Jesus. A stater was worth four times a drachma.

Though the story is a controversy of sorts, and though it does appear in our Bibles, wise ministers will preach on the Caesar/God passage and avoid tangling with this odd passage for obvious reasons: the setting of the story is ambiguous; the story requires too much historical reconstruction to grasp and, thus, will risk tedium; and the magic fish-with-coin story simply seems too far-fetched to credit. Some years ago, there was a splendid T-shirt with the motto, "I fish, therefore I lie." Fish stories that stretch credulity too far do not usually contribute to faith.

CONFLICT OVER RESURRECTION

Mark 12:18–27 (also Matthew 22:23–33 and Luke 20:27–40)

[18]The Sadducees, who claim there is no resurrection, came up to Jesus and questioned him, saying, [19]"Teacher, for us Moses wrote, 'If someone's brother dies and leaves behind a wife, but no child, the man must take his brother's widow as a wife and produce children on behalf of his brother.' [20]Now there were seven brothers and the first took a wife but he died without having children. [21]The second took her, but he also died before having children; the third, likewise. [22]All seven [married her], but left no children. [23]In the resurrection, when they all rise again, whose wife will she be—for all seven had her as a wife?"

[24]Jesus said to them, "You're wrong again; you don't understand Scripture or the power of God! [25]When the dead rise they neither marry nor are given in marriage, but live like angels in the heavens.

[26]"As for the dead, they are raised, for have you not read in the scroll of Moses how God spoke to him at the [burning] bush, 'I am God of Abraham and God of Isaac and God of Jacob.' [27]God is not a God of the dead but of the living. So you're completely wrong."

Other Versions

Matthew draws on Mark's version with only minor changes. Luke, on the other hand, has expanded the end of Mark's verse 25 from "but live like angels in the heavens" to "they can't die anymore, for they are like angels; as children of God they are children of the resurrection." Both Matthew and Luke rewrite Mark's rather abrupt ending, "So you're completely wrong." Matthew adds a stock phrase: "the crowd heard and was astonished by his teaching." Luke, however, uses a conclusion drawn from Mark's controversy over the Great Commandment: "Then some of the scholars replied, 'Teacher, you have spoken well,' for they no longer dared ask him anything."

Mark's Story

For the first time, Mark has a dialogue with Sadducees. As a group they denied the resurrection, viewing it as a Pharisaic false doctrine for which there was no basis in Torah. The story seems to feature a somewhat ridiculous stock question and some well-worn stock answers. Many scholars view the entire story as an apologetic product of the early church as it debated those who questioned resurrection faith.

The question is based on the idea of levirate marriage as set forth in Scripture. Here is the text from Deuteronomy 25:5–6:

> When brothers dwell together and one of them dies and leaves no son, the wife of the deceased shall not be married to a stranger, outside the family. Her husband's brother shall unite with her: he shall take her as his wife, and perform the levir's duty. The first son that she bears shall be accounted to the dead brother, so that his name may not be blotted out in Israel.

The custom prompts a ridiculous question. Suppose a man dies leaving a childless wife and the man's brother marries her but again dies leaving her childless. Still another brother is enlisted, but the sad situation happens again; this occurs for all seven brothers. In the resurrection, when they all meet, whose wife will the woman be? It is a silly question, like the one about how many angels can dance on the head of a pin. But, according to David Daube's scheme, the second son on Passover eve voices a ridiculous question. Stripped of levirate repetition, the question could be reduced to "Is marriage kept in the resurrection?"

Jesus replies somewhat abrasively, "You're wrong again; you don't understand Scripture or the power of God!" Harsh words for Sadducees, who relentlessly adhere to Scripture. Then Jesus explains, "When the dead rise they neither marry nor are given in marriage, but live like angels in the heavens." Some scholars suppose that here Jesus denies the idea of bodily resurrection. Not necessarily. At the end of a long section contrasting earthly life and heavenly life (1 Cor. 15:42–50), Paul writes that "flesh and blood cannot inherit the kingdom; neither can the perishable inherit the imperishable." Nevertheless, Paul also speaks of a *soma pneumatikon,* "a body given by the Spirit." So Jesus' sweeping statement does not preclude some paradoxical mode of embodiment. As W. H. Auden once quipped, "I wouldn't be caught dead without a body!" All Jesus is saying is that God's new order will be decidedly new.

Then Mark's Jesus adds a "proof of the resurrection" by drawing on Torah itself. He cites the famous story of God's appearance to Moses from the mysterious blazing bush and God's saying, "I am God of Abraham and God of Isaac and God of Jacob." Thus, from God's own "I am" voice, Jesus deduces, "God is not a God of the dead but of the living." He concludes with a fairly unfriendly "You're completely wrong." So much for Sadducees! The arguments sound well-worn, the strategies of early Christian defense put on the lips of Jesus. Nevertheless, though sounding stock, unpacked they may be an encouragement to faith. Plus, an argument involving Abraham, Isaac, and Jacob should put a stop to Christians who try to deny Jews the eternal promise of God: "I will be your God; you will be my people."

The Controversy

What about the shape of the controversy? Here the controversy is quite different. There is a somewhat labored, ridiculous question about levirate marriage and the resurrection. Does Mark suppose that the Sadducees assume Jesus is a Pharisee? Though the question was probably a stock Sadducee-Pharisee debate ploy, it was no doubt aimed at early Christians as well.

Though there is immediate criticism of the questioners—"Wrong again!" —there is no direct counterquestion. Nonetheless, "You don't understand Scripture or the power of God" does show a mind-set of the Sadducees; they were early-day fundamentalists. Scripture, like "a lamp unto our feet," casts light *ahead of itself,* light to walk by through life. Scripture was light for the Sadducees as well, but, as I have suggested, it was a light shining down to form a circular prison cell without doors. We can't walk anywhere led by light; we must live inside the circle of light.

Is there a final pronouncement? Jesus ventures two answers to his opponents—one to the specific question of levirate marriage ("They neither marry nor are given in marriage") and another to rebut the case against resurrection ("God is not a God of the dead but of the living"). If God is a living God, and at the same time the God of Abraham, Isaac, and Jacob, then they too live. The final statement, though part of a logical argument, is an epigrammatic pronouncement and serves to wrap up the controversy.

Homiletic Theology

Though the story is ridiculous, involving levirate marriage laws multiplied absurdly, it does raise a question: Will relationships forged on earth be bound in a life to come? Beyond the question of marriage ties is the harder question of resurrection per se. In Jesus' day the subject was debated by Sadducees, who denied any resurrection, and Pharisees, who affirmed a life after death. Job's blunt question, "If a man die, will he live again?" is mostly answered in the negative by the Hebrew Scriptures—"Not a chance!" Though there is mention of Sheol in the Bible, sheol can be defined as no more than a subzero existence. Later writings, for example Daniel and Maccabees, do affirm a resurrection.

Nevertheless, the "oral Torah," namely writings of the Jewish sages, seems to support some sort of resurrection. Jacob Neusner sums up the position simply in a series of authoritative statements:[6]

1. We are judged.
2. We are rewarded or penalized for our life on earth by being sent to either the garden of Eden or Gehenna.
3. When Messiah comes we will all be raised from the dead.

There are many variables, metaphors, and meanings, but underlying the statements Neusner poses is a clear belief system. Notice the first statement, "We are judged." For Protestant Christians, it is helpful to remember that though we are saved by grace through faith, we are nonetheless judged by works. Judaism affirms God's moral seriousness. God's grace is never cheap. In a way, if we do revere the merciful justice of God, we must speak of accountability before God.

The second statement seems to show up in the teaching of Jesus where Gehenna is also used metaphorically (Matt. 5:22, 29; 10:28). But both terms "garden of Eden" and "Gehenna" are images, suggestive of the seriousness of judgment and the alternative ways of human life. But watch out for reading metaphors literally.

The third statement, "When Messiah comes we will all be raised from the dead," seems to override the finality of the second statement, and indeed it does. Responding to Messiah, Israel will repent and be a faithful covenant people. Though God is assuredly just, God's justice lives within God's purposes and, above all, God's covenant promises. God is merciful. Appropriately, Neusner quotes the wonderful synagogue prayer:

> Your might, O Lord, is boundless. Your loving kindness sustains the living, your great mercies give life to the dead. You support the falling, heal the ailing, free the fettered. Keep your faith with those that sleep in the dust. Whose power can compare with yours? You are the master of life and death and deliverance. Faithful are you in giving life to the dead. Praised are you, Lord, master of life and death.[7]

Christianity inherited resurrection faith from Israel. The apostle Paul shapes the pattern and then records the first testimony to the resurrection in 1 Corinthians 15:2–11.

> I handed on to you as most important what I myself had received; namely,
>   that Christ died for our sins as in the scriptures;
>   that he was buried, and he was raised on the third day
>   as in the scriptures;
>   that he was disclosed to Cephas, to the twelve,
>   and then, to more than five hundred brothers [and sisters] at once,
>   most of whom are still around, although some have fallen asleep.
> He was then disclosed to James,
>   to all the apostles, and, last of all, as if to someone born unexpectedly,
> He was also disclosed to me.

I have translated the Greek *ophthe* as "disclosed," acknowledging the revealing action of God. Paul's introductory statement, "I handed on to you as most important what I myself had received," seems to indicate a tradition he received in Jerusalem. The stylized nature of the material he quotes seems to indicate a liturgical or creedal formulation crystalized from an earlier time, perhaps in the mid-forties. Though the material is formulaic, it constitutes the first Christian testimony to the resurrection of Jesus. The later resurrection stories that conclude the Gospels are like Easter carols; they are more theological than historical.

Preaching the Passage

The question posed by the Sadducees is ridiculous; most test questions designed to show up an opponent are. But underneath a silly question is often something human and even troubling. Are the covenants we make in life honored in the hereafter? We have lots of questions about the possibility of life after death that trouble us.

In a world where "ignorant armies clash by night," death is more and more a daily news break. The sheer scale and dreadful repetition of daily military death tolls seem to devalue life and turn human dying into mere statistics. Then when, on top of daily death tolls we witness a sudden tsunami in which hundreds of thousands of lives are simply swept away, how hard it is to believe God cares or that there is any future beyond R.I.P. gravestones. Resurrection isn't easy to credit when death dominates our news. Many of us worship in Christian congregations where once in a while we stand to recite the Apostles' Creed, which includes the statement "I believe in the resurrection of the body" (a phrase that actually may refer to "the body of Christ," as an ultimate communion of saints, small "s"). How do we explain such belief to ourselves? Moreover, how can we conceive of the reality of the resurrection promise?

The conflict story offers a counterstatement: "When the dead rise they neither marry nor are given in marriage, but live like angels in the heavens." The statement has general meaning beyond marriage. The life to come will be a new order beyond conventions of here and now—a good thing! There was a wonderful, blunt, old Anglican lady who quite systematically moved herself into a hospital (including a small bar) when she figured it was time to die. She then commanded a minister to arrive and discuss the matter. Said Belle, "I do not believe in resurrection. I don't want to go on being me forever." The minister answered sweetly, "I don't blame you." If a life beyond our lives isn't somehow free from the cruel inter-involvement of our sinful selves, it's not much of a prospect. Hereafter may still be a continuing pilgrimage, but we should be freed from the compulsions of damaging sin as well as the hurts and fierce struggles of our aging flesh. Who wants to go on being us forever? We look to be renewed selves in some glad renewed company. Jesus seems to be saying that the new order of God will be decidedly new, quite beyond our human imagining.

The only way we mortals have penetrated the mystery is with metaphors that are consistent with our dim knowledge of God. Israel ventured those wonderful images of worldwide partying on Mount Zion. Christianity, with its breaking bread and hoisting wine on a regular basis, has delighted in the same sweet image; hereafter will be eucharistic, "They stand, those halls of Zion, all jubilant with song . . . the song of them that triumph, the shout of them that feast."[8] Metaphors always aim at essential meaning but leave room for the improvisations of God.

Then Jesus adds a decisive word: The God of Abraham, Isaac, and Jacob is "a God of the living." His great one-liner that could only be improved by adding Sarah and Deborah, Leah, and others. God is the creator, the life-giver, and the lover of us all. The pronouncement gives all the reassurance any of us could ask. The image is inclusive, drawing together Jewish and Christian communities. "Party" is a modest term for what God has in mind![9]

CONFLICT OVER THE GREAT COMMANDMENT

Mark 12:28–34 (also Matthew 22:35–40 and Luke 10:25–28)

[28]One of the scribes approached. He had been listening to them debate and had seen how well [Jesus] answered them. He asked, "Which is the most important commandment of all?" [29]Jesus answered, "The first is 'Hear O Israel, the Lord your God is one Lord, [30]and you shall love the Lord your God with all your heart, with all your soul, [with all your mind], and with all your energy.' [31]The second is this: 'You are to love your neighbor as your [own].' There is no commandment greater than these."

[32]The scribe said to him, "Right, Teacher, you are correct. There is one and no other, [33]and to 'love him with all one's heart and with all one's mind and with all one's energy' and to 'love your neighbor as your [own]' is greater than all burnt offerings and sacrifices." [34]Jesus, seeing how wisely he replied, said to him, "You are not far from the new order of God." From then on, nobody questioned him.

Other Versions

In Luke, the story appears earlier in the Gospel and, compressed, is used as an introduction to the parable of the Good Samaritan. In both Matthew and Luke, the scribe who quizzes Jesus is a lawyer. Matthew makes three other changes: (1) He writes verse 34 as a transition from the previous story; (2) he adds "The second is the same thing" to link the two commandments; and (3) he adds a conclusion, "On these two commandments hang all the law and the prophets." Probably Luke and Matthew have a version of the story from Q. But Matthew may have collated Q and Mark to produce his own distinctive version.

Mark's Story

What happened to the controversy? There is little apparent controversy in Mark's version. The question is asked from simple piety, as is the third son's question in Daube's scheme. Actually, there was debate over the question, Which is the most important command? Jewish fundamentalists of the time insisted that no command was more important than any other command because they were all from the voice of God. In Matthew 5:19 there is a warning against those who would rank commandments as greater and lesser. But with more than 600 commandments, there was naturally a debate over whether there was a most important command from which all others would follow.

Rabbi Hillel (25 BCE) offered such a summary: "What you yourself hate, do not do to your fellow; this is the whole law; the rest is commentary; go and learn." But here Jesus answers by reciting the Shema from Deuteronomy 6:4–5: "Hear O Israel, the Lord your God is one Lord, and you shall love the Lord your God with all your heart, with all your soul, and with all your energy." Mark, providing what may be a Hellenistic emphasis, has added "with all your mind" to Deuteronomy, though his addition is dropped from some manuscripts. The Shema was Israel's traditional "credo," recited morning and evening by pious Jews, so Jesus' answer would satisfy almost any critic. But then Jesus adds another command, "You shall love your neighbor as your [own]," from Leviticus 19:18. Then he adds, "There is no commandment greater than these."

Two comments are in order. First, some preachers claim that Jesus was the first to couple the two commands together—loving God and loving neighbors—but Jesus was speaking from his own Jewish tradition in doing so. For example, the *Testament of the Twelve Patriarchs, T. Issa' 5:2* (2nd century BCE) has "Love the Lord and your neighbor, and show compassion for the poor and weak." Philo claimed the two loves were one in the tablets of the Decalogue, the first calling for "God lovers" (*philotheoi*) and the second tablet for "human lovers" (*philanthropoi*). The two commands were already linked in Jewish thought.

Second, I have translated Leviticus 19:18 as "You are to love your neighbor as your own." Years ago David Noel Freedman argued that "self" simply could not have been the original command, even though it is found in the Septuagint translation. Instead, we could substitute "own," meaning our own kinfolk—we are to love neighbors as if they are members of our own family. There have been too many misconstrued sermons on self-love as a basis for neighbor love, even though the Bible has virtually nothing about self-love anywhere.

Responding to Jesus, the scribe approves, saying, "Teacher, you are correct," and adding that to love God and love one's neighbor is "greater than all burnt offerings and sacrifices" (1 Sam. 15:22; Hos. 6:6; Prov. 21:3). Jesus tells him he is "not far from the new order of God." The passage ends in happy unanimity with a final conclusion: "From then on, nobody questioned him."

The Controversy

Evidently Mark has turned his version of the story from a controversy into catechetical instruction for his Christian audience. His questioner has become a "son of simple piety." Matthew's version (22:35–40), from the Q source, shows the shape of controversy much more clearly:

When they heard that he had silenced the Sadducees, the Pharisees got together to quiz him. One of them, a lawyer, tested Jesus by questioning him, "Teacher, what commandment is most important in the law?" And he answered him, "'You shall love the Lord your God with all your heart, and with all your soul, and with all your understanding.' This is the first great commandment. The second is the same thing: 'You shall love your neighbor as yourself.' On these two commandments hang all the law and the prophets."

Matthew, a Jewish Christian, knows that the lawyer's question "What commandment is most important in the law?" is a tricky test question designed to get Jesus into trouble. Jesus' answer is safe enough, for he quotes the Shema as the first great commandment. But then, unexpectedly, he adds, "The second is the same thing: 'You shall love your neighbor as your own.'" The usual translation, "is like unto it," does not give full force to Jesus' words—that to love your neighbor is the same as loving God! Douglas R. A. Hare observes, "We should probably see 'like' as meaning more than 'similar in structure' or even 'similar in importance.' What is implied is a similarity in theological depth and an interrelationship"[10]—thus, "the same thing." The notion also shows up in 1 John 4:7–12.

Finally, Matthew's Jesus announces, "On these two commandments hang all the law and the prophets." But, in a sense, they are no longer two; they are one, thus bypassing the trick question.

Homiletic Theology

The Shema ("Hear") is rather like a creed for Israel. Pious Jews recited the words three times daily. As God's chosen covenant partner, Israel is called to respond with active love. Here is the full command in Deuteronomy 6:4–9:

> Hear O Israel, the Lord is our God, the Lord alone. You shall love the Lord your God with all your heart and with all your soul, and with all your might. Take to heart these instructions with which I charge you this day. Impress them upon your children. Recite them when you stay at home and when you are away, when you lie down and when you get up. Bind them as a sign on your hand and let them serve as a symbol on your forehead. Inscribe them on the doorposts of your house and on your gates.

Early Christianity adopted the "Great Commandment" along with the verse on neighbor love from Leviticus 19:18b as a helpful summary of the law. But, in Matthew, the assembling of the two commands with "the second is the same thing" is theologically surprising.

The word "love" in Jewish and Christian contexts needs some explanation. When Denis de Rougemont came to America for the first time, he said he heard the word "love" sung so often on the radio, he was thinking of sending in for a free sample. We bandy the word about carelessly. In our songs, love is mostly a feeling. Sometimes on bumper stickers "love" expresses enthusiasm toward cities or animals: "I love New York," or "I love Sheepdogs." Such love is an emotion that also fills the hymns we sing. But in the Shema as in Leviticus 19:18b, love is action. Love is something you do, and not merely a genial sense of general affection. No wonder that Jesus' command to love enemies is so troubling. Love requires active doing for, giving to, helping out. In the Shema we are actively to serve God with all our willpower, our life, and every ounce of strength we can muster. According to Jesus, we do so by devoting ourselves in the same way to our neighbors. Given the fact that, in consciousness, we are centered selves and others always seem peripheral, the commandment will take some doing. But, happily, love is always a gift of God's grace.

If love is action, then the command to love God requires a knowledge of God and of God's will. Otherwise, the idea of loving God implies an orientation toward what? Some years ago, a theologian confessed that whenever he tried to focus on God, something like a blank page formed in his mind. Once in a while a cut-out camel left over from church school would cross the page, but for the most part, when he tried to think about God, he drew a blank. How can we focus on a consciousness that is conscious of us, a consciousness "in whom we live and move and have our being"? Here then is the question: How can we know God?

Lately, Protestant "Word of God" theology has tried to lock revelation up inside the Bible, denying any display of God in the natural world or in the area of interactive human experience. The narrowing of revelation to the Bible page is no doubt a reaction to natural sciences that explain matters without recourse to God, and to a psychology that analyzes human experience in much the same way. Thus, ideas of "general revelation" seem to have disappeared these days in favor of finding God in the Book alone. Too bad, for a past tense "God in print" is apt to seem somewhat remote.

Can we ignore the strange, numinous wonder of the natural order and the rather surprising transformations in ourselves and others that only make sense under the heading of "being redeemed"?[11] Such experiences may be authentic moments of God-awareness. But once we stumble on surprising moments of God-awareness, they seem to multiply. God-awareness can happen retroactively, as we think back on our lives and discover previously unnoticed grace. Sometimes, odd to say, we may sense presence in hope-filled anticipation of

God's promises. Nevertheless, we are creatures, and must learn to be content with hints.

Problem: A general awareness of God may not teach us anything more than mystery, although awareness of mystery is a huge gift. What we need is a true knowledge of God and God's will. And we cannot spot God's goodness in creation or in redemptive transformation of our common lives without some sort of prior faith. No wonder we rely on public worship, where we feed on the testimonies of Scripture, speak words of praise, hear regular preaching of the "Word" that shapes our faith, and share the Eucharist. Without public worship, there can be no meaningful beyond-the-page knowledge of God.

So how do we love God? Remember, love is activity. With a head full of clues from traditional faith, and from such "theonomous" moments as we are given, we try to go where God goes, usually wherever redemptive movements and ministries occur. To go where God goes almost always means being involved with God's special friends the poor and the needy. The failure in many of our churches is that they have rather systematically helped us to avoid direct involvement with the poor and needy. Of late, we offer classes in spirituality instead.

I live in a city known as "the buckle on the Bible Belt," where again and again I am moved by conservative Christian friends who meet with inmates in prison, feed the hungry, teach classes for immigrants, comfort the elderly in public nursing facilities, aid the handicapped, and serve the poorest of the poor in splendid fashion. Apparently, they have caught up with the idea that "you shall love your neighbor as your own" and have merged it with the wonder of Shema.

A Sermon

Here's a brief homily preached to a monastic community in 1980.

Introduction   Some years ago a suburban church was disrupted by militants. They claimed to speak for the poor. Right in the middle of worship the front door slammed open and they barged into the building. Up the aisle they raced and into the chancel. Of all things, they swept the Communion bread onto the floor. "My people are hungry," cried the leader of the group. "My people are hungry," says the Lord. Police were called in to restore order, but oddly enough no charges were pressed: "My people are hungry," says the Lord.

1 Let's begin with fact. *Religion can get in the way of neighbor love.* Strange to say, piety can be perverse. Piety can turn us away from the world where weak folk wonder, hunger, and die, particularly piety that launches private desert trips! Wasn't it Alfred North Whitehead who defined religion as "what a man does with his solitude"? Somehow the definition doesn't ring true to the Bible. In Scripture, religion has to do with our checkbooks, our time. So private devotion that remains private isn't devotion at all; it's simply a nasty little religious perversion. If personal faith remains personal, if it has no room for neighbors, it can end like the *New Yorker* cartoon that shows a man kneeling by his bed in prayer, saying, "Thank you, God, for being me!" So let's begin with honesty. Religion, our love of God, can get in the way of neighbors. Fact is, religion can forget the hungry.

2 Of course, *God himself made no such mistake: he loved the human world.* God lived among us, flesh with suffering flesh. Perhaps God could have locked himself in glory, dancing in the Trinity, admiring God's own perfect attributes. But, no, God came among us with Jesus. See the high and holy God dunking in a muddy river with a tub full of sinners. See God rubbing human fur with tax-collecting racketeers and professional girls in some boozy backroom in Galilee. And, oh, see, see God-with-us hung up to die on a bad Friday, with clanking soldiers all around, and a carnival crowd in town for the season, clapping at his agony. A few years ago a New York City society artist painted an artful crucifixion, as a gilded cross set against a satin-black background. The artist's social-worker brother then improved the painting. He pasted all over the bottom half of the canvas headlines, case reports, pictures from the papers. Our God did not cling to solitary glory. God was with Christ, with human flesh among us. God-in-Christ was with the hurt people of earth.

3 So what do we do? *We take our faith into the world where God is!* We go with God into the human world, for we can't get away with splitting the Great Commandment. The God of an isolated self is no god; pray to him and you pray to the great god Nothingness. True religion begins in the gutters of Calcutta with Mother Teresa, or perhaps in the anguish of a Birmingham jail where Martin Luther King Jr. said he learned to pray, or maybe in the whirl and weeping of a parish ministry. Private prayer is never private, for your mind must be papered over with the faces of the poor, the belly-bloated hungry folk of the world. So old Ulrich Zwingli, teetering on a stepladder, painted over the icons and statues of his Zurich church, shouting "The true images for Christian worship are the faces of the poor!" Of course, a whitewashed wall is not much better than an icon is it? You've got to be there. You've got to care. Our faith lives out in the world where God is.

Conclusion   So here we are. And Christ the living bread is with us now. Listen! You cannot spread Christ with the marmalade of your own sweet, private pieties. No. You break him for the world, O God, for the hungering world.

Discussion

Here is a brief homily written in 1980 for a monastic community. The homily may seem altogether inappropriate for a contemplative community, but they were Benedictine, and the wonderful Rule of St. Benedict calls for a balance between the *opus Dei* of the monastic life and forms of outgoing neighbor love. So the monks were involved in all sorts of useful ministries. In our present-day, broken, agitated world, we could do with much more of the disciplined life of the Benedictine monks. I was honored for some years to live among them at St. Meinrad Abbey and its splendid school of theology.

The homily is brief so as to fit into the monastic schedule–three moves with an introduction and an even briefer conclusion. Brief homilies are more difficult than developed sermons because a preacher can afford few if any mistakes. They require exact definition and highly imaged language. But inasmuch as it takes around three-and-a-half minutes to form even a single simple idea, homilies need to be long enough to make a movement of meanings. (The dear Anglican bishop who once insisted that "no souls are saved after ten minutes" was not helpful. I reviewed his homilies and guessed few souls were saved after thirty seconds!) At St. Meinrad, I was delighted with my Catholic students. They came without preconceptions, worked exceptionally hard to be able preachers, and seemed to have a more lively available language. Do middle-class Protestants lean more readily on heard sermon styles and linguistic cliches? Hard to say.

Introduction   The introduction was done in about eight sentences, which is about as short as possible. The repetition of "My people are hungry" was crucial to balance the rather shocking story. Eucharistic bread should not be manhandled.

1 The first move seems rather unsettling for a monastic community, and probably was. The aside about "desert trips" picks up a then-recent, somewhat fashionable option in spiritual formation. The *New Yorker* cartoon works well as an end-of-the-line example.

2 The language adds force to the second move. If God is involved in our messy human world, the clutter of images is essential: "muddy river," "tub full of sinners," "racketeers and professional girls," "boozy backroom," "hung up to die," "clanking soldiers," "carnival crowd." The visual illustration of additions to the painting also fits.

3 The deliberate illustration about Ulrich Zwingli was used because Zwingli, for a time, was homiletician at the monastery theological school at Einseiden, Switzerland, from which St. Meinrad evolved.

Conclusion   The "marmalade of your own sweet, private pieties" was probably too vivid a negative image, but "for the hungering world" takes a lis-
tener back to the introduction.

The homily broke style with the usual monastic homily. Was that a good
thing? I am unsure. My personal gratitude for the hospitality of the St. Meinrad Benedictine community is huge.

CONFLICT OVER THE SON OF DAVID

Mark 12:35–37 (also Matthew 22:41–46 and Luke 20:41–44)
³⁵While teaching in the Temple, Jesus would ask, "How come
scribes say that Messiah is the Son of David? ³⁶David himself, by the Holy
Spirit, said:

> 'The Lord said to my Lord, "Sit here at my right
> until I put your enemies under your feet."'

³⁷David himself calls him, 'Lord,' so how can he be his son?" A huge
crowd was listening to him with delight.

Other Versions

Both Matthew and Luke drop the reference to "scribes." Matthew mentions
"Pharisees" and Luke simply has "them." Luke reduces the story to a minimum and replaces "feet" with "footstool." Matthew elaborates beginning
and end to produce a more developed controversy dialogue: Jesus questions
the Pharisees, "About the Messiah, what seems correct? Whose son is
he?" When they answer, "The Son of David," he then questions them about
Psalm 110:1. Matthew ends the passage (and the series of controversies) with
"No one could answer him, nor from that day on would anyone ask him more
questions."

Mark's Story

I noted in the discussion of the controversy over taxes to Caesar that Mark 12
has four controversies that match questions asked at Passover eve: a point of
law, a matter of ridicule, a question asked by a pious son, and an unanswer-
able question put by the head of the family. Here is the last controversy in the
set of four, and Jesus himself initiates the question: "How come scribes say
that Messiah is the Son of David?"

The passage is murky and has occasioned considerable scholarly flap. Most scholars agree that debate over the first verse of Psalm 110 was probably a postresurrection concern. Given Jesus' reticence, the so-called messianic secret in Mark, such a discussion by Jesus does not seem likely. To understand the passage, we need to agree on three prior assumptions—namely, that Jesus believed (1) David was the author of all the psalms; (2) that David wrote Psalms under the inspiration of the Holy Spirit, and (3) that Psalm 110:1 contains a specific reference to the Messiah.

The idea of Messiah as a son of David was prompted by a number of biblical texts, most notably 2 Samuel 7:12, Jeremiah 30:9, and Ezekiel 34:23. The *Psalms of Solomon,* a writing from the first century BCE, developed the idea:

> Behold, O Lord, and raise up unto them their king, the Son of David, at the time known to you, O God, in order that he may reign over Israel your servant. And gird him with strength that he may shatter unrighteous rulers, and that he may purge Jerusalem from gentiles that trample her. . . . He shall destroy the godless nations with the word of his mouth. . . . And he shall reprove sinners for the thoughts of their hearts. And he shall gather together a holy people. (*Psalms of Solomon*, 17)

Evidently, the Son of David would be a political leader who, armed with the power of God, would drive out godless nations (read, the Romans) and restore Israel's monarchy to glory years, obviously a popular hope.

But here, though Jesus himself might have been descended from David, he seems to be debunking the hope of a powerful, armed Son of David. He cites the first verse of Psalm 110: "The Lord said to my Lord, sit here at my right until I put your enemies under your feet." If David wrote the verse under the inspiration of the Spirit, how could the Messiah, whom he calls "my Lord," be the Son of David? Besides, God says, "I put your enemies under your feet"; thus, our trust is in God and not in the military power of a son of David. The argument that if David calls the Messiah, who is to be seated at the right hand of God, "my Lord," then Messiah is not "Son of David," does seem a bit labored.

All the way through his Gospel, Mark has been playing with the idea of Jesus' hidden kingship; Jesus is the king who dies in weakness. Nevertheless, as the Roman soldier at his cross declares, "This man really was God's son" (15:39). For Matthew, it is important to affirm Jesus as "Son of David" and "Son of Abraham" (Matt. 1:1), but for Mark the only crucial thing is faith in Jesus, the Christ, the Son of God. Why in Psalm 110 does David himself call Messiah "my Lord"? Because David is bowing before the true Messiah, namely, God's son.

The Controversy

Once more Matthew's version demonstrates the shape of controversy more clearly:

> When the Pharisees assembled, Jesus quizzed them, asking, "What seems to you the correct understanding of Messiah? Whose son is he?" They answered him, "The son of David." He said to them, "How then, in the Spirit, could David call him 'Lord,' saying,
>
>> The Lord said to my Lord, sit to the right of me,
>>   until I put your enemies under your feet.
>
> If David called him 'Lord,' how can he be his son?" No one was able to say anything, nor from that day on did anyone ask him more questions.

Here we have a question, a reply, and another question, so we sense the conflict involved. We are dealing with two issues: the true character of Messiah and the true stature of Jesus, the Christ, whom Christians call "Lord."

In Mark, the question of Jesus' identity is a central mystery. Remember, in Mark 8–10, the question is definitely raised: "Who do you say I am?" (8:29). Peter answers, "You are the Messiah!" Then Jesus tells his disciples that the son of humanity must suffer and die. But angrily, Peter bawls him out, because in Peter's mind Messiah is a triumphant conqueror. Then in chapter 9, Jesus appears glorified on top of a mountain along with Elijah and Moses. Peter says in effect, "Great. Let's build." But along comes a dark cloud saying sternly, "This is my son; listen to him." What was it he said? Why, another blunt prediction of suffering and death (9:30–31). Then Jesus' glory fades and he marches off to Jerusalem and his death. Finally, there is a story we have previously examined, about the sons of Zebedee who want to get in on political power even though Jesus has made a third passion prediction (10:33–34). Yes, Jesus is Messiah, but a messianic king who is rejected, who suffers and dies. Here, in the controversy over David's son, the same issues are involved. Jesus does not flex military might to drive out the pagan nations, nor does he guarantee automatic prosperity. Rather, he is rejected and dies, and Mark knows his followers will likely be rejected and die as well. But in his dying Jesus displays the obedience of a true son of God and, in so doing, defeats the deadly "powers that be."

Homiletic Theology

Early Christians had a problem: they wanted to connect Jesus to messianic prophecies. But, embarrassingly, Jesus died disgraced on a cross. Yet their own experience seemed to support Jesus' messianic credentials. They testi-fied to his resurrection and to the resurrection of their own being-redeemed community with the gift of the Spirit. Naturally they turned to the Servant Songs in Isaiah, singularly to the Suffering Servant in Isaiah 53. They also drew on the agonies voiced in Psalm 102. These still were received and under-stood as messianic prophecy. After all, militant, political, messianic images did not seem to support the nonviolent Jesus. So to Israel they announced that Jesus was the Christ, the anointed, promised Messiah, and they rallied texts from Scripture to support the claim. Some listeners responded; many did not.

But as more and more Gentiles were recruited, the term "Christ" was emp-tied of messianic meaning and almost became a second name. While Israel had an ancient and varied messianic tradition, Gentiles did not. Thus, apolo-getic strategies changed. Gradually, almost inevitably, Christianity, begun as a Jewish sectarian option, became a Gentile social movement. While still affirming the one God, who was surely the God of Abraham, Isaac, and Jacob, theological adjustments were made to shape Gentile Christianity.

But the aligning of the Jesus story with messianic texts, particularly texts from Second and Third Isaiah, was part of the Christian understanding. Chris-tians discovered that such messianic prophecies spoke to Gentile converts. Prophecies lined up with Jesus' cruel death but at the same time seemed to speak to general human pathos and human longing. No wonder that Isaiah 61:1–3 is implied throughout the so-called Sermon on the Mount. Early Chris-tians discovered that the nonviolent messianic prophecies they had gathered around the figure of Jesus from the prophets—Hosea, Isaiah, Jeremiah, Micah, Joel, Zechariah—spoke most meaningfully to peoples everywhere. In the process then of moving out of Israel and into the wider Gentile world, the iden-tification of Messiah with Israel dissolved, but messianic hopes were general-ized and offered apologetically. Apostles, like Paul in Athens, preached the new order of God as liberating hope to a world overburdened and strangely enslaved by the Pax Romana. Around the figure of Jesus, Christianity grew.

Preaching the Passage

The linguistic trickiness of the passage is scarcely convincing to modern pew sitters. Perhaps its forced cleverness worked in Jewish communities, but even then the argument is somewhat dubious. Here's my judgment call: Jesus never said it, and we would do well not to preach it. The passage requires too much background information to be useful. Plus, it is not easy to lead contemporary congregations, even highly conservative congregations, into the mind-set of a first-century Jewish scribe.

If preachers insist that the passage become sermon fodder, then a topical sermon on the role of Messiah and its meaning for our world might be in order. Otherwise, the text can best be left to keep contemporary biblical scribes busy.

CONFLICT OVER THE ANOINTING OF JESUS

Mark 14:1–9 (also Matthew 26:6–13 and John 12:1–8; but see also Luke 7:36–50)

[1]Now in two days it would be the Passover and the festival of Unleavened Bread. The chief priests and scribes were looking for ways to nab him surreptitiously so as to kill him. [2]But they said, "Not during the festival, lest there be rioting among the people."

[3]When he was in Bethany in the house of Simon the leper, while he relaxed at table, a woman came with an alabaster jar of perfume, pure expensive nard. Smashing the alabaster jar, she poured [the perfume] over his head. [4]Some of the people grumbled among themselves, "Why was there this waste of perfume? [5]The perfume could have been sold for more than fifteen thousand dollars to give to the poor!" They were furious with her.

[6]But Jesus said, "Let her be. Why are you giving her a hard time? She has done a wonderful thing for me. [7]For you will always have the poor with you, and whenever you want you can be good to them, but you will not always have me. [8]What she could, she did; she anointed my body ahead of time for burial. [9]Amen, I'm telling you, wherever the gospel is preached through all the world, what she did will be told in her memory."

Other Versions

Luke 7:36–50 has the story of an anointing in the home of Simon the leper, but, though it may show Markan influence, probably the story is from some independent source. Matthew follows Mark rather closely, although he changes those people who complain to disciples. Matthew also reduces Jesus' reply, omitting "and whenever you want you can be good to them." John schedules the event six days before the Passover and tells us the woman was Lazarus's sister Mary and that their sister Martha is waiting on table. As a true disciple, Mary pours the nard on Jesus' feet. (In the following chapter Jesus washes his disciples' feet and then urges his disciples to wash one another's feet.) John also has the complaint over cost lodged by Judas who, he tells us, used to steal from the common purse. John omits Mark's final tribute to the woman's memory.

Mark's Story

As he begins his passion narrative, Mark tells of the "chief priests and scribes" plotting Jesus' arrest and death, thus setting up a contrast between those who reject Jesus and a woman who honors him.

Passover is the celebration of Israel's liberation from Egypt. In spite of a series of plagues, the pharaoh refused to free the enslaved Israelites. Finally, God vowed to go through the land striking down the firstborn of the Egyptians, but the Israelites, with their doorways marked, were "passed over" (Exod. 12:1–28). Subsequently, the Israelites left Egypt so rapidly that their bread did not have time to rise. From the dough, the people baked unleavened bread in the desert. Thus, the feast of Unleavened Bread became part of the Passover celebration. During the festival no leavened bread could be eaten, and houses were swept of any leavened crumbs. Passover, an eight-day celebration, was Israel's great festival. Pilgrims crowded Jerusalem for the occasion. To Mark, the first day of Unleavened Bread was of special symbolic significance as the day on which the Passover lambs were sacrificed (14:12). Though the dating of Holy Week is difficult—the Gospel of John has a different, possibly Essene, schedule—Mark dates the passage "in two days it would be the Passover."

The event takes place in the home of Simon the leper, presumably so named because he once had had some sort of skin condition (there was no Hanson's disease in those days) and was now certifiably cured. Apparently Simon was wealthy enough to throw a formal, late afternoon dinner party. Suddenly an unnamed woman shows up with an alabaster jar filled with pure nard, an expensive perfume. She shatters the jar dramatically and pours the perfume over Jesus' head, anointing him in an impromptu coronation. In Israel, kings were anointed (2 Kgs. 9:3–6), and Mark has hinted Jesus' hidden kingship throughout his Gospel.

The people around grumble among themselves, "Why was there this waste of perfume? The perfume could have been sold for more than fifteen thousand dollars to give to the poor!" They are quite correct. The text sets the value at "three hundred denarii." A denarius was pay for a farm worker's twelve-hour day (Matt. 20:2). If nowadays we guess a figure of fifty dollars a day, the value would be fifteen thousand dollars! Rates of exchange across two thousand years are uncertain, but the nard was enormously expensive. People looked and grumbled, "What a waste!"

Jesus counters them: "Why are you giving her a hard time? She has done a wonderful thing for me." The woman has honored Jesus with a spontaneous act of love. Though giving to the poor was especially approved during Passover, Jesus speaks directly to the grumblers, "You will always have the poor with you, and whenever you want you can be good to them." Matthew and John only have the first clause, but Mark has the full saying, which may be a version of Deuteronomy 15:11: "For there will never cease to be needy ones in your land, which is why I command you: open your hand to the poor and needy kinsman in your land." Jesus' words "You will always have the poor with you" have often been quoted cynically to justify a benign neglect, but, in Deuteronomy as in Mark, the phrase ends in a command to be generous in giving to the poor.

Jesus then turns the moment into a passion prediction. "You will not always have me," he says, and adds a wry comment: "What she could, she did; she anointed my body ahead of time for burial." In spite of the testimony in the Gospel of John, Mark supposes Jesus' body was buried unceremoniously without usual anointing. Subsequently, women come to the tomb with spices to anoint him (16:1).

Finally, there is a tribute to the woman: "Wherever the gospel is preached through all the world, what she did will be told in her memory." But while the event has been recorded, ironically her name seems to have been omitted.

The Controversy

The situation provokes a dialogue. The grumblers slap a price tag on the woman's passionate action. "Fifteen thousand dollars!" they exclaim, appalled at the extravagance. Jesus answers, "She has done a wonderful thing." The word in Greek (*kalos*) is often translated "good" but can also be "beautiful." I have used "wonderful" in an attempt to put both meanings together. The shape of the conflict is apparent: moral calculation versus expressive self-giving love.

Because Jesus speaks sharply to the woman's critics, many preachers join the game and roundly upbraid the moralists in favor of elaborate ecclesial spending to celebrate Jesus. But Jesus handles the matter more wisely by telling the critics that they will have an ongoing opportunity to give and give generously to the poor. Then he adds a new meaning to the woman's astonishing gesture: "She anointed my body ahead of time for burial."

The controversy ends, but not with a final saying. The woman's action is praised and said to be memorable, but then Mark immediately turns to tell of taking money to betray Jesus. The account (14:10–11) is abrupt:

> One of the twelve, Judas Iscariot, went to the chief priests to turn him over to them. When they heard him, they were delighted and promised to give him money. So he was on the lookout for the right moment to betray him.

Thus, Mark has bracketed the woman's tribute between leaders who are plotting Jesus' death and a disciple who is willing to take money for the betrayal. Perhaps irony is Mark's style.

Homiletic Theology

Controversies over money spent on church decor when there are needy folk nearby have been with us for centuries. The Cathedral of St. John the Divine in New York City was begun overlooking a slum area. With the money that has been poured into the building the entire area could have been rebuilt luxuriously. What is the answer?

The story of the woman with the jar of nard is cited frequently: "She has done a beautiful thing" (RSV). The argument: Expensive aesthetic tributes to God are always warranted. But the issue has been a matter of controversy for centuries. Holy things are frequently expensive things. The stuff we use in the worship of God—silver chalices, custom-designed clergy stoles, carved baptismal fonts—are costly. But a nagging question lingers: What honors God, and what is simply ecclesial triumphalism? Wasn't it Luther who criticized architectural splendor by reminding us that Christ was born in a cow stall? Luther also drew a contrast between what he termed a "theology of glory" and an authentic "theology of the cross."[12]

Yes, to honor God we do want to set out our best, but in God's name we are called to reach out to God's special friends, the poor. Maybe "*our* best" is a clue. A ceramic chalice made by a church member might be a better gift than expensive silver communion ware. Stoles made by church members may also be good gifts. And an attractive bowl will do nicely for baptisms. Gifts we ourselves make will always be better. In a world where the poor are getting poorer, in God's name, prosperous American churches must review and remove excessive budget items.

The story may offer a clue. Said Jesus, "You will not always have me." Remember the great Easter confession: "He is not here; he is risen" (Mark 16:6). Piety tries to claim that Jesus, though unseen, is with us still, whatever such a statement may mean. But early Christianity affirmed, "He is not here." Our theology should be precise: The Holy Spirit, the same Spirit that was with Jesus, is here among us, though Jesus is not. Early Christians cried out, "Lord come!" for, as Theodore Jennings has observed, Christian worship began with a profound longing for the gone-away Christ![13] Though Jesus is not here in flesh, the poor are. In the same Spirit of Christ with us, we can serve them. Purchasing expensive church furnishings when there are poor folk who need us is never a Christian virtue. What's more, such extravagance can never be justified by appealing to the wonderful woman who so lavishly anointed Jesus.

A Sermon

The sermon, preached at a Holy Week service in the late 1980s, is based on John 12:1–8:

> [1]Six days before the Passover, Jesus came to Bethany, where Lazarus lived, whom Jesus raised from the dead. [2]They gave a dinner party for him there; Martha served while Lazarus was with those at table. [3]Then Mary took a pound of perfume, expensive pure nard, and poured it on Jesus' feet, wiping it off with her hair. And the house was filled with the fragrance of the perfume. [4]One of the disciples, Judas Iscariot, who was about to betray him, protested: [5]"Why wasn't this perfume sold for twelve thousand dollars and the money given to the poor?" [6]He didn't say this because he cared anything for the poor, but because he was a thief and kept his hand in the purse where money was put. [7]"Let her alone," said Jesus. "She has kept the perfume for the day of my burial. [8]You will always have the poor with you, but you will not always have me."

Introduction   The anointing at Bethany is a dramatic story. The story gets better year by year—with inflation. According to the Bible, the perfume Mary dumped on Jesus' feet was worth three hundred denarii. In today's market, each coin would be worth around forty dollars. So how much perfume did Mary pour out on a pair of dusty feet? About twelve thousand dollars' worth! Think of it! Twelve thousand dollars spilled in a moment of passion. If nothing else, you'll have to admit, hers was an extravagant gesture.

I

1 Nowadays, we read the story and we're embarrassed. Mary is too much for us; twelve thousand dollars tossed away in an instant without even thinking. Well, our love is seldom so careless. Even though we're in church on Sunday, to us religion is not all in all. It's only a part of our lives, along with other interests—play and politics, sex, the arts, good books, and a few hours every week in front of the TV. How did a Hollywood actress put it? "I believe in being religious," she said. "I just don't want to get carried away." There's the motive: we don't want to get carried way. So we believe in peace, but not enough to get carried away in an antiwar protest. And we believe in justice, but not enough to stand up and say so when we're in the midst of injustice. And we believe in Jesus Christ, but not enough to talk about him out of church in public without a blush and a stammer. We never, no never, get carried away. So no wonder we find it hard to understand wild, irrepressible Mary. We are embarrassed.

2 *What did Mary do? Here's what she did: she gave herself away.* Twelve thousand dollars isn't small change spilled over calloused feet, soaking away through the earthen floor, lost and gone forever. There was nothing calculating about Mary. She might have thought it over and chosen a lesser gift; after all, as we say, "It's the thought that counts." Did you see that cartoon in a magazine last Christmas? It showed a well-dressed man in a department store going over his Christmas list. "Do you have something for a five dollar relative?" he said. There was no such calculation in Mary; she didn't put price tags on people or dollar signs on deeds. She didn't sit down with a checkbook and ask how much she could afford to give; she simply gave—pouring out priceless perfume to honor her priceless Savior. If nothing else, you'll have to admit hers was an extravagant gesture!

II

3 Extravagant? *An extravagant waste! That's what Judas thought.* "It should have been given to the poor," said he, indignantly. Some Christians do have a way of killing joy, don't they? They will stamp out love in the name of propriety, morality, or sometimes even social action. "It should have been sold and the money given to the poor," snarled Judas. By Judas' logic, what good is worship? Worship time could better be given to community service. Or what good is bread and wine in Holy Communion? There are hungry people in Somalia who crave bread and drink. Morally Judas had all the logic on his side; his arithmetic was unassailable. Wasn't it Queen Victoria who at the age of eleven stood up in a public assembly and announced, "I will be good!" According to a biographer, she kept her vow through a long and tedious life! Of course it was tedious. Morality without some great devotion dries up and becomes mere moral calculation. Judas was a moralist, a social action man, who had lost faith in Jesus Christ. "It should have been given to the poor," said Judas, dollar signs blinking in his eyes.

4 *What did Jesus say? How did Jesus answer?* "Let her alone," Jesus snapped. "She has saved her perfume for my burial." We hear the words and simply do not understand. What on earth has Mary's gift got to do with Jesus' death? If there's a connection it clearly escapes us. Mary's gift and Jesus' death—what's the tie-in? The one was a costly gift poured out in love, and the other . . . Why that's it, isn't it? The other, Christ's death on the cross, was the same thing! A costly gift of God's love, extravagant and utterly self-

less; Godlove poured out for all us poor, broken sinners. Old James Denny, a British cleric, once climbed into a pulpit lugging an eight-foot-tall cross. He stood it up and pointed to it, shouting, "All this he has done for us! Can we hold back?" Can we hold back? "Love so amazing, so divine, demands my soul, my life, my all." "She has saved her perfume for my burial," said Jesus. Love for love, gift for gift, outpouring for outpouring, she gave.

III

5 Well, *here's the question: what are we saving ourselves for?* "The poor," said Jesus quoting the Hebrew Scriptures, "the poor you will always have with you." Listen, Jesus was not laying down a logic of benign neglect— since you will always have the poor hanging around you can safely ignore them. That's been our nation's economic policy for the past dozen years. And, maybe it's been church policy too. We build our Christian Family Life Centers, casting shadows on the slums. No, "You will not always have me with you," says Jesus, "but you will always have the poor"—to serve! Christ is no longer with us in flesh—"He is not here; he is risen," sang the angel at his tomb—but his special friends the poor, the hassled, the hurt, the homeless, and the victims, they are with us, and we can pour out ourselves in love for them. Faith that forgets the poor isn't faith at all; it's merely a private little religious perversion. Did you ever read John Calvin's advice on planning your budget? You give one-fourth of your money to the poor, he says, and one-fourth to the education of the clergy, and another fourth to the mission of the church. And with the last fourth what do you do? Why, you give that to the poor as well. Was Calvin serious? Well, he was never widely known for a sense of humor. Jesus would have approved with high, holy laughter. The poor we have with us and, lately, while the rich have been getting richer the poor have multiplied. How do you celebrate Holy Week in response to the sacrificial love of God? Why, you give yourself away—extravagantly.

Conclusion   The anointing at Bethany is a strange, strange story: twelve thousand dollars poured out in love. The story is shocking. Well, wouldn't it be wonderful if the churches were both as careless and as loving? Then, perhaps, the shocked world would say, "See those crazy Christians! Look, they give themselves away."

Discussion

Introduction   The introduction takes little more than eight sentences, which is about right. It picks up the action of the story and then immediately calculates worth. Then the last sentence engages the congregation. So the introduction does no more or less than it should.

1 The first move features Mary's extravagance and, by contrast, our controlled dedication to God—"Our love is seldom so careless." The quote from a Hollywood actress sets the tone, "I just don't want to get carried away."

2 Now I turn and appreciate Mary's passion: "She gave herself away." Again, I draw a contrast between Mary and us—namely, we calculate cost. No, Mary was "pouring out priceless perfume to honor her priceless Savior."

3 Here I represent Judas but, like the passage, reject his position. Morality without great devotion dries up and becomes mere moral calculation. I draw a contrast between Mary's passion and Judas's rational-moral calculation.

4 The move features a rhetorical trick. I deliberately delay the meaning I am trying to get at by musing a question: What has a self-giving gesture got to do with Jesus' death? I make the congregation think it out and, along with the preacher, finally hit on the meaning. (This happened nicely when the sermon was preached.) The James Denny illustration then follows to clinch the meaning: "All this he has done for us! Can we hold back?"

5 The final move is surprising. I have run down Judas as a calculating moral killjoy. But now I focus on the poor. Christ is no longer with us in flesh, so we can turn to serve Christ's special friends—the poor. The illustration from Calvin caught the congregation with surprise, and then laughter. Good. We want extravagant joy connected with giving to the needy.

Conclusion I turn the Bethany story into our story. Wouldn't it be wonderful if because of our generosity, the world would react, "Look, they give themselves away"—a phrase used earlier in the sermon to describe Mary's action. The sermon was originally written for a Holy Week service.

STILL ANOTHER ANOINTING STORY

Luke 7:36–50

[36]A certain Pharisee had asked [Jesus] to dine with him. He went to the Pharisee's house, and was relaxing at table with him. [37]A local woman, a sinner, heard that Jesus was dining at the Pharisee's house and came with an alabaster [jar] of myrrh. [38]She stood behind him at his feet, crying. She wet his feet with her tears and then wiped them with her hair; she kissed them and anointed his feet with the myrrh. [39]Watching this, the Pharisee who had invited him was thinking to himself, "If he were any kind of prophet, he'd have spotted her, seeing what sort of woman was touching him. She's a sinner!"

⁴⁰Jesus addressed him, "Simon, I have something to say to you." "Teacher, say on," he replied. ⁴¹"Two persons owed money to the same creditor; one owed twenty thousand dollars and the other two hundred. ⁴²When they couldn't pay, he forgave them both. So which one will love him the most?" ⁴³"I suppose," Simon answered, "the one who was forgiven more." He said to him, "Right you are!"

⁴⁴Then, turning to the woman, Jesus said to Simon, "See this woman. I walked into your house and you didn't give me water for my feet, but she wet my feet with her tears and dried them with her hair. ⁴⁵You didn't greet me with a kiss, but from the moment she entered she hasn't stopped kissing my feet. ⁴⁶You didn't anoint my head with oil, but she anointed my feet with myrrh. ⁴⁷I tell you, her sins, which are many, have been forgiven, because she loves so much. Who is forgiven little, loves little."

⁴⁸He said to her, "Your sins have been forgiven." ⁴⁹Those at table with him began murmuring to one another, "Who is this who can even forgive sins?" ⁵⁰Jesus said to the woman, "Your faith has saved you. Go in peace."

Luke's Story

The story of the woman with the alabaster jar of perfume in Luke does not seem to be dependent on Mark. Luke has set his story early in the Gospel and has skipped Mark's story of the anointing at Bethany. No doubt Luke realized he had a different version of Mark's anointing at Bethany.

Luke's story is very different. It may be a patched-together controversy, for it includes amazement over Jesus' declaration of pardon—"Who is this who can even forgive sins?"—similar to the crowd reaction when Jesus forgives the paralytic. And it has reference to an alabaster jar, as does Mark. But whereas Mark has an anointing of Jesus' head, a coronation of sorts, here in Luke (and in John) the woman anoints Jesus' feet. There is no moral debate over the cost of the perfume or its value, if sold, to the poor. Instead, the woman's moral standing seems to be the issue.

The woman is splendidly excessive. She is a lover. With Jesus stretched out, reclining at table, the woman comes behind him and leaning over wets his feet with her tears, and wipes them with her hair. She kisses his feet and then perfumes them with myrrh. Jesus' host, Simon, is embarrassed and disturbed: "If he were any kind of prophet, he'd have spotted her, seeing what sort of woman was touching him."

Jesus' answer is to tell a little parable of a creditor who forgives debtors, one of whom owes twenty thousand dollars and the other two hundred. "Who," Jesus asks, "will love him the most?" Simon acknowledges the larger debtor. Then Jesus lines out the contrast: "I walked into your house and you didn't give me water for my feet, but she wet my feet with her tears and dried them with her hair. You didn't greet me with a kiss, but from the moment she entered she hasn't stopped kissing my feet. You didn't anoint my head with oil, but she anointed my feet with myrrh." Then Jesus announces his final formula: Those forgiven much, love much. Those forgiven little, love little. By implication, Simon is forgiven little.

Is There a Controversy?

The passage discloses the usual structure of a controversy. Simon thinks to himself, "If he were any kind of prophet, he'd have spotted her, seeing what sort of woman was touching him. She's a sinner!" This thought voices a question: "What kind of prophet so lacks moral discernment?"

In Luke, Jesus is often a mind reader. So Jesus, psyching Simon out, poses a parable along with a question: "Two persons owed money to the same creditor; one owed twenty thousand dollars and the other two hundred. When they couldn't pay, he forgave them both. So which one will love him the most?"

Jesus concludes his words to Simon with a pronouncement: "I tell you, her sins, which are many, have been forgiven, because she loves so much. Who is forgiven little, loves little." More tersely, here's the formula: Who is forgiven much, loves much. Who is forgiven little, loves little.

Chapter Eight

The Controversial Jesus

Conflict stories are hard to preach. Almost all of them are products of an early Christianity struggling for identity between a Jewish heritage and Gentile possibilities. Debates, accusations, dismissals—the period was filled with painful contention. In many cases, the contentiousness was written back into the stories of Jesus. As a result, many of the conflict stories are quite contrived. And yes, many seem unnecessarily combative with regard to Jewish opponents. Somehow we must manage to adjust the stories and at the same time preach their true gospel message. A daunting homiletic task.

We have two projects:

1. We must rediscover a Jesus to redeem the stories.
2. We must develop a homiletic to preach them.

Jesus in the Conflict Stories

At the outset, let us underscore the obvious: Jesus was a Jew. The God he worshiped was the unspoken, YHWH, God of Israel, "whose name be blessed." Jesus was circumcised as an infant. He grew up in a small village, perhaps populated with Hasmonean descendants and thus religiously conservative. We can assume his family ate kosher, observed hours of prayer, Sabbath regulations, and those special days—Yom Kippur and Passover—that undergird Jewish life. In sum, Jesus was brought up as a faithful Jew.

As for Jesus' education, instruction was provided by the village. While archaeologists have found no evidence of a separate school or synagogue building in Nazareth,[1] certainly education would have been provided for children in the village, as well as an ordered religious life. Jesus appears to be familiar with Jewish scriptural tradition. Did he work with his father in construction? Possibly. Sepphoris, the provincial capital, was next door to Nazareth, and Herod Antipas, the appointed ruler, was hiring huge numbers of construction workers at the time.

We can suppose that when Jesus was around nineteen, he was attracted by the apocalyptic, renewal preaching of John the Baptist. Jesus was baptized, and for a while, he seems to have been one of John's disciples. Sometime after John's murder by Herod Antipas, Jesus moved to Capernaum, gathered his own disciples, and with them began preaching, teaching, and healing in the villages of Galilee.

His message was an announcement of God's coming new order, when the poor would be raised up, the hungry fed, the powerless empowered, and those who grieve for the way of the world would rejoice. Evidently, he called people to live in God's coming new order ahead of time. Jesus welcomed his followers to meals that may have symbolized the promised eschatological feast on Mount Zion (Isa. 25:6–10). The author of Matthew seems to have supposed that Jesus' message was thematically the same as John's, namely, an apocalyptic call to repentance, but Luke 7:33–34 draws a line between the two figures: "John the Baptist came not eating bread or drinking wine, and you said, 'He's crazy'; the son of humanity came eating and drinking, and you say, 'He's a glutton and a wino.'" While John called converts to a baptism of repentance, apparently Jesus did not baptize but instead welcomed followers to table. So though both John and Jesus announced that an eschatological new order was on the way, they seem to have called for somewhat different responses. But both men anticipated an end to the present age with the arrival of God's new order. And both may be labeled "restorationist," for they were urgently seeking to renew Israel's covenant obedience to God.

We may not portray Jesus as antinomian. Jesus was not opposed to the commandments given on Mount Sinai. If the so-called Sermon on the Mount is any gauge of Jesus' teaching, he upheld the commandments rigorously and, if anything, urged followers to better the commandments in their righteousness. In Matthew 5 there is a specific statement, "Don't think I have come to undercut the law" (v. 17), followed by an exacting defense of the statutes of the law. Then, in the so-called antitheses (vv. 21–48), Jesus cites the ancient commandments and then demands his followers exceed them in their righteousness. The law of God is in no way subverted by Jesus.

Moreover, in Matthew 6 he upholds the usual Jewish pattern of piety, namely, almsgiving, fasting, and prayer. Yes, he warns against ostentatious praying in public, but he does so as a Jewish man of prayer. Again, though Jesus condemns showy almsgiving, he supports true generosity toward the poor. And while he advises those who fast not to advertise their fasting, he certainly doesn't condemn fasting per se. Thus, we cannot picture Jesus as opposed to the law or critical of usual Jewish ritual piety. Instead, we must search the issues involved in each of the conflict stories. In doing so, we must never picture Jesus as anything but a respectful Jew debating issues with other devout Jewish colleagues. Remember, Mark deliberately pictures Jesus as confrontational by retrojecting harsh conflicts back into the biblical record. Mark is no doubt overdrawing a contentious image of Jesus. To set the record straight, we should begin by insisting that Jesus was a faithful Jew dedicated to YHWH, the holy God of Israel.

But if Jesus was a faithful Jew, why do we have conflict stories? Why does Jesus seem to duke it out verbally with Pharisees and scribes? Actually, Jesus and the Pharisees were both dedicated to renewing the covenant faithfulness of Israel, and, to push the matter further, both he and the Pharisees sought a righteousness exceeding the law. We could argue that Jesus always put neighbor love forward as the true interpreter of God's law. But, obviously, Jesus' position is not that simple. Jesus was concerned with neighbor love, but he did not pit Leviticus 19:18 against Deuteronomy 6:4–9, the Shema. Such a division, with one side of the Great Commandment against the other, is quite unthinkable. Jesus was a pious child of God. He could not step out of his faith into an unexamined commitment to neighbor love that might banish the awesome mystery of God. Jesus was not a one-man Ethical Culture Society. We are dealing with a more profound pattern of faith than can be summed up by turning Leviticus 19:18 into a banner.

A solution: We must take Jesus' new-order preaching seriously. Most biblical translations use "kingdom" language, but clearly Jesus was talking about a new social order, indeed God's new order that he believed was on the way. Like the prophets Amos, Hosea, Isaiah, Micah, and Zechariah, Jesus envisioned a peaceful world, a *shalom*, in which human beings are devoted to serving one another, a world with no more poverty, hunger, injustice, ungoverned greed, or armed conflict. The world he envisioned is described by his Beatitudes. Jesus' social dream of God's new order is the backdrop for all his parables, and the cutting edge of his teachings. Inevitably, his new-order vision prompts disagreements with opponents in the conflict stories.

We must be careful not to read Jesus as a modern utopian futurist. Utopian thought begins with hints of human achievement and then, by enlarging them, projects a triumphant superworld. No wonder sci-fi utopias these days are jam-packed with technological wonders and superbrainy human beings. But, inevitably, every utopian dream founders on the hard fact of our persistent human sinfulness. Years ago the New York World's Fair featured a building that put visitors back into the nineteenth century—complete with cobblestone streets, gaslights, and carriages—but then via a dark tunnel let them step through time and come out in the world of the future, which featured bubble cars, glass skyscrapers, and rocket ships. Within the first month, someone had a purse snatched in the "World of Tomorrow." Jesus was realistic: human beings are fallen and will always corrupt their utopian projects. Jesus' vision is not utopian but eschatological; he is word-painting an impressionistic portrait of God's ultimate world.

Basileia (often translated "kingdom") is an end-term notion that Jesus uses to depict the human social world God intends. He prays fervently, "Your kingdom come, your will be done," which might be translated, "You, make your kingdom come; you, make your will be done." When we recite Jesus' prayer, we do not suppose for a moment that human energies can accomplish God's purposes. We are finite, sinful, and, when it comes to kingdom building, hopelessly incompetent. But the prayer does suggest that, in spite of our recalcitrant human nature, a wonderfully innovative God is striving to bring about ultimate purposes among us—"Your will be done." Thus *basileia,* God's intended social order, is a "happening" in which we live and at the same time an eschatological future-perfect coming toward us. Analyze the parables of Jesus: half seem shaped by a future-oriented eschatology, while the other half appear to suggest a new order forming among us now.[2] The mix is not surprising, because the God of the eschatological future is our God *now.* Thus, Jesus' talk of *basileia* is always both an eschatological ultimate and a present-tense mystery.

If, as C. H. Dodd insists, all Jesus' parables are kingdom parables,[3] must we not argue that behind all of Jesus' epigrammatic conflict-story sayings is a similar vision of God's new order, the coming *basileia?* Scribal wisdom seems to be generated by prudence and worthy piety, both designed for here and now. But Jesus is looking beyond the immediate world at hand to the horizon of God's promised new order, as well as to the possibility of human communities striving to live as new-order citizens ahead of time. If Jesus seems outraged by regulations that prevent healing a crippled man, surely it's because he envisions a world where the handicapped are not only healed but welcomed. And if he resents exclusions on the part of an exclusive few, surely it's because he sees God's new order drawing into itself all God's children. Conflict stories, no less than parables, are all about the coming realm of God.

Jesus and the Poor

If we are to understand Jesus, we must also acknowledge his social context. Generally, Jesus appears to align himself with the poor. He and his disciples seem to preach in a circuit of Galilean villages and not in Herod Antipas's showcase cities: Sepphoris and, later, Tiberias. Rural Galilee was in some economic distress. People were being taxed toward poverty and farmers were losing property to land brokers in the cities, property they believed God had given their forefathers. Some were ending up as sharecroppers on land that once had been their own. In addition, the tax burden was extreme. There were taxes to cover the substantial annual tribute to Rome, and taxes to support Herod Antipas's overambitious city building program, which included luxurious Roman manor houses amid Roman style public buildings, arenas, and theaters.[4] There was also the requisite temple tax, with the prospect of a lavish temple building program. On top of everything else, there were all sorts of extraneous tolls imposed somewhat randomly. The result was that people were tumbling into bankruptcy and bandits roved trade routes raiding unwary travelers.[5] Why had the province not rebelled? Perhaps because some decades earlier more than a thousand protesting Galileans were publically crucified all at once—a blunt, bloody message from Rome to be told and retold in the province of Galilee.

Though Jesus may have visited in homes of the wealthy, for example, Zacchaeus and Simon the leper, for the most part he and his disciples seem to have moved among the village people of Galilee. They preached a *basileia* vision, urging folk to live faithfully in God's coming empire even if, overtly, they were no-account subjects under Roman domination. Jesus was leading a liberation movement, as defined by Isaiah 61:1–2, preaching

> joy to the humble,
> binding for the wounded heart,
> release to the captives,
> liberation to the imprisoned,
> and proclaiming a year of God's favor.

If food laws seemed to be a rich privilege and a burden for the poor, Jesus feasted with the poor. His vision of *basileia* was inclusive and no doubt disturbing to "gated-community" wealth. Why is context important? Though Jesus proclaimed God's new order, the nature of this new order implied an over-against critique of his current social order.

Jesus' awareness of his social context shows up in the Beatitudes. In God's new order the poor will be raised up, the hungry fed, the powerless empowered, and peacemakers honored. But the first phrase in every Beatitude implies that right now the opposite is true, scathingly true. Social orders can create poverty, hunger, social helplessness, warfare, and grief. Ours certainly does. Galilee, with a huge disparity between wealth in Herod's cities and poverty elsewhere, was also a picture of social injustice. The contrast is written in the rhetoric of the Beatitudes. Social injustice is an underlying, unspoken issue in conflict stories as well.

The Freedom of Jesus

Anyone who reads the Gospels is bound to be struck by Jesus' astonishing freedom. He does not seem to be inhibited by inner rigidities. There is no sense of guilt on display. Jesus seems quite free from the constraints of what we call "public opinion"; evidently he didn't feel he must either conform to social pressures or compulsively defy them. Further, he is depicted as having chased the devil by refusing stock messianic temptations—to be a bread provider, a miracle worker, or a power politician—and thus being free from their tug and pull.

Often preachers explain Jesus' freedom as being free in the Spirit from the burden of the law. But such a reading poses an impossible theological conundrum. Jesus' spirit was surely one with the free Spirit of God, but, please note, the same God who established the law. Should we then suggest that God's Spirit can be opposed to God's law? Never! We can say that God's Spirit may enable us to fulfill the law, but we cannot make law an enemy to be overthrown by a clap-hands, free God-given Spirit. Above all, we must never say that the law is a Jewish proclivity but that we Gentiles have been liberated from the law by the Spirit of God. I fear that such a proposal has been preached more often than we might suppose.

Sometimes Christians have announced that love is the fulfilling of the law and, further, that love can make legal restriction quite unnecessary. We have seen that Jeremiah promises a "new covenant" in which the law will be scribbled on human hearts so humans will need no further instruction, because everyone will "know the Lord" (Jer. 31:31–34). Jeremiah is not alone in his hope. The same renewed covenant theme shows up in Isaiah (49:8) as well as Ezekiel (34:25) and Hosea (2:18). As for the idea of an outpouring of the Spirit on all Israel, enabling free obedience, such an outpouring is anticipated in Isaiah (32:15; 44:3), Ezekiel (39:29), and, of course, Joel (2:28–29). The Spirit is a Spirit of faithful obedience so that all Israel will do God's law naturally. Christians read the prophecies and imagine that they are fulfilled in Jesus and in Christian communities after the wondrous day of Pentecost. But, led by the Spirit, a Spirit of love, are Christians now free from the law?

Psychiatrist Karen Horney wrote about internal "oughts" that can be crushing and from which human beings should be liberated.[6] Crushing "oughts" are pathological in extreme obsessive-compulsive disorders, but Horney was not discussing the pathological. Rather, she was referring to oughts most people struggle with to some degree, particularly as we emerge from childhood and pass through adolescence. Most of us internalize oughts, often unexamined, formed in us by family standards and/or by social disapprobations that can trouble most human beings even after they reach adult years. Of course, internalizing oughts is not all bad. We do so and thus become good citizens in society. But what about those internalized rules we barely recognize, inhibitions that prevent us from living in cheerful freedom or loving those who love us? From such internal bondage Christianity promises liberation. The good news of God's justifying love can set us free. The phrase "saved by grace through faith" applies to such inner bondage. But can we extend the notion of freedom from internalized "oughts" to mean that we are liberated from the laws that govern our social orders?

The Reformers, Luther and Calvin, claimed that we are delivered from a burden of guilt because of God's love; they preached Paul's gospel that while we were sinners, indeed sinning, Christ died for us. Thus, we are justified by God's free grace alone (Rom. 5:1–8). But both reformers insisted that the Ten Commandments still govern the human social world, and Calvin, week after week, following a bold declaration of pardon, had his congregation hear the Ten Commandments as a guide for holy living. In God's mercy we may be free from the self-accusing "oughts," but we are still guided by the covenant commandments given Moses. So though we are justified by grace, we are still judged under the law.

The Ten Commandments are written for our social good. They are sane and helpful. They call us to worship the one true God. The second commandment turns us from idolatries. The third can free us from claiming God's endorsement of our nation's economic system or religious practices. We honor the Sabbath day with gratitude because no one should be forced to work a seven-day week. We honor fathers and mothers by designing social programs to secure their needs. We know we cannot kill and be part of a stable society, nor can we be sexually aggressive, preying on other people's husbands or wives. We cannot steal without disrespecting neighbors. And we should never bear false testimony against neighbors. The final commandment, against coveting, seems to condemn the advertising industry ("Madison Avenue" doesn't exactly perch on moral heights) but, nonetheless, is designed to protect our neighbors from us, that is, from covetous invasions. Though they are basic, the Ten Commandments project a social order in which we can live together in peace and with mutual respect.

Because the Ten Commandments are basic, in a way they are minimal, Israel had to enact secondary laws to interpret and sustain the commandments. No wonder that in Israel there was both a written and an oral Torah. The internalization of hundreds of subordinate dos and don'ts in Jewish culture or in any human society may well be a burden. There were more than six hundred subordinate laws in Jewish society. In conflict stories, Jesus never rejects basic covenant commandments, but sometimes he takes issue with misapplied restrictions that can seem disconnected from the covenant, or with oral traditions that seem to subvert neighbor love. But his taking issue usually occurs over matters still open and up for debate among faithful Jews. Jesus is not attempting to tip over the whole weight of Jewish tradition, the oral Torah, or cancel the useful guidance of subordinate laws. He is not rejecting his own Jewishness or his faith in the one, holy God of Israel.

But Jesus certainly seems free. He was free, as were the prophets, to call Israel to covenant faithfulness. Above all, he was free, as he was grasped by a vision of God's coming new order, a social order that could fulfill all the covenant promises of God. He was also free in his profound bond with other human beings, reflected in his calling himself a "son of humanity." He enacted neighbor love and bridled against any suggestions that appeared to inhibit neighbor love. God's new order was a vision of human interinvolvement: we human beings will serve neighbors and neighbors will serve us in a kind of bemused but glad exchange under the blessing of God our true Parent. In sum, Jesus was free, for he was already living in the freedom of God's coming new order.

The Impatience of Jesus

On occasion, Jesus seems to flash with anger. There is the "woe to you" condemnation of three cities—Chorazin, Bethsaida, and Capernaum—whose residents saw miracles but would not repent. What's more, Jesus adds a cutting comment, remarking that pagan strongholds Tyre and Sidon would have repented! Matthew has attached the passage to talk of John the Baptist, whereas Luke patches in the same material after the disciples return from their mission. Some scholars suspect the tirade is not Jesus' material but reflects a postresurrection Galilean composition. There is another, still harsher denunciation of scribes and Pharisees in Matthew 23:1–6, but again, except for a few verses, many scholars consider the passage suspect. Most of the material is found only in Matthew, and the style is distinctively Matthean, so, though the words are placed on Jesus' lips, they probably reflect harsh controversies within Matthew's own troubled situation. Evidently Matthew's peculiar "Jesus synagogue" has drawn persecution from traditional synagogues in the area. His zealous critics may well have been both scribes and Pharisees.

Though these "woe to you" passages appear to be later additions, undoubtedly Jesus was critical of scribes and Pharisees. His famous phrase "Judge not" is a clue. Interpreters usually try to weaken Jesus' words, suggesting that, after all, human beings do have to judge, assessing others if only for self-protection. But the command is sweeping. There are many stories in which Jesus is rankled by righteous, or usually self-righteous, condemnation of others. For example, there is the strange, perhaps misplaced story of the adulterous woman in John 8:1–11.[7] The woman has been caught in the act of adultery. She is hauled off and stood up before a crowd. The scribes and Pharisees quiz Jesus: "Moses commanded us to stone such a woman. What do you say?" For awhile Jesus says nothing. He seems to be looking down while idly scribbling in the dirt, perhaps not wishing to add to the woman's embarrassment. Finally he straightens up: "Whoever's without sin among you, let him throw the first stone." One by one the crowd dissolves. "Where are they?" asks Jesus. "Has no one condemned you?" She answers, "No one, sir." "Neither do I," says Jesus. "Go on, and don't sin again."

Then there's a somewhat similar story involving a woman who disrupts a dinner party in the home of Simon the leper. She wets Jesus' feet with tears and wipes them with her hair, then she anoints his feet with costly myrrh. Simon, Jesus' host, is irate. He looks at Jesus, thinking, "If he were any kind of prophet, he'd have spotted her, seeing what sort of woman was touching him. She's a sinner!" Jesus traps Simon with a parable and then firmly discusses his lack of love. The same reaction seems on display in the story of Jesus' dining with "tax collectors and sinners." The scribes and Pharisees lift their eyebrows with displeasure. Then Jesus announces, "I didn't come to recruit the upright, but sinners." (The Jesus Seminar translates the phrase, "I didn't come to enlist religious folk but sinners.") The implication is that the accusers are self-righteous.

Another example of Jesus' admonition not to judge is the peculiar story in Luke 13:1–5. A crowd asks Jesus to name the sin of persons whom Pilate had recently executed, assuming that people who die tragically must have been sinners. Jesus goes after them: "Do you think they were the worst sinners in Galilee? No way, but unless you repent you will perish!" He draws the same conclusion with regard to eighteen people crushed by a tumbling tower at Siloam. "Do you think they were the worst sinners in Jerusalem? No way, but unless you repent you'll perish the same way." In both cases the crowd is judging sinners from the stance of their own assumed righteousness, and Jesus reacts. Though the Gospels tell us Jesus came preaching, "Repent, for God's new order is on the way!" (Mark 1:15), Luke 13 is about the only occasion when Jesus actually goes after listeners with the word "repent." Why? Because they were prejudging their neighbors and, in so doing, were usurping God's prerogative. Said Jesus, "Judge not."

There is another situation in which Jesus seems to get his back up. Several stories recount Jesus taking action to heal the sick or handicapped on the Sabbath day. Again, there may be the lurking assumption that physical disability or long-term illness is a punishment for sin. When such a person could be helped but Sabbath law prevents healing, Jesus is usually angry. Later the Rabbis agreed with Jesus' position, but presumably in Jesus' own day the prohibition was sometimes imposed. If law prevents compassionate care one for another, then Jesus is quick to question such interpretation of the law.

There still may be another issue that seems to draw Jesus' irritation. When the law is read to prohibit a natural sharing of human pleasures, then Jesus tends to counter such interpretations. Thus, when disciples are reprimanded for the rather natural act of tasting kernels of wheat while they are moving through a wheat field, Jesus defends their altogether innocent human actions. Likewise, when his own disciples get in the way of children, Jesus intervenes. Enjoying the remarkable candor of free-spirited kids should be a natural pleasure.

These are not merely examples of Jesus being humane, nor are they acts of obedient neighbor love, of putting Leviticus 19:18 into action. Once again, what underlies all the stories is a Jesus who is looking toward God's new order and seeking to represent in action the new order ahead of time. The Ten Commandments, as Calvin noted, are prohibitions, that is, "shall nots," but they imply a social order envisioned by prophets and seers. Jesus was similarly far-sighted, for he expected the new order of God and, gripped by a vision of God's future, lived accordingly. His vision may have been apocalyptically abrupt or prophetically intense—such distinctions are gradations on a scale—but though he spoke in the style of a wise seer, he spoke with the passion of a man impatient for the renewal of all things in an imminent divinely designed social order.

Jesus: Judgment and Laughter

Does Jesus anticipate a coming judgment of God? Yes, absolutely. Anyone who looks toward the coming of God's new order assumes it will counter the corruptions of our present world. When John the Baptist preached, "Repent, God's *basileia* is on the way," he was calling Israel to change its usual ways of living. Passing through the waters of baptism, Israel was to become a new, faithful people of God, sealed against the coming judgment. Both John and Jesus were thinking of something bigger than a one-by-one personal conversion to God; their preaching had a social dimension, because the word *basileia* designates a new God-designed and installed social order. But to preach a new order of God is precisely a judgment on the old order it is to replace.

Matthew is convinced that Jesus and John preached the same message (Matt. 3:2; 4:17). But Jesus seemed to focus on the liberation in the coming new order, as represented by the Beatitudes. Nevertheless, if we look at the teachings of Jesus, the theme of God's judgment is certainly present. John called Israel to pass through the waters of baptism, waters of renewal, in advance of the coming fire of judgment. Did Jesus? At the outset, he did not baptize, though presumably he could have done so. And though the language of John is clearly distinguished by apocalyptic vigor—looking for the "wrath to come," with images of slashing down morally "barren trees" and consigning them to fire—Jesus seemed to speak a language closer to the wisdom tradition, with ethical concern, parables, epigrammatic style, and obvious wit. Jesus is abruptly critical at times; his one-liners aimed at the self-righteous are rough stuff. But usually Jesus is not strident, and sometimes in parables he can be downright funny. He often tells stories of rogues, and does so with a degree of affectionate bemusement that scarcely adds up to judgment. Nonetheless, his message of a coming *basileia* does imply the judgment of God on our present age. And, yes, Jesus definitely did use the suggestive metaphor of Gehenna.

But, overall, Jesus does not employ a rhetoric of threat. He does not billboard the wrath to come and then preach an intimidating "or else" gospel. Such a message would appeal to prudent self-interest, and such self-concern is not an adequate basis for the Christian life. What Jesus does do is invite us to become citizens of God's wondrous new order ahead of time. The coming new order is inevitable, but it is not hedged around with threat, at least not in Jesus' preaching. Ultimately, God's new order is great and good and, compared to our world, positively liberating. For power brokers and profit chasers, the message of a new order may be bad news, but for most of us confused, broken sinners, the new order, though scary, is graceful news indeed.

So how do we portray Jesus in the conflict stories? Above all, we must retain images of Jesus' Jewishness. If he is locked in dispute with scribes and Pharisees, we must not picture the scene as mortal combat, with our man Jesus against villainous opponents. These are in-family debates that, however strident, do not necessarily fracture family ties. Instead, Jesus is a free and visionary Jewish figure; his eye is on the coming future of God. He enjoys being with all sorts of folk. He does not foster exclusiveness but proclaims an open invitation to join God's coming new order. People can by choice exclude themselves, and people do, but Jesus does not. His vision of God's coming *basileia* is startlingly egalitarian.

Jesus was likeable. He had wit, energy, and compassion. In parables his humor comes through. Though humor doesn't show up in conflict stories, we should keep Jesus' humor in mind, for clearly a sense of humor is part of who he was. At times, Jesus' counterquestions can be sharp-edged, but his pronouncements are witty, epigrammatic, and thus memorable. Jesus was smart. He was an attractive leader who had an astonishing way with words. In the freedom of God, Jesus is free to love his neighbors even in the midst of conflict stories.

On Preaching the Conflict Stories

How do we preach the conflict stories? How can we design sermons faithful to the theological meaning of the texts yet be aware of the scandal of our inherited anti-Judaism? Anti-Judaism is a Christian problem, and conflict stories are clearly part of the problem. Therefore, we must preach them with care. The Gospel of Mark has shaped the stories as confrontations, but they must never be preached as win/lose engagements. Debates are scored by points, but except for occasional conflicts in which Jesus' opponents try to trap him with questions, the stories are not competitive debates. Images of a triumphant Jesus are not helpful, for his pronouncements are never gloating. Instead, we have described Jesus' pronouncements as "nonlegal waves toward the purposes of God." Because the language is nonlegal, Jesus and his opponents end up considering their particular conflict within a broader theological frame of reference. So can we.

At the outset, we must always look beneath the surface of the text, to discover the "theological field" in which the dialogue moves. There are matters of specific debate, but always there is a wider ethical controversy with regard to God's will and our responsibilities toward one another. The underlying theological fields are frequently perennial issues that are still with us today. Pronouncements that conclude the stories are designed to let us see contending issues within the grand purposes of God, namely, the coming of a reconciled new order.

Among the controversies are stories where the underlying issue is the circumscribing of our human relationships to family, or nation, or those morally approved. In these stories Jesus widens the definition of his family, approves the Syrophoenician woman, and enjoys a meal with tax collectors and sinners. Clearly, the attempt to circumscribe human affections is still a contemporary issue. There are also stories where the issue seems to be tension between ritual practices designed to guard the holiness of God and compassionate concern for neighbors in need. Among these are several Sabbath healing stories, which may speak to the social disapprobation experienced by AIDS victims in our own society. There are stories in which the basic issue seems to be religious authorization and/or free compassion. Can anyone forgive sins on God's behalf? Can anyone cast out demons? Can anyone in our churches serve and receive the Eucharist? Finally, there are issues over the nature of discipleship. Are children disciples? Can disciples be wealthy? Can disciples seek political power? Can disciples be divorced? The issues are perennial. Each story has particular details, but preachers must uncover the basic issues, most of which still trouble us.

I have said that the counterquestions disclose the mind-set of Jesus' questioners. They also define positions, often entirely legitimate positions that still divide religious communities. Just because Jesus may seem to be on one side of an issue does not mean that the other side cannot have sincere defenders. What's more, the sincere defenders are often us. Desire to respect the holiness of God with religious observance is clearly honorable. Therefore, we must not treat Jesus' counterquestions as attacks. They may define sides, but the sides are frequently legitimate positions. Above all, we must be careful that our Christian tendency to set free grace up against law does not deform the stories. The Pharisees' desire to extend the law of God to all areas of human life is a worthy notion. God's law is good, and we must respect defenders of the law. If Jesus asks, "What does Moses tell you?" he is not belittling the law, even though he may seek to set the law within God's purposes for the whole creation.

As for the pronouncements, I have described them as "waves toward the purposes of God." Thus, they move conflicts into theological consideration. The concise style of the pronouncements encourages exploration. Here again are some of the punch lines:

> "The Sabbath was made for humanity, not humanity for the Sabbath."
> "Give to Caesar, Caesar's; [but] give to God, God's."
> "Whoever does the will of God is my mother, brother, sister."
> "What God has joined together, let no one rip apart."
> "Whoever wants to be great among you must be your servant."
> "Who is forgiven little, loves little."
> "I didn't come to recruit the upright, but sinners."
> "No one puts new wine into old wineskins."
> "There is nothing from outside a person that can defile, but from inside a person are things that can defile."
> "Whoever will not accept God's rule like a child cannot enter the new order."
> "How hard it is for monied people to get into God's new order."
> "God is not a God of the dead, but of the living."

These are sweeping statements that invite consideration. We must try to explore their meaning, which, even when the word "God" is not included, is always theological. Every conflict story must perforce move Jesus and his conversation partners—namely, us—before the mystery of God's purposes for humanity. And, to Jesus, God's purposes are always defined by the images of a coming new order. "Whoever wants to be great among you must be your servant" is interpreted by Jesus' images of a social order in which we are all mutual servers. "How hard it is for monied people to get into God's new order" is interpreted by a beatitude: "Congratulations you poor, for yours is the kingdom of God." Obviously, if the poor are to be raised up, the wealthy must become hugely generous. How do preachers interpret the often enigmatic pronouncements? We set the words of each pronouncement before the horizon of God's coming new order.

Do you sense that the conflict stories provide a basis for sermon design? They do. Begin with the question being asked. If possible, you will demonstrate that the questioner—scribe, Pharisee, elder, Sadducee, or even Herodian—is asking a valid question. Usually, the question is very much alive—a question we ask in our churches. The counterquestion will give us a clue as to our own assumptions, positions we should understand and explore. Finally, the concluding pronouncement, often puzzling, can lead us into God's purposes for us and all humanity. The conflict stories show us how our sermons can move. Moreover, in their movement, the conflict stories can change our minds, which, after all, is their purpose.

In every sermon, we must picture Jesus not as an opponent but as a faithful Jew among faithful Jews debating open issues. At the same time, we can see Jesus addressing us in our religious communities, for almost always the issues involved are still live issues. Jesus helps resolve issues that trouble us by setting them within the horizon of "Your kingdom come." A vision of God's new order can transform conflict stories into gospel. Come, Jesus invites us, enter God's future now and become new people—brave, astonishing, and graceful.

A Special Problem: Law/Grace Preaching

Again and again, conflict stories have been preached under the rubric of law versus grace. In such sermons, law is regarded as an enemy of Christian freedom. If law is not an enemy, it is pictured as judgment that can reduce us to helpless sinners who cry for mercy. The pattern seems to be connected with an *ordo salutis*, a sequence of salvation, in which (a) we face the demands of the law (b) that force us to admit our hopeless locked-in-sin situation, so (c) we repent before God and (d) are able to receive the good news of free, justifying grace. The pattern seems to match Martin Luther's own struggle for God's approval. But, in spite of law/grace preaching, fixed patterns of salvation are seldom helpful homiletic designs. There is no doubt that some law/grace preaching ends up battering us sinners with demands of the law, demands that can dominate a sermon with mounting intensity while ministers keep an eye out for signs of heartfelt repentance in their bruised if somewhat dazed congregations. In such preaching, the law is always bad news from which we are saved by grace. Some preachers may suppose that the worse the news, the more sincere our cries for mercy.

What is the danger with such law/grace preaching? The good covenant law of God may become nothing more than a whip to lash the vagrant conscience of Christians who need a firm dose of repentance on a weekly basis? But stop and analyze the when's and where's of human repentance. Here are a few of the moments: We may be awed by the wonder of the world around us—sun in the morning, stars in the night—and sense that somehow we have not been as grateful as we should. Relaxed and alone, we can think back on our lives and be filled with a vague sense of somehow having failed. Lying awake at night beside the man or woman with whom we share a bed, we may realize his or her needs and know we have never expressed our love enough. Then there are fleeting moments when we know we should have said something but were silent. In middle-class America these days, repentance seems to be occasional, an unexpected discomfort that passes almost as soon as it is felt. Seldom does such momentary guilt happen to us under the strictures of God's law, even when the category of law is broadly conceived. Yes, an offhand sense of "ought" does seem to be involved, but it is an almost absent-minded ought. For many middle-class Americans, any oughts are momentary, felt, then filed away on the fringes of consciousness. We go on living without even recognizing the free grace in which we all live and move and have our being.

In many cases, what gets us is not recited law but awe or gratitude that prompts residual religious feelings. Instead of finding God at the end of an *ordo salutis*, we may begin with God known in a moment of delight and then sense our undeserving selves. There may be times when we are swept with a sense of sin before the demands of almighty God. But as a repeated homiletic strategy, first the judgment and then the good news of justification, the pattern may wear thin to the average pew sitter. Quite simply, it doesn't always align with the astonishing variety of human religious experience.

More disturbing, law/grace preaching may treat the law of God as something to be rid of, to be replaced in Christian lives by cheerful grace. The law was a gift to humanity from the covenant-keeping God, a gift given to and through Israel. Thus, antinomian preaching is always a mistake. While antinomian impulses are bound to appeal to our lurking adolescence, Christian preaching should help us grow up. We are free in the Spirit, free to embrace God's good law without noticing it is law. But are we ever free from the law? No, because we are never free from the God of our lives.

Undeserved justification by God is a grand Protestant gospel message. And we receive the message by God-given faith. Though unacceptable, we have been accepted.[8] But here are some caveats: First, the famous phrase "justification by grace through faith" should be parsed with care. We often shorten the phrase to "justification by faith," as if our faith has earned justification and, in fact, has exempted us from ultimate judgment. In such a scheme, believing has become a work, a work that abolishes all moral considerations.

Before God, we suppose, believing is all. Second, we are justified by God's free, undeserved love—"amazing grace" indeed. Who can believe such wondrous love? No one. But God forms faith in us to embrace the wonder. If justification is by grace alone, so also, miraculously, is our receptive faith. Third, though we are justified by God, ultimately we will be judged by God on the basis of works. Will we have to see ourselves in the undistorted lens of God's truth? That would be fierce judgment indeed. Our hope is that the God who judges is also our justifier.

The secret meaning of every conflict story is not law versus grace, with grace a guaranteed winner. If the law is involved, and Jesus appears critical, the law itself is never the problem. Rather, there may be a misapplication of law involved. The law that requires us to keep the Sabbath day holy is a good gift, but is the law properly applied if it prevents God's own power of healing? Thus, in the repeated conflicts over Sabbath law, we must honor the law, but, if critical, be critical of its misapplication. If law inhibits God's own compassionate goodness, then Jesus is not critical of the law per se but of a misappropriation of the law. The distinction is not nitpicky, but homiletically crucial. The same logic applies to laws of ritual cleanliness. Such laws not only provide for good health, but they may be useful ways to honor the holiness of God. Again, the purity laws can be applied overscrupulously, cramping moments of splendid human interaction. But the law itself is never our enemy; the interpretation or misapplication of law is the usual problem.

But do we preach grace? Absolutely. As Karl Barth reputedly said, "Everything is grace." Does grace liberate us from ourselves? Yes. Does grace liberate us from the law? No. Grace can lead us into an all but unnoticed fulfilling of the law, of our better selves, and of God's purpose for our lives. Amazing grace indeed!

Conflict Stories: They Are Us

I have suggested that the conflict stories are about us. We still debate similar issues in our churches. Deeper still, the conflict stories can represent the struggles that human beings may experience within themselves. The preacher's problem is how to show us to ourselves in the stories.

Almost all the conflict stories seem to involve a concern for the holiness of God and the humanness of humanity. I have argued that in the so-called Great Commandment (Matt. 22:34–40), the Greek word *homoia* usually translated "like" could be rendered "same," implying that loving God (the Shema) is fulfilled in loving neighbors. But more often than not, within ourselves we set one side of the commandment against the other. How can we love God with-

out foregoing our other human loves? For some Christians the choice seems
to set St. John of the Cross against Dame Julian of Norwich. For John, loving
God required him to abnegate all other loves, but for Julian, God was loved
through her other loves.[9] (Jean-Paul Sartre drew the line more harshly: either
we deny God with Nietzschean courage so as to love humanity, or, cleaving
to God, we reject humanity altogether, including our own humanity).[10] The
choice is something we may sense within ourselves. Conflict stories get to us
because, frequently, they happen within us.

We must not denigrate our concern for the holiness of God. Ritual acknowledgments of God are profoundly necessary particularly in a culture where
blasé disinterest in God is often considered fashionable. So we can bow our
heads and say grace at table. We may genuflect before entering a pew. We can
stand to honor God, or humble ourselves by bowing down. We can respond
to Scripture by touching brow, lips, and heart—may God's word be in my
mind, on my lips, in my heart! Such ritual acknowledgments are not Romish
inventions created to annoy free-church sensibilities; they can be useful ways
to respect the holiness of a holy God. The impulse to do such ritual actions is
a profound part of many lives. They show up in conflict stories as ritual hand
washing, respecting the Sabbath day, or refusing to break bread with blatant
racketeers. If, on occasion, Jesus seems to act in opposition, he is not being
cavalier about the holiness of God or trying to debunk empty rituals. We
should be clear that Jesus stands in awe before the holiness of God. After all,
did he not teach us to pray, "hallowed be your name"?

If we preachers are wise, we will empathize with the Pharisees, evoking
our own respect for the holiness of God. If we grasp a genuine concern to protect the Sabbath from erosion, we will preach the conflict stories not only with
sensitivity but with meaning. After all, see what has happened to Sundays. If
there is league football in our cities, or sales in our stores, church attendance
plunges. Ever so gradually, the holy day is no longer holy except as a form of
odd nostalgia. The Pharisees were properly concerned. And if we are sincere
about revering the holy God, inwardly we should be too. A good preacher will
find dimensions within us where the strange once-in-a-while shiver of God's
presence is still felt. Then and there, we must contend with the Jesus who contends within us.

Preaching the Gospel in Conflict Stories

Some years ago, in a little book about Christology, I drew a distinction.[11] I
suggested that we know Jesus Christ in two ways. First, we know him as a
character in the Bible. The Bible, from Genesis to Revelation, is a story of

God and humanity. The story is peopled with characters—Abraham, Sarah, Isaac, Jacob, Leah, Moses, the prophets, the sages, and, of course, Jesus of Nazareth. To know Jesus within the story is to meet a human being under God. But we seem to know Jesus in another way: I used the term "Living Symbol." In our preaching we hold him up before the mystery of God. We say that we know God and pray to God "through Jesus Christ." Apparently Jesus has become a symbol who mediates the present nature of God. But as a symbol for God, Jesus seems to take on a kind of divinity for us. So Jesus of Nazareth in our preaching is both a character in the story of God and humanity, and a disclosure symbol for God-with-us.

Let's apply this pattern to the conflict-pronouncement stories. All the conflict stories occur within the larger story of the Gospels, and the Gospels happen within the whole sweep of the biblical story, a story of God and humanity. So, in a way, the conflict stories begin with Jesus of Nazareth as a human being quizzed by other human beings. Question and counterquestion seem entirely natural human activities—Jews debating religious issues in public. To grasp the questions and counterquestions, we turn to historical research. What were the issues and why were they issues? We may discover a kind of double meaning if the issues seem still viable nowadays. What is the shape of the issues in our churches today?

The pronouncements, however, seem different. The instant we turn toward the purposes of God, we step into the gospel message. Suddenly, Jesus is not simply a smart human being arguing with other smart human beings; he becomes the mediator of God's purposes, indeed, of God's nature. We have seen that the pronouncements are never legal in character. They penetrate the law to the gracious, loving, author of law. God's good purposes shaped the law, and Jesus' pronouncements open to us God's purposes for all humanity. The final pronouncements are frequently mysterious or paradoxical. We have to puzzle them out not only by setting them within the story of God and Israel but by reading them in the light of Jesus' life, death, and resurrection. In the pronouncements, Jesus, the living symbol, discloses the mystery of God-with-us.

If you want to preach conflict stories, above all, you must picture a Jewish Jesus who has grown up eating kosher, remembering the Sabbath day, and annually observing Yom Kippur and Passover. You must picture Jesus with Israel's story scribbled in his mind. Imagine a witty Jew with a brilliant feel for language and a devout sense of the unseen God-with-us. Above all, catch the glory of God's promised future reflected in his eyes.

Notes

INTRODUCTION

1. In presenting this material, I have modified examples previously used in my *Homiletic: Moves and Structures* (Philadelphia: Fortress Press, 1987), 298–300.

2. See Martin Albertz, *Die synoptischen Streitgespräche: Ein Beitrag zur Formengeschichte des Urchristentums* (Berlin: Trowitzsch, 1921).

3. See Rudolf Bultmann, *The History of the Synoptic Tradition*, rev. ed., trans. John Marsh (New York: Harper & Row, 1968), and Martin Dibelius, *From Tradition to Gospel* (New York: Charles Scribner's Sons, 1934).

4. See Vincent Taylor, *The Formation of the Gospel Tradition*, 2nd ed. (London: Macmillan, 1964).

5. Arland J. Hultgren, *Jesus and His Adversaries: The Form and Function of the Conflict Stories in the Synoptic Tradition* (Minneapolis: Augsburg, 1979), 39.

6. David Buttrick, "A Fearful Pulpit, a Wayward Land," in *What's the Matter with Preaching Today?* ed. Mike Graves (Louisville, KY: Westminster John Knox Press, 2004), 17–50.

CHAPTER ONE: THE SHAPE OF THE FORM

1. See Arland J. Hultgren, *Jesus and His Adversaries* (Minneapolis: Augsburg, 1979), chaps. 3–4.

2. Joanna Dewey, *Markan Public Debate: Literary Technique, Concentric Structure, and Theology in Mark 2:1–3:6*, SBL Dissertation Series 48 (Chico, CA: Scholars Press, 1980).

3. David Daube, "Four Types of Question," in *The New Testament and Rabbinic Judaism* (Peabody, MA: Hendrickson Publishers, 1998), 159–69.

4. H. Richard Niebuhr, *Christ and Culture* (New York: Harper, 1954).

CHAPTER TWO: PROBLEMS, PROBLEMS, PROBLEMS

1. Rudolf Bultmann, *The History of the Synoptic Tradition*, rev. ed., trans. John Marsh (New York: Harper & Row, 1968), 61.

2. Vincent Taylor, *The Formation of the Gospel Tradition*, 2nd ed. (London: Macmillan, 1964), 26.

3. See David E. Aune, "Pseudepigraphy," in *The Westminster Dictionary of New Testament and Early Christian Literature* (Louisville, KY: Westminster John Knox Press, 2003), 387–88.

4. Some of the material and language in the following two paragraphs have been drawn (and then modified and expanded) from an earlier article I wrote, "On Preaching from Romans 9–11," in *Ex Auditu* 4 (1989): 113–22.

5. See Rosemary Radford Ruether, *Faith and Fratricide: The Theological Roots of Anti-Semitism* (New York: Seabury Press, 1974), which served up the issue of anti-Judaism in the Christian tradition for open discussion.

6. For example, see Paula Fredrickson, "The Birth of Christianity and the Origins of Christian Anti-Judaism," in *Jesus, Judaism, and Christian Anti-Judaism: Reading the New Testament after the Holocaust*, ed. Paula Fredrickson and Adele Reinhartz (Louisville, KY: Westminster John Knox Press, 2002), 8–30; and the rather conservative defense in Robert A. Guelich, "Anti-Semitism and/or Anti-Judaism in Mark?".

in *Anti-Semitism and Early Christianity*, ed. Craig A. Evans and Donald A. Hagner (Minneapolis: Fortress Press, 1993), 80–101.

7. For example, see Joseph B. Tyson, "Anti-Judaism in the Critical Study of the Gospels," *Anti-Judaism and the Gospels,* ed. William R. Farmer (Harrisburg, PA: Trinity Press International, 1999), 219–51.

8. See Douglas R. A. Hare, *The Theme of Jewish Persecution in the Gospel according to St. Matthew* (Cambridge: Cambridge University Press, 1967); and, more recently, Amy-Jill Levine, "Anti-Judaism and the Gospel of Matthew," in Farmer, ed., *Anti-Judaism and the Gospels,* 9–36.

9. See J. Louis Martyn, *History and Theology in the Fourth Gospel* (Nashville: Abingdon Press, 1968), part 1.

10. See John Dominic Crossan, *Who Killed Jesus? Exposing the Roots of Anti-Semitism in the Gospel Story of the Death of Jesus* (San Francisco: HarperSanFrancisco, 1995), for a strong argument that Rome killed Jesus but that the Gospels, appealing to a Gentile audience, shifted blame to Jewish leaders.

11. See Amy-Jill Levine, "Matthew, Mark, and Luke: Good News or Bad?" in Fredrickson and Reinhartz, eds., *Jesus, Judaism, and Christian Anti-Judaism*, 77–98.

12. Arthur Miller, *After the Fall* (New York: Bantam Books, 1965), 1, 21, and 162.

13. For recent discussion of Galatians, see Mark D. Nanos, ed., *The Galatians Debate: Contemporary Issues in Rhetorical and Historical Interpretation* (Peabody, MA: Hendrickson Publishers, 2002), in particular Paula Fredrickson, "Judaism, the Circumcision of Gentiles, and Apocalyptic Hope: Another Look at Galatians 1 and 2," 261–81; and the exceptional essays in part 3: "The Galatian Situation(s)."

14. In 1543, three years before his death, Martin Luther, age 60, wrote *On the Jews and Their Lies* (see *Luther's Works*, vol. 47, trans. Martin H. Bertram [Philadelphia: Fortress Press, 1955]) advising that Jewish synagogues and schools be burned, that the houses of Jews be destroyed, that their prayer books and Talmudic writings be taken from them, and that their rabbis be forbidden to teach. "This is to be done," wrote Luther, "in honor of our Lord and Christendom" (268–69).

15. This survey of Hebrew Scripture texts was modeled after similar charts provided by the Jesus Seminar and by Walter Wink.

16. The significance of the Ezekiel material has recently been revived in Walter Wink's intriguing *The Human Being: Jesus and the Enigma of the Son of Man* (Minneapolis: Fortress Press, 2002).

17. Douglas R. A. Hare, *The Son of Man Tradition* (Minneapolis: Fortress Press, 1990), is particularly strong on Mark's use of the term. See chap. 6.

18. For a blunt warning that Jewish communities may be fearful of Christians who come to dialogue, see Steven Leonard Jacobs, "Jewish-Christian Relations: After the Shoah," in *War or Words*, ed. Donald W. Musser and D. Dixon Sutherland (Cleveland: Pilgrim Press, 2005), 58–74.

19. The act of standing for the reading of the Gospel goes back to Byzantine worship when, in a dramatic liturgy, the Gospels were paraded through a church to symbolize the coming of Christ. The custom does not mean that the Gospels should be preached 75 percent of the time. Lectionaries provide three readings so that preachers may preach across the full range of biblical books. Obviously, the letters of Paul declare the gospel message as much as the Gospels. Because the God of Israel is our God, so do many great readings from the Hebrew Bible. If we never reach beyond the Gospels, we slide into a "Jesus cult" in which the word "God" could disappear.

CHAPTER THREE: PROBLEM SOLVING

1. Here I draw on Joel Marcus, "The Scribes and the Pharisees," in *Mark 1–8: A New Translation with Introduction and Commentary* (New York: Doubleday, 2000), 519–24; Anthony Saldarini, *Pharisees, Scribes, and Sadducees in Palestinian Society* (Grand Rapids: Wm. B. Eerdmans Publishing Co., 2001); E. P. Sanders, *Jesus and Judaism* (Philadelphia: Fortress Press, 1984); and Günter Stemberger, *Jewish Contemporaries of Jesus: Pharisees, Sadducees, Essenes* (Minneapolis: Fortress Press, 1995).

2. Sanders, *Jesus and Judaism*, 170–82.

3. See Jacob Neusner, *Mishnah: A New Translation* (New Haven, CT: Yale University Press, 1988).

4. Herbert W. Basser, *Studies in Exegesis: Christian Critiques of Jewish Law and Rabbinic Responses 70–300 C.E.* (Boston: Brill Academic Publishers, 2002), 19.

5. I've made up examples. Therefore, they display peculiarities of my imagination and my style. Your style and the resources of your imagination will serve you better.

6. E. P. Sanders, *The Historical Figure of Jesus* (New York: Penguin Books, 1993), 217.

7. See David Friedrich Strauss, *The Life of Jesus, Critically Examined*, trans. George Eliot, ed. Peter C. Hodgson (Philadelphia: Fortress Press, 1973).

8. But see the critical article by James Barr, "Revelation through History in the Old Testament and in Modern Theology," in *New Theology No. 1*, ed. Martin E. Marty and Dean G. Peerman (New York: Macmillan, 1964), 60–74.

9. See Paul Ricoeur, *The Symbolism of Evil*, trans. Emerson Buchanan (Boston: Beacon Press, 1969).

10. "Sociology of knowledge" is associated with the thought of Alfred Schutz. See his *The Phenomenology of the Social World* (Evanston, IL: Northwestern University Press, 1967). On the notion of revelation through social symbols, see Avery Dulles, *Models of Revelation* (Garden City, NY: Doubleday, 1983), 257–59.

11. There is a third use of the term in another conflict story (Mark 10:45): "The son of humanity didn't come to be served, but to serve." The added phrase "and give his life as a ransom for many" tips the phrase in the direction of a passion prediction.

12. From the "Brief Order for Confession and Forgiveness" of the Evangelical Lutheran Church in America.

13. These options are presented and discussed in Walter Wink, *The Human Being* (Minneapolis: Fortress Press, 2002), 68–69.

CHAPTER FOUR: AN INAUGURAL SET

1. The rhetorical character of this set of stories is studied by Joanna Dewey in *Markan Public Debate: Literary Technique, Concentric Structure, and Theology in Mark 2:1–3:6*, SBL Dissertation Series 48 (Chico, CA: Scholars Press, 1980).

2. In Sartre's play *The Flies*, the god Zeus strives to keep guilt firmly fixed so that he may continue in the ritual forgiveness business. The play is available in Sartre, *No Exit and Three Other Plays* (New York: Vintage Books, 1955), 49–127.

3. Helen Flanders Dunbar, MD, was an early researcher in psychosomatics. Her first work, *Emotions and Bodily Changes: A Survey of Literature on Psychosomatic Interrelationships,* was published in 1936. Her major study, *Psychosomatic Diagnosis*, was published in 1943. For an introduction to her thought, see Dunbar, *Mind and Body: Psychosomatic Medicine* (New York: Random House, 1947).

4. See the difficult but brilliant article by Edward Farley, "Psychopathology and Human Evil: Toward a Theory of Differentiation," in *Crosscurrents in Phenomenology,* ed. R. Bruzina and B. Wilshire (The Hague: Nijhoff, 1978).

5. Erich Fromm, *The Sane Society* (New York: Rinehart & Co., 1955), 205.

6. Jeanne D'Orge, "Red Seed," in *Voice in the Circle* (Santa Barbara, CA: Noel Young Printer, 1955), 59.

7. W. H. Auden, "For the Time Being: A Christmas Oratorio," in *The Collected Poems of W. H. Auden* (New York: Random House, 1945), 459.

8. I am rather sure the line is from a poem by Peguy, but I have been unable to locate the source.

9. Such words are said by the ship's captain in Nicholas Monsarrat's *The Cruel Sea,* as quoted in Alexander Miller, *The Renewal of Man* (Garden City, NY: Doubleday, 1955), 101.

10. I have written several times on the meaning of "kingdom of God." In particular, see *Preaching the New and the Now* (Louisville, KY: Westminster John Knox Press, 1998), a book on preaching the kingdom; and chap. 2 of *Speaking Parables: A Homiletic Guide* (Louisville, KY: Westminster John Knox Press, 2000), which is on the kingdom in parables.

11. *Poems of James Thompson—B.V.*, ed. Gordon Hall Gerould (New York: Henry Holt & Co., 1927), 121.

12. The story is based on a scene in Frederick Buechner's *Love Feast*, but then improvised.

13. The idea of the two ways can be traced back to the mystic theology of Pseudo-Dionysius. For a dramatic presentation that favors the *via negativa*, see T. S. Eliot, *The Cocktail Party* (New York: Harcourt, Brace & Co., 1950). For literature that in general favors the way of affirmation, see the novels of Charles Williams, a contemporary of Eliot's.

14. For a discussion of Sabbath law with respect to the passage, see Herbert W. Basser, *Studies in Exegesis: Christian Critiques of Jewish Law and Rabbinic Responses, 70–300 C.E.* (Boston: Brill Academic Publishers, 2002), 26–30.

15. Ibid., 28n39.

16. In my discussion of the Jewish Sabbath, I have drawn on Jacob Neusner, *Judaism When Christianity Began: A Survey of Belief and Practice* (Louisville, KY: Westminster John Knox Press, 2002), chap. 6.

17. The first question in the Shorter Catechism is "What is the chief end of man?" The answer: "Man's chief end is to glorify God, and enjoy him forever."

18. Hannah Arendt, *The Human Condition* (Chicago: University of Chicago Press, 1958), sections 3 and 6.

19. See Basser, *Studies in Exegesis,* 20–26.

20. Geza Vermes, *The Authentic Gospel of Jesus* (New York: Penguin Books, 2004), 46–50.

21. The subtitle of Jim Wallis's recent book describes the current controversy succinctly: *God's Politics: Why the Right Gets It Wrong and the Left Doesn't Get It* (San Francisco: HarperSanFrancisco, 2005).

22. C. S. Lewis, *The Screwtape Letters* (New York: Macmillan, 1948), 135.

CHAPTER FIVE: TWO BY TWO

1. See Trevor Ling, *The Significance of Satan: New Testament Demonology and Its Contemporary Relevance* (London: SPCK, 1961).

2. Denis de Rougemont, *The Devil's Share*, trans. Haakon Chevalier (New York: Pantheon Books, 1944), 17. De Rougemont attributes the remark to Baudelaire.

3. The notion that Jesus was an unauthorized healer and thus regarded as a dangerous magician is argued in Morton Smith, *Jesus the Magician: Charlatan or Son of God?* (Berkeley, CA: Seastone, 1998).

4. Graham Greene, *A Burnt-Out Case* (New York: Viking Press, 1961), 90.

5. This is from an old Cornish prayer cited in Gordon Rupp, *Principalities and Powers: Studies in the Christian Conflict in History* (Nashville: Abingdon-Cokesbury, 1952), 16.

6. Joel Bakan, in a carefully argued book, *The Corporation: The Pathological Pursuit of Profit and Power* (New York: Free Press, 2004), claims that without legal regulation corporations are amoral and, thus, ultimately "socially psychotic."

7. See the following two resources on preaching about the family: Elizabeth Achtemeier, *Preaching about Family Relationships* (Philadelphia: Westminster Press, 1987); and David Buttrick, "Preaching and the Family," in *Preaching In and Out of Season*, ed. Thomas G. Long and Neely Dixon McCarter (Louisville, KY: Westminster John Knox Press, 1990). These works put forth two quite different positions.

8. See Walter Harrelson, *The Ten Commandments and Human Rights* (Philadelphia: Fortress Press, 1980), 92–105, 122–33.

9. Gerd Theissen, *Sociology of Early Palestinian Christianity* (Philadelphia: Fortress Press, 1977), 11–12.

10. For discussion of the image of "household," see Paul S. Minear, *Images of the Church in the New Testament* (Philadelphia: Westminster Press, 1960), 165–72. The word "household" is more extensive than our intimate definitions of family.

11. I have reproduced material in this section from my article "Preaching and the Family."

12. Ernest Renan, *The Life of Jesus* (New York: Carleton Publisher, 1863), 210–11.

13. Quoted in John Brown, *John Bunyan* (North Haven, CT: Archon Books, 1969), 178.

14. The song, "Mutual Admiration Society," is from the 1956 Broadway show *Happy Hunting*, with music by Harold Karr and lyrics by Matt Dubey.

15. Alan Paton, *Cry the Beloved Country: A Story of Comfort in Desolation* (New York: Charles Scribner's Sons, 1948), 269.

16. Lewis Sherrill told this story to a class at Union Theological Seminary.

17. Arthur Miller, *All My Sons*, in *Arthur Miller's Collected Plays* (New York: Viking Press, 1947), 127.

18. Jacob Neusner, *The Mishnah: A New Translation* (New Haven, CT: Yale University Press, 1988), 1123.

19. See Jacob Neusner, *Judaism When Christianity Began: A Survey of Belief and Practice* (Louisville, KY: Westminster John Knox Press, 2002), chap. 2, "Revelation and Scripture: The Oral Torah."

20. From *Antiquities*, 13:297, cited in Geza Vermes, *The Authentic Gospel of Jesus* (New York: Penguin Books, 2004), 52.

21. From *The Collected Poems of A. E. Housman* (New York: Henry Holt & Co., 1940), 81–82.

22. Cited in Harry Emerson Fosdick, *On Being a Real Person* (New York: Harper & Brothers, 1943), 149.

23. Franz Kafka, "A Hunger Artist," in *The Complete Stories*, ed. Nahum N. Glatzer (New York: Schocken, 1971).

24. I have been unable to locate my source for this quote from Lewis; I suspect it was a BBC interview. For a discussion of the same subject, see C. S. Lewis, "Revival or Decay?" in *God in the Dock: Essays on Theology and Ethics*, ed. Walter Hooper (Grand Rapids: Wm. B. Eerdmans Publishing Co., 1970), 250–53.

25. Moss Hart, *Act One: An Autobiography* (New York: Random House, 1959), 287.

26. Graham Greene, *Our Man in Havana* (New York: Bantam Books, 1955), 140.

27. Boris Pasternak, *Doctor Zhivago* (New York: Pantheon Books, 1958), 42.

28. See the sophisticated treatment of the story of the Syrophoenician woman in Johannes Munck, *Paul and the Salvation of Mankind* (Richmond, VA: John Knox Press, 1959), 260–64; and also two excellent essays in Amy-Jill Levine, ed., *A Feminist Companion to Mark* (Sheffield: Sheffield Academic Press, 2001): Sharon H. Ringe, "A Gentile Woman's Story Revisited: Rereading Mark 7.24–31," 81–100, and Ranjini Wickramsaratne Rebera, "The Syrophoenician Woman: A South Asian Feminist Perspective," 101–10.

29. The quote from William Lyon Phelps is drawn from a sermon by Paul L. McKay, "Christmas and Meaning," *Pulpit Magazine* 26, no. 12 (December 1955): 8.

CHAPTER SIX: ON DISCIPLESHIP

1. On terms for "divorce," see David Daube, *The New Testament and Rabbinic Judaism* (Peabody, MA: Hendrickson Publishers, 1998), 362–72.

2. Elisabeth Schüssler Fiorenza, *In Memory of Her* (New York: Crossroad, 1985), 143.

3. Most of the material in this section is drawn from my article "Marriage and the Marriage Service," *Reformed Liturgy and Music* 14, no. 1 (Winter 1980): 5–14.

4. John Calvin, *Institutes of the Christian Religion*, ed. John T. McNeill and Ford Lewis Battles (Philadelphia: Westminster Press, 1950), 2:1481.

5. Most marriage customs have solid pagan sources. The wedding ring may have signified the satisfactory conclusion to a dowry deal; the giving of the bride, a father's acceptance of the contract; the joining of hands, the tribal trading of a woman to her husband's clan. In addition, bridesmaids were dressed up to deceive demons who might otherwise abduct the bride; the veil may have been a similar disguise, or a representation of curtains to be opened to a bridal bed. Rice goes back to a fertility cult custom, and the hoisting of a bride over a threshold is "a last remnant of marriage by capture." See W. K. Lowther Clarke, "Solemnization of Matrimony," in *Liturgy and Worship*, ed. W. K. Lowther Clarke and C. Harris (London: SPCK, 1932).

6. John Dominic Crossan, *Jesus, A Revolutionary Biography* (San Francisco: HarperSanFrancisco, 1998), 54.

7. Oscar Cullman, *Baptism in the New Testament* (London: SCM Press, 1950), argues for an early practice of infant baptism, but his position is rejected in Kurt Aland, *Did the Early Church Baptize Infants?* (Philadelphia: Westminster Press, 1963). I concur with Aland.

8. David Noel Freedman believed that Jesus could not have said "as yourself." See his article "The Hebrew Old Testament and the Ministry Today: An Exegetical Study of Leviticus 19:18b," *Perspective* (Pittsburgh Theological Seminary) 5 (1964): 9–14.

9. Ignazio Silone, *Bread and Wine*, trans. Gwenda David and Eric Mosbacher (New York: Harper & Brothers, a Signet Book, 1937).

10. Ched Myers, *Binding the Strong Man: A Political Reading of Mark's Story of Jesus* (Maryknoll, NY: Orbis Books, 1994), 272–73.

11. John R. Donahue, *The Gospel of Mark* (Collegeville, MN: Liturgical Press, 2002), 303.

12. On God's preferential option for the poor, see Norbert F. Lohfink, *Option for the Poor: The Basic Principle of Liberation Theology in the Light of the Bible* (Berkeley, CA: Bibal Press, 1987); George V. Pixley and Clodovis Boff, *The Bible, the Church, and the Poor* (Maryknoll, NY: Orbis Books, 1986); and Elsa Támez, *The Bible of the Oppressed* (Maryknoll, NY: Orbis Books, 1982). On the theme of wealth in Christian Scriptures, see David L. Mealand, *Poverty and Expectation in the Gospels* (London: SPCK, 1980).

13. See Charles Williams, *He Came Down from Heaven and The Forgiveness of Sins* (London: Faber & Faber, n.d.), chap. 7.

14. For a fuller treatment of the subject of money, see my *Speaking Jesus: Homiletic Theology and the Sermon on the Mount* (Louisville, KY: Westminster John Knox Press, 2002), chap. 9.

15. Theodore J. Weeden, *Mark: Traditions in Conflict* (Philadelphia: Fortress Press, 1971).

16. See Barnabas Lindars, *New Testament Apologetics: The Doctrinal Significance of the Old Testament Quotations* (London: SCM Press, 1973); and Ben Witherington III, *The Gospel of Mark: A Socio-Rhetorical Commentary* (Grand Rapids: Wm. B. Eerdmans Publishing Co., 2001).

17. John Dean, *Blind Ambition: The White House Years* (New York: Simon & Schuster, 1979).

18. Bushnell believed that every nation received an evangelical commission from God with respect to its own time and place.

19. Frederick Buechner, *Love Feast* (New York: Atheneum, 1974), 229–30.

CHAPTER SEVEN: FINAL CONFLICTS

1. E. P. Sanders, *The Historical Figure of Jesus* (New York: Penguin Books, 1995), 184–87.

2. See Allan A. Boesak, *Finger of God: Sermons on Faith and Socio-Political Responsibility*, trans. Peter Randall (Maryknoll, NY: Orbis Books, 1982).

3. Second Helvetic Confession, chap. 18: "Of the Ministers of the Church, Their Institution and Duties."

4. Daube, *The New Testament and Rabbinic Judaism*, part 2, chap. 7.

5. On the creation of church-state policy, see Kathleen Flake, *The Politics of American Religious Identity: The Seating of Senator Reed Smoot, Mormon Apostle* (Chapel Hill: University of North Carolina Press, 2004).

6. Jacob Neusner, *Judaism When Christianity Began: A Survey of Belief and Practice* (Louisville, KY: Westminster John Knox Press, 2002), 164.

7. From the *Mahzor for Rosh Hashanah and Yom Kippur*, edited by Rabbi Jules Harlow (New York: The Rabbinical Assembly, 1972), p.D7.

8. This is from a twelfth-century hymn, "Jerusalem the Golden," by Bernard of Cluny, translated by John M. Neale in 1851.

9. I have written often on resurrection. See esp. "Preaching on the Resurrection," *Religion in Life* (Autumn 1976); *Preaching Jesus Christ: An Exercise in Homiletic Theology* (Eugene, OR: Wipf & Stock, 2002), chap. 5; and *The Mystery and the Passion: A Homiletic Reading of Biblical Traditions* (Eugene, OR: Wipf & Stock, 2002), 15–95.

10. Douglas R. A. Hare, *Matthew,* Interpretation: A Bible Commentary for Teaching and Preaching (Louisville, KY: John Knox Press, 1993), 260.

11. For a description of the numinous in nature, see chap. 7 of Kenneth Grahame, *The Wind in the Willows* (New York: Charles.Scribner's Sons, 1961).

12. For a contemporary reflection on Luther's theology of the cross, see Douglas John Hall, *Lighten Our Darkness: Toward an Indigenous Theology of the Cross* (Philadelphia: Westminster Press, 1976).

13. Theodore T. Jennings, *Life as Worship* (Grand Rapids: Wm. B. Eerdmans Publishing Co., 1982), section 1.

CHAPTER EIGHT: THE CONTROVERSIAL JESUS

1. John Dominic Crossan and Jonathan L. Reed, *Excavating Jesus: Beneath the Stones, Behind the Texts* (San Francisco: HarperSanFrancisco, 2001), 26.

2. See G. R. Beasley-Murray, *Jesus and the Kingdom of God* (Grand Rapids: Wm. B. Eerdmans Publishing Co., 1986), 71–80.

3. C. H. Dodd, *The Parables of the Kingdom* (New York: Charles Scribner's Sons, 1961), 19–20.

4. Crossan and Reed, *Excavating Jesus*, 66–70, 108–15.

5. On the economy in Galilee and the effects of taxation, see K. C. Hanson and Douglas E. Oakman, *Palestine in the Time of Jesus: Social Structures and Social Conflicts* (Minneapolis: Fortress Press, 1998), chap. 4.

6. See Karen Horney, *Neurosis and Human Growth: The Struggle toward Self-Realization* (New York: W. W. Norton, 1950), chap. 3, "The Tyranny of the Should."

7. The story is skipped in Bultmann's commentary and dealt with in an appendix by Barrett, Hosyns, and others. Its problems are three: (1) It does not appear in early manuscripts of the Gospel, (2) its style is clearly more Synoptic than Johannanine, and (3) its location seems to interrupt the structure of the Gospel. In addition, there is no mention of such a story before the third century.

8. See Paul Tillich's sermon "You Are Accepted," in *The Shaking of the Foundations* (New York: Charles Scribner's Sons, 1955), chap. 19. Tillich makes it quite clear that we are accepted even though, as sinners, we are unacceptable.

9. See St. John of the Cross, *Dark Night of the Soul*, trans. Mirabai Starr (New York: Riverhead Books, 2002); and Julian of Norwich, *Revelations of Divine Love*, trans. Elizabeth Spearing (New York: Penguin Books, 1999).

10. Jean-Paul Sartre, *The Devil and the Good Lord and Two Other Plays* (New York: Alfred A. Knopf, 1960), 141.

11. David Buttrick, *Homiletic: Moves and Structures* (Philadelphia: Fortress Press, 1987), chap. 1.

Bibliography

THE CONFLICT-PRONOUNCEMENT STORIES

Albertz, Martin. *Die synoptischen Streitgespräche: Ein Beitrag zur Formengeschichte des Urchristentums.* Berlin: Trowitzsch, 1921.

Bultmann, Rudolf. *The History of the Synoptic Tradition.* Rev. ed. Translated by John Marsh. New York: Harper & Row, 1968.

Daube, David. "Four Types of Question." In *The New Testament and Rabbinic Judaism,* 159–69. Peabody, MA: Hendrickson Publishers, 1998.

Dewey, Joanna. *Markan Public Debate: Literary Technique, Concentric Structure, and Theology in Mark 2:1–3:6.* SBL Dissertation Series 48. Chico, CA: Scholars Press, 1980.

Dibelius, Martin. *From Tradition to Gospel.* Translated by Bertram Lee Woolf. New York: Charles Scribner's Sons, 1934.

Hultgren, Arland J. *Jesus and His Adversaries: The Form and Function of the Conflict Stories in the Synoptic Tradition.* Minneapolis: Augsburg, 1979.

Kingsbury, Jack Dean. *Conflict in Mark: Jesus, Authorities, Disciples.* Minneapolis: Fortress Press, 1989.

Mack, Burton L., and Vernon K. Robbins. *Patterns of Persuasion in the Gospels.* Sonoma, CA: Polebridge Press, 1989.

Taylor, Vincent. *The Formation of the Gospel Tradition.* 2nd ed. London: Macmillan, 1964.

THE GOSPEL OF MARK: COMMENTARIES

Anderson, Hugh, *The Gospel of Mark.* London: Oliphants, 1976.

Cranfield, C. E. B. *The Gospel according to Saint Mark: An Introduction and Commentary.* Cambridge: Cambridge University Press, 1960.

Donahue, John R., and Daniel J. Harrington. *The Gospel of Mark.* Collegeville, MN: Liturgical Press, 2002.

Dowd, Sharyn. *Reading Mark: A Literary and Theological Commentary on the Second Gospel.* Macon, GA: Smyth & Helwys, 2000.

Gundry, Robert H. *Mark: A Commentary on His Apology for the Cross.* Grand Rapids: Wm. B. Eerdmans Publishing Co., 1993.

Hare, Douglas R. A. *Mark.* Louisville, KY: Westminster John Knox Press, 1996.

Hooker, Morna D. *The Gospel according to Saint Mark.* London: A. & C. Black, 1991.

Juel, Donald H. *The Gospel of Mark.* Nashville: Abingdon Press, 1999.

Kee, Howard Clarke. *Community of the New Age: Studies in Mark's Gospel.* Philadelphia: Westminster Press, 1977.

Marcus, Joel. *Mark 1–8.* Garden City, NY: Doubleday, 2000.

Myers, Ched. *Binding the Strong Man: A Political Reading of Mark's Story of Jesus.* Maryknoll, NY: Orbis Books, 1988.

Nineham, D. E. *The Gospel of Saint Mark.* Baltimore: Penguin Books, 1964.

Schmidt, Daryl D. *The Gospel of Mark with Introduction, Notes, and Original Text.* Sonoma, CA: Polebridge Press, 1990.

Schweizer, Eduard. *The Good News according to Mark.* Atlanta: John Knox Press, 1977.

Taylor, Vincent. *The Gospel according to Saint Mark.* 2nd ed. London: Macmillan, 1966.

Tolbert, Mary Ann. *Sowing the Gospel: Mark's World in Literary-Historical Perspective.* Minneapolis: Fortress Press, 1989.

Witherington, Ben, III. *The Gospel of Mark: A Socio-Rhetorical Commentary.* Grand Rapids: Wm. B. Eerdmans Publishing Co., 2001.

THE GOSPEL OF MARK: GENERAL STUDIES

Anderson, Janice C., and Stephen D. Moore, eds. *Mark and Method: New Approaches in Biblical Studies.* Minneapolis: Fortress Press, 1992.

Blount, Brian K. *Go Preach! Mark's Kingdom Message and the Black Church Today.* Maryknoll, NY: Orbis Books, 1998.

Blount, Brian K., and Gary W. Charles, *Preaching Mark in Two Voices.* Louisville, KY: Westminster John Knox Press, 2002.

Kelber, Werner H. *The Kingdom in Mark: A New Place and a New Time.* Philadelphia: Fortress Press, 1974.

———. *Mark's Story of Jesus.* Philadelphia: Fortress Press, 1979.

———. *The Passion in Mark: Studies on Mark 14–16.* Philadelphia: Fortress Press, 1976.

Kingsbury, Jack Dean. *The Christology of Mark's Gospel.* Philadelphia: Fortress Press, 1983.

Levine, Amy-Jill, with Marianne Bickenstaff. *A Feminist Companion to Mark.* Sheffield: Sheffield Academic Press, 2001.

Marcus, Joel. *The Mystery of the Kingdom of God.* SBL Dissertation Series 90. Atlanta: Scholars Press, 1986.

Perrin, Norman. *A Modern Pilgrimage in New Testament Christology.* Philadelphia: Fortress Press, 1974.

Rhoads, David, Joanna Dewey, and Donald Michie. *Mark as Story: An Introduction to the Narrative of a Gospel.* 2nd ed. Minneapolis: Fortress Press, 1999.

Senior, Donald. *The Passion of Jesus in the Gospel of Mark.* Collegeville, MN: Liturgical Press, 1984.

Waetjen, Hermen C. *A Reordering of Power: A Socio-Political Reading of Mark's Gospel.* Minneapolis: Fortress Press, 1989.

Weeden, Theodore J. *Mark: Traditions in Conflict.* Philadelphia: Fortress Press, 1971.

JUDAISM IN THE FIRST CENTURY

Chilton, Bruce, and Jacob Neusner. *Judaism in the New Testament: Practices and Beliefs.* New York: Routledge, 1995.

Crabbe, Lester L. *An Introduction to First Century Judaism: Jewish Religion and History in the Second Temple Period.* Edinburgh: T. & T. Clark, 1996.

Daube, David. *The New Testament and Rabbinic Judaism.* Peabody, MA: Hendrickson Publishers, 1998.

Hengel, Martin. *Judaism and Hellenism: Studies in Their Encounter in Palestine during the Early Hellenistic Period.* Translated by John Bowden. Philadelphia: Fortress Press, 1974.

Malbon, Elizabeth Struthers. "The Jewish Leaders in the Gospel of Mark: A Literary Study of Markan Characterization." *Journal of Biblical Literature* 108, no. 2 (1989): 259–81.

Marcus, Joel. "The Scribes and the Pharisees." In *Mark 1–8: A New Translation with Introduction and Commentary,* 519–24. Anchor Bible. New York: Doubleday, 2000.

Neusner, Jacob. *Judaism When Christianity Began: A Survey of Belief and Practice.* Louisville, KY: Westminster John Knox Press, 2002.

Rivkin, Ellis. *A Hidden Revolution.* Nashville: Abingdon Press, 1978.

Saldarini, Anthony J. *Pharisees, Scribes and Sadducees in Palestinian Society.* Grand Rapids: Wm. B. Eerdmans Publishing Co., 2001.

Sanders, E. P. *The Historical Figure of Jesus.* London: Penguin Books, 1993.

———. *Jesus and Judaism.* Philadelphia: Fortress Press, 1984.

Stemberger, Günter. *Jewish Contemporaries of Jesus: Pharisees, Sadducees, Essenes.* Minneapolis: Fortress Press, 1995.

Vermes, Geza. *The Authentic Gospel of Jesus.* New York: Penguin Books, 2004.

ANTI-JUDAISM IN THE GOSPEL OF MARK

Basser, Herbert W. *Studies in Exegesis: Christian Critiques of Jewish Law and Rabbinic Responses 70–300 C.E.* Boston: Brill Academic Publishers, 2002.

Charlesworth, James H. *Jesus' Jewishness: Exploring the Place of Jesus in Early Judaism.* New York: Crossroad, 1991.

———. *Jews and Christians: Exploring the Past, Present, and Future.* New York: American Interfaith Institute, 1990.

———, ed. *Overcoming Fear between Jews and Christians.* New York: American Interfaith Institute, 1992.

Evans, Craig A., and Donald A. Hagner. *Anti-Semitism and Early Christianity: Issues of Polemic and Faith.* Minneapolis: Fortress Press, 1993.

Farmer, William R., ed. *Anti-Judaism and the Gospels.* Harrisburg, PA: Trinity Press International, 1999.

Fredriksen, Paula, and Adele Reinhartz, eds. *Jesus, Judaism, and Christian Anti-Judaism: Reading the New Testament after the Holocaust.* Louisville, KY: Westminster John Knox Press, 2002.

Gagner, John. *The Origins of Anti-Semitism: Attitudes toward Judaism in Pagan and Christian Antiquity.* New York: Oxford University Press, 1985.

Kee, Howard C., and Irvin J. Borowsky, eds. *Removing Anti-Judaism from the Pulpit.* New York: Continuum, 1996.

Lohfink, Norbert. *The Covenant Never Revoked: Biblical Reflections on Christian-Jewish Dialogue.* Translated by John J. Scullion. New York: Paulist Press, 1991.

THE SON OF MAN TRADITION

Borsch, Frederick Houk. *The Son of Man in Myth and History.* Philadelphia: Westminster Press, 1967.

Burkett, Delbert. *The Son of Man Debate: A History and Evaluation.* Cambridge: Cambridge University Press, 1999.

Hare, Douglas R. A. *The Son of Man Tradition.* Minneapolis: Fortress Press, 1990.

Lindars, Barnabas. *Jesus Son of Man: A Fresh Examination of the Son of Man Sayings in the Gospels in the Light of Recent Research.* London: SPCK, 1985.

Tödt, Heinz E. *The Son of Man in the Synoptic Tradition.* Philadelphia: Westminster Press, 1959.

Wink, Walter. *The Human Being: Jesus and the Enigma of the Son of Man.* Minneapolis: Fortress Press, 2002.

OTHER BOOKS CONSULTED

Beare, Francis W. *The Earliest Records of Jesus.* Nashville: Abingdon Press, 1968.

Funk, Robert W., and Ray W. Hoover, with the Jesus Seminar. *The Five Gospels: What Did Jesus Really Say?* San Francisco: HarperSanFrancisco with the Polebridge Press, 1993.

Funk, Robert W., and the Jesus Seminar. *The Acts of Jesus: The Search for the Authentic Deeds of Jesus.* New York: HarperCollins, 1998.

Hanson, K. C., and Douglas E. Oakman. *Palestine in the Time of Jesus: Social Structures and Social Conflicts.* Minneapolis: Fortress Press, 1998.

Horsley, Richard A., ed. *Christian Origins.* Vol. 1 of *A People's History of Christianity.* Minneapolis: Fortress Press, 2005.

Malina, Bruce J., and Richard L. Rohrbaugh. *Social Science Commentary on the Synoptic Gospels.* 2nd ed. Minneapolis: Fortress Press, 2003.

Moxnes, Halvor. *Putting Jesus in His Place: A Radical Vision of Household and Kingdom.* Louisville, KY: Westminster John Knox Press, 2003.

Smith, Morton. *Jesus the Magician: Charlatan or Son of God?* Berkeley, CA: Seastone, 1998.

Index of Biblical Citations

Index of Personal Names

Index of Subjects

213

Conflict Stories in the Synoptic Gospels

	Mark	Matthew	Luke	Page
Forgiveness of Sins	2:1–12	9:1–8	5:17–26	38
Eating with Sinners	2:13–17	9:10–13	5:29–32	48
Fasting	2:18–20	9:14–17	5:33–39	56
Picking Grain on the Sabbath	2:3–28	12:1–8	6:1–5	60
Healing on the Sabbath	3:1–6	12:9–14	6:6–11	67
Jesus' Healings	3:20–30	12:22–37	11:14–23	73
Jesus' Family	3:20, 31–35	12:46–50	8:19–21	79
Washing before Eating	7:1–23	15:1–20		88
The Syrophoenian Woman	7:24–30	15:21–28		98
Asking for a Sign	8:11–13	16:1–4		105
Coin in a Fish		17:24–27		151
Woman Bent from Birth			13:10–17	70
Man with Dropsy			14:1–6	71
Divorce	10:2–12	19:1–12		107
Children	10:13–16	19:13–15	18:15–17	113
Wealth	10:17–31	19:16–30	18:18–30	117
Power	10:35–45	20:20–28	22:24–27	125
Authority	11:27–33	21:23–27	20:1–8	134
Taxes	12:13–17	22:15–22	20:20–26	144
Resurrection	2:18–27	22:23–33	20:27–40	152
The Great Commandment	12:28–34	22:34–40	10:25–28	158
The Son of David	12:35–37	22:41–46	20:41–44	165
The Anointing of Jesus	4:1–9	26:6–13	7:36–50	169